HOUSTON TO COOPERSTOWN

The Houston Astros Biggio & Bagwell Years

FOREWORD BY BILL BROWN

Indianapolis, Indiana

Houston to Cooperstown

The Houston Astros' Biggio and Bagwell Years
Copyright © 2017 by Greg Lucas

Published by **Blue River Press**
Indianapolis, Indiana
www.brpressbooks.com

Distributed by **Cardinal Publishers Group**
Tom Doherty Company, Inc.
www.cardinalpub.com

ISBN: 978-1-68157-053-2

Cover Design by Scott Lohr
Cover Photos: Astos Cubs Baseball by David Durochick /
    Associated Press
Editor: Dani McCormick
Book design by Dave Reed

Printed in the United States of America

10 9 8 7 6 5 4 3 2 1

Contents

Foreword

In the pages to follow, Greg Lucas takes you through many of the most important times in the history of the Houston Astros, especially the teams of two Astro career Hall of Famers, Craig Biggio and Jeff Bagwell.

Greg has lived in Houston for thirty-five years and he has as good a sense of what has mattered to Houston as well as anybody. In his position as play-by-play broadcaster, field commentator, and studio host in his long career, he has been devoted to chronicling what matters to fans of many sports especially baseball fans. He is well equipped to take us on the long trip through the best era in the team's fifty-five years.

He incorporates stories from the beginning of the franchise to give the reader perspective in this comprehensive look at the owners, managers and players who have moved through our decades of memories. This book offers a terrific collection of the most memorable times in Houston from Colt Stadium to Minute Maid Park.

Years ago Greg and I were in Washington, D.C. on a road trip with the Astros. They had never played in the city until the Montreal Expos moved to our nation's capital. But Greg had studied baseball history extensively and combed through countless baseball books, making him well aware of the history of baseball in every city. Naturally, he thought of old Griffith Stadium. Greg had packed with him a book of many of the historic ballparks with diagrams of each. He opened the book and we looked at the information inside, with some notes about various features including dimensions of the playing field and arrows pointing to where historic moments had occurred, such as a tape measure homerun hit by Mickey Mantle of the New York Yankees.

It was not unusual to see Greg walking the streets of any major league city, sometimes for more than two hours. As with many long time baseball fans, he seemed to be literally turning back the clock to a time when automobiles were a luxury and time was not so pressing. He loved to find the location of old ballparks in places like Chicago, New York, Pittsburgh, Philadelphia, Boston, and Montreal for example. With the time for thinking those long walks could bring, a baseball fan can at times play mind games and see what his memory can conjure, with no need for television highlights and game analysis to be entertained.

Part of being a good baseball analyst/reporter is mastering the constant challenge of incorporating new information into each broadcast while reporting the exploits of the same small core of star players with grace over and over. The main characters remain the same, but facing daily challenges. The story lines can change gradually over long periods of time. Greg approaches this book in the same way, weaving previously unknown personal stories about Craig Biggio and Jeff Bagwell to help us understand them as people as well as athletes. He digs back into their high school and college years to allow us to embrace the foundations of their Hall of Fame careers. We learn how Craig's compassionate side surfaced early in his life when he helped a friend deal with tragedy. Decades later, he became a permanent part of the Sunshine Kid's charity, helping families deal with their children's battles with cancer. We also learn how the sudden and shocking death of a teammate on the baseball field affected Craig's life.

As the life stories of Biggio and Bagwell became intertwined, they steamed forward at full speed on course for Cooperstown. You will see how their blue collar work ethic instilled them in their quest for excellence. You will also see the forces in professional sports that tug at players' and owners' career choices.

There were many conversations with the media about the Biggio-Bagwell era, a rarity in modern pro sports, with two Hall of Famers both playing their entire career with one team and being teammates during that exciting era. They were both great players as well as great leaders.

It was not unusual for one media member to ask another, "What do you think '7' and '5' will do about this?" when a teammate of theirs failed to hustle. Referring to Biggio and Bagwell by their uniform numbers, as every day media members often did, was a way of honoring their professional ethics and treating them as the team leaders they were. When players like Derek Bell or Carl Everett brought some baggage to Houston from their previous stops, "7" and "5" made sure they stayed in line on the team and clubhouse while respecting their individuality.

Astro fans had a large presence at Cooperstown in 2015 when Craig Biggio became the first player to enter the Hall of Fame wearing as Astros cap. They lined the streets and cheered loudly, yelling out enthusiastic greetings to anybody they recognized from the Astros organization. The voices were heard by the nationwide TV audience from the grassy field in Cooperstown on induction day. Having been selected to join that honored body in early January 2017, it will be Jeff Bagwell's turn in the summer. Craig Biggio will be on the stage with returning Hall of Famers that day. Number "5" and "7" will be linked again forever.

– Bill Brown

The primary Astro television play-by-play announcer from 1987 through 2016, which encompassed the full careers of both Craig Biggio and Jeff Bagwell. He is also the author of three books: *My Baseball Journey*, *Houston Astros-Deep in the Heart* and *Breathing Orange Fire* with Jose Altuve.

"We're enjoying the moment for what it is right now, so I don't even want to think about that factor."

— Jeff Bagwell when asked about how the Biggio-Bagwell era may be near an end

Author's Introduction

In 2015 the Houston Astros got their own Hall of Famer. Two years later, they got their second. No two Houston players in the history of Major League Baseball more deserved to be the first two honored in Cooperstown more than Craig Biggio and Jeff Bagwell. Not only do the pair own almost all the hitting records for the Colt45/Astro franchise, but no players have ever appeared in more games wearing a Houston uniform than those two. In fact, according to the Elias Sports Bureau, the official keeper of Major League Baseball records, Craig Biggio and Jeff Bagwell played in 2029 games together, which is the most ever for two Hall of Fame teammates. Their fifteen seasons together as future Hall of Famers is only equaled by the pairs of Roberto Clemente and Bill Mazeroski of the Pirates, Carl Hubbell and Mel Ott of the Giants, and Mickey Mantle and Whitey Ford of the Yankees. During the fifteen years they played together over a twenty-year period, the Astros had the best teams in franchise history. They were in pennant races thirteen of those seasons, including six in the postseason with a World Series appearance. It was the Golden Era of Houston Major League Baseball. It took some time to get there and has taken some time to get back. Houston has an interesting if not fully successful history.

The team we now know as the Houston Astros was born into the National League as the Houston Colt 45s when major league baseball expanded in 1961 and 1962. This was the first expansion since four teams from the disbanded American Association were added to the National League in 1891. Since then quite a bit had changed. In 1891 the automobile had not yet been invented. Electricity and indoor plumbing in every house was only a dream. Forget radio, television, computers, or the internet. The latter two weren't even around in 1962,but by 1962 we had lots of cars, jet airplane travel, and were even starting to consider the exploration of space. The National Aeronautics and Space Administration had been created in 1958. By 1961 thanks to the political influence of Vice-President Lyndon Johnson, a Texas native, the Manned Spacecraft Center opened in the Houston suburb of Clear Lake, Texas. NASA made the Houston area the capital of space exploration. In 1962 the city would also join the Major Leagues of Baseball.

Baseball had expanded in the American League in 1961 with the Los Angeles Angels and the second version of the Washington Senators. Houston would be the only "new" market joining the major leagues the next year.

This book will cover the seasons major league baseball has been played in Houston but especially the careers of the best two baseball players ever to wear a Houston major league uniform—Craig Biggio and Jeff Bagwell. After having to wait a while, both were finally recognized with election to and induction into the Baseball Hall of Fame in Cooperstown, NY in 2015 and 2017 respectively. However, it was their actual playing careers that made those inductions possible. Neither played for any major league team other than the Houston Astros. Biggio lasted from midway through the 1988 season until the final out in 2007—twenty years. He had more than 3000 hits and a number of other special achievements. Bagwell was an Astro for 15 straight seasons. He had a lifetime batting average of .297 with a lifetime on base percentage of .408. He hit 449 homeruns. Had he not spent the first nine years of his career playing home games in the Astrodome with its dead air and long distances, that total could reasonably have been much closer to 600. Even so, all were Houston records. Biggio and Bagwell were teammates and close friends for all of those fifteen and remain so today.

As the regular right side of the Houston infield for more than a decade, they were, in the words of former manager Larry Dierker, "Absolutely the best. When both were at their peak defensively, that was not only a great offensive right side of the infield, but superb defensively as well. In all the fifty years I watched virtually every game of the season, I never saw a right side of the infield like that. Bagwell's instincts were beyond Biggio's, but that is not a knock. Bagwell's instincts to me were on a par with Willie Mays. And I can't think of another player better than those two instinctually."

Biggio and Bagwell are both of different temperament and never were off the field "hang-out" buddies. However, from the first day they met they both knew the other had a burning desire to win and to succeed in the sport they love.

Biggio and Bagwell were the best players during the best era of Houston Major League Baseball. For a franchise that had a .489 win-loss percentage over its 54 -year history through 2016, the club played at a winning percentage of 52% during Biggio's twenty seasons and 53% during Bagwell's fifteen. They were also a postseason team six times including the only Houston appearance in a World Series in 2005.

Individually, Biggio and Bagwell hold most Houston hitting records, won Gold Gloves on defense, and were willing to make personal sacrifices by changing defensive position to help the team.

Biggio and Bagwell were the most prominent members of Houston's famed "Killer B's" which at different times also included Lance Berkman, Derek Bell, Geoff Blum, Sean Berry and Carlos Beltran, plus any other player who happened to be with the team with a last name starting with the letter "B". Biggio and Bagwell were the constants. When players had questions, Biggio and Bagwell had the answers. They ran the team in the clubhouse. Woe to the player that did things wrong, or worse, failed to hustle.

I was lucky to be part of the Astros television announcing crew during most of their careers. I saw them get the big hits, make the great plays, and be true team leaders. Always co-operative whenever I needed an interview, I have nothing but fondness in remembering the Biggio-Bagwell years. I will never forget the first time I met Jeff. In 1995 I began working on Astro telecasts after six years of being part of the Texas Rangers TV crew. Since interleague play had not begun yet, the two teams never met. The Astros opening game was in San Diego, California. Seeing Bagwell on the bench, I went over to introduce myself. "Hi, Jeff, I'm Greg..." was as far as I got. Jeff interjected, "I know who you are. I've seen you on TV many times announcing basketball and Texas Ranger games." We had a nice conversation and relationship from then on. Jeff Bagwell, the reigning NL MVP actually knew who I was before I had introduced myself!

My first introduction to Biggio had actually come in Tokyo, Japan. He was part of the MLB team that was in Japan to play the Japan All-Stars in a series of games in 1992. I was there to announce four of the games for a number of regional sports networks in the United States. Biggio had just converted from catcher to second baseman prior to the 1992 season, so he served as a super utility man for Tom Kelly's MLB team that fall. Other than introducing myself and mentioning that, while I was a Ranger's announcer, I still lived most of the year in Houston so I was very much aware of his adventures in changing positions, we didn't say much. But that was the first time.

The importance of Craig Biggio and Jeff Bagwell wearing Astro caps on their plaques in Cooperstown cannot be minimalized. Until they got to the Hall, Houston had a team in Major League Baseball for fifty-three years with no Hall of Famers and only one World Series appearance. Their elections were very significant.

Some Astros players, like Cesar Cedeno and J. R. Richard, were on a Hall of Fame track early in their careers, but injuries and lower production, or, in Richard's case a stroke, cut short his career. Others like pitcher Don Wilson saw their lives end early. And two others, who did make the Hall, Joe Morgan and Nolan Ryan, had their biggest career moments elsewhere. Hall of Famers Nellie Fox, Robin Roberts, Eddie Mathews, Don Sutton, Pudge Rodriguez, Randy Johnson and Leo Durocher wore Houston colors, but were more remembered for their play or managing careers for other cities. Biggio and Bagwell never played anywhere else. They also put up numbers and were the leaders of the best run of success in Houston baseball history. The Hall of Fame voters could not ignore them forever.

Before Biggio and Bagwell arrived, the major leagues had been in Houston for more than twenty-five seasons, but with only a couple short periods of success. Craig Biggio and Jeff Bagwell led the way to major improvement. This book will cover Houston major league history from the birth of the franchise past the end of the Biggio-Bagwell era, but will also focus on the years the duo was the heart of the Astros. I hope Astro and baseball fans enjoy it.

Houston to Cooperstown

The Houston Astros
Craig Biggio & Jeff Bagwell Years

1 Craig Biggio Achieves Baseball Immortality

"A Lot of things have happened here over the course of my twenty-year career, but tonight, I think was the best."

— Craig Biggio after reaching the 3000 hit milestone and the crowd reaction

On June 28, 2007, the Houston Astros were hosting the Colorado Rockies in what would ordinarily have been a routine game in a so far dismal season. The Astros, only two seasons removed from their first National League pennant, were only 32-46 and in fifth place in the National League Central and 14 games off the lead.

Yet a sellout standing room only crowd of 42,537 fans filled Minute Maid Park. They had a good reason to be there. Craig Biggio entered the game with 2,997 career hits. With just three more he would become only the ninth player in Major League Baseball's history to achieve 3,000 hits while playing for only one team. The magic number of 3,000 would almost certainly guarantee Biggio election to Baseball's Hall of Fame a few years after he retired.

While at the advanced age of forty-one and hitting just .238, expecting Biggio to reach 3,000 by getting three hits that night was a long shot, and fans were taking no chances. One of Biggio's best friends on the team, catcher Brad Ausmus, didn't expect the big hit that night. When his wife in San Diego asked whether she should get a flight to Houston for the first game, Ausmus told her to stay home and wait. As Biggio remembered, Brad told her, "Hey he hasn't had three hits all year. There is no way he's getting three hits." Liz Ausmus missed out. Of course many fans were hedging their bets. Fans who had purchased tickets for the next two home games sold the place out in advance. The games had actually been sold out more than two weeks earlier, prior to an Astros nine game road trip which would precede a long home stand.

The race to 3,000 was somewhat precarious since owner Drayton McLane wanted the achievement to take place in front of the home fans. For manager Phil Garner, keeping Biggio out of some games on the trip was not the sacrifice it would have been two or three years earlier. Craig was not the same player now and keeping him rested was key. At this point, his number one replacement Mark Loretta was having a better year with a solid .300 batting average.

Before the road trip began that led into the big night, Biggio played Saturday night at home and was one for five at the plate. Garner held him out of Sunday's afternoon sellout, which likely upset owner McLane a bit. Resting vets for day games after night games is not uncommon in baseball, but while Biggio was still well short of 3,000, he hated to see any of his stars rested before large home crowds no matter how old they were.

When the team hit the road playing two interleague series in Anaheim and Arlington and winding up in Milwaukee, Garner and Biggio were hoping things would work out so that Craig would be only a handful of hits short of 3,000 before coming home for a long eleven game home stand. They had worked out his playing schedule in advance.

Biggio started six of the nine road games. He was used as a pinch hitter in two others and did not play at all in one. He collected just eight hits and returned to Houston only three shy of 3,000 with eleven games to make it. The quest for 3000 was on a good track. The team wasn't. Ten games under .500 at 30-40 and nine games off the lead when the trip started, they returned home 14 games under .500 and now 14 games behind.

The record mattered little to the fans that jammed the park. Among the number and sitting in a box above the field was Jeff Bagwell. Before the game, Bagwell, an on-field partner of Biggio's for 15 consecutive seasons, told his buddy that he had better get to 3,000 within the next two nights or Bagwell wouldn't be there. He had a long awaited travel vacation set to begin over the weekend.

Tonight would be the night.

In the first inning with the crowd roaring as his name was announced, Biggio, perhaps uncommonly nervous, swung over the top of the second pitch from Rockie starter Aaron Cook and dribbled an easy grounder to third baseman Garrett Atkins who easily threw him out.

By the time Biggio faced Cook again, Chris Iannetta had hit a solo homerun off Astro starter Roy Oswalt and the Rockies led 1-0. When Biggio came to the plate in the third, Oswalt had just singled with one out. Biggio took a 2-2 pitch and lined it to centerfield for career hit 2,998. Oswalt made it to second, but both Lance Berkman and Hunter Pence were retired to end the inning.

Biggio really got the crowd going in the bottom of the fifth. With one out and no one on base, Biggio hit an 0-1 pitch down the line at third. Garrett Atkins fielded the ball, but seemed to have a problem getting a good grip, causing a slight pause. When he cut loose, the throw carried the ball above first baseman Todd Helton's reach. It was ruled Biggio would have beaten the throw anyway and he was safe with a hit. His second hit of the night in just the first five innings of the game gave him 2,999 and a real shot at making history that very evening. The crowd was again on its feet as Biggio wound up at second base following the over-throw. Up in the suites Bagwell was smiling broadly as the play was ruled a hit. So was the entire Biggio family: his wife Patty, sons Cavan and Conor, and daughter Quinn.

Meanwhile the game was still in favor of the Rockies and both Oswalt and Cook were turning hitters away regularly.

The biggest moment of the night came in the last of the seventh. Still trailing 1-0, Astro catcher Brad Ausmus led off the inning with a line drive single to center on a 2-1 pitch. He was sacrificed to second base by Eric Bruntlett. Orlando Palmeiro was called on to pinch hit for Oswalt, but all he could do was bounce a ball up the middle to pitcher Cook, who threw him out.

With two out and the tying run on second base, Biggio, wearing his pine tar and dirt stained Astro batting helmet, strode to the plate. Few times, if ever, in the history of Minute Maid Park was the crowd louder. Had the roof not been closed, drillers on the oil rigs in the Gulf of Mexico might have been able to hear them. Forty-one year old Craig Biggio had played in bigger games, but never a bigger individual moment than what was coming up now. The man who had devoted his entire major league career to the Houston Astros, had raised his family in Houston, had elected to stay with the Astros despite larger monetary offers elsewhere, had devoted hours and hours toward working with the Sunshine Kids in Houston to help them ease the pain of having to battle cancer, the man with over 42,000 fans in the stands and his at-bat to be televised nationally was coming to bat.

Craig Biggio disappointed no one. Working the count to two balls and no strikes Biggio got the one he wanted on the third pitch and drove it into right-center field. It was hit number 3,000 and it drove in Ausmus with the tying run. But Biggio wanted more. Always known for his ability to hit doubles, he thought he could beat the throw from former teammate Willy Taveras to second base and put himself into scoring position with two out. He was wrong and was tagged out by shortstop Troy Tulowitzki. Biggio later emphasized he tried for the double not because it was his signature hit, but to get into scoring position with two out—a sound baseball play. It may have been for the best that he was thrown out, though. The inning was over and Biggio could be rightly honored for what he had just achieved.

In the suite Jeff Bagwell was thrilled. "I'm sitting there and when he got the hit I thought I've got to go see him. I just wanted to go down there and give him a hug. I cried when I went down from the box because I was so freaking happy for him. That's a big deal. I didn't want to be part of it, just to give him a hug in the dugout before he went back on the field."

When the out was recorded at second base, the Astro dugout led by Brad Ausmus raced out to second base. Biggio's wife Patty and daughter Quinn ran onto the field from their box seats while both sons, Cavan and Conor , only had to come out from the dugout. They had been serving as additional batboys for the game. As Patty told MLB.com reporter Alyson Footer, "It was definitely a release. He looked so determined out there tonight. He was super-focused. I didn't move from my seat, didn't stop chewing the gum I was chewing. I didn't do anything different than when he got his first hit." The possible superstition tied to that decision should have been no surprise. Biggio, himself, had many superstitious quirks, although he preferred to refer to them as regular routines or rituals and not superstition. Even so, he never allowed the gunk to be cleaned off his batting helmet. He had a regular warm up schedule and partner before games plus many other routines that caused many of his teammates to call him the most superstitious player on the club. He would not talk about the 3,000 hit drive when he was on his way. That made him a post-game cliché expert in many interviews. Former teammate Ken Caminiti let some of Biggio's secrets out when he revealed, "He's got baseball cards in his back pocket. He's got crosses. He's got a lot of crazy stuff." Craig, of course, like most with superstitions, wouldn't reveal what they were because he always pointed out that everybody has them and it was superstitious to talk about them. Biggio would always point out that if players say they don't have some routines, rituals or superstitions, they are not being truthful.

After the 3,000[th] hit and the outpouring of congratulations from his teammates and family, Biggio moved toward the dugout but stopped near first base, and with the crowd still cheering, motioned to the dugout. He had spotted someone he wanted to share the moment with.

Although trying to wave it off because, as Bagwell later said, "It was Craig's moment," Biggio would have none of that. Biggio had to almost pull Bagwell onto the field. When the crowd saw that, there were a lot of tears in a lot of eyes. Bagwell hugged Biggio and both waved to the crowd.

Later Biggio reflected, "I couldn't have scripted it any better. As a baseball player the way the fans treated me. I've said this for a long time, I love these guys. I love this city. I worked hard here and they appreciated that."

After the season, Biggio retired and the first golden era of Houston Major League Baseball was over. It took a while to get there, and it took two Hall of Famers to lead the way, but Craig Biggio and Jeff Bagwell were up to the task. Houston fans had waited a long time.

2 Houston's Major League Start Is Unimpressive

Courtesy of The Sporting News Archives

"All I know is that I could play on any team on this list."

– Colt 45 General Manager, fifty-three-year old Paul Richards upon seeing the expansion list the Colt 45 and Mets would choose from

Before Craig Biggio and Jeff Bagwell could lead the Houston Astros into multiple postseason appearances and ultimately to a World Series, the original expansion franchise that started with a different name and played in the outdoor heat and humidity of Houston had a long road to ride. And it was bumpy road. Little about the early years was smooth. Major League Baseball was opening up a territory that had to adapt.

How Major League Baseball Got to Houston in the First Place

Cities all over the United States and Canada were growing rapidly after the end of World War II. The big change showed up in the 1960 census. The top five were the same but a city in Texas jumped into the top ten in seventh place with 938,024 citizens. That city was Houston.

There were many other cities that were showing population jumps as well. Yet Major League Baseball in 1950 was playing in the same cities it had been since just after the turn of the century. There were sixteen teams but only ten cities or regions. None of them were further south or west than St. Louis. The New York area had three teams with two in New York proper and the third in Brooklyn, now a borough of New York, but once an independent city. Philadelphia, St. Louis, Chicago, and Boston had two teams each.

In the early 1950s things started to change as franchises left Boston, Philadelphia, and St. Louis for Milwaukee, Kansas City, and Baltimore. After the 1957 season, two teams from New York departed. The Giants to San Francisco and the Brooklyn Dodgers to Los Angeles.

Baseball had more cities and had expanded West for the first time. But there was a void in the nation's most populous city. New York had no team in the National League. Plus, cities like Houston, Minneapolis, Atlanta, Dallas, Denver, and like Montreal and Toronto in Canada were growing rapidly. They were large enough to support Major League Baseball, but how could they get it? For a while a new league, the Continental League, was proposed by longtime baseball executive Branch Rickey. Plans even started to move forward until the current owners in the National and American Leagues decided it might be better to stave off competition by expanding and taking four of the proposed cities into Major League Baseball.

Leaders in Houston led by promoter George Kirksey and oilman Craig Cullinan had long lobbied hard with Major League Baseball for their city to get a shot. In the early 1950s when the St. Louis Cardinals were in a tight financial spot, Houston had been considered a possible new home either for the club to be transferred or sold. Any plans died when August Busch and the Anheuser-Busch brewery bought the team to keep it in St. Louis. It was the St. Louis Browns who would relocate not to Houston, but to Baltimore. The Philadelphia Athletics also moved to Kansas City, but not before Houston had tried to become an option.

Houston Wasn't Really Ready in the 1950s and Barely So When MLB Did Come

In reality Houston would not have been ready for the major leagues in the 1950s. Texas was still linked in tradition with the deep South. That meant Negroes were not allowed in many white establishments including hotels and restaurants, had to use separate drinking fountains and rest rooms, and, as far as athletic events were concerned, had to sit in separate areas. College education, and specifically athletics, were segregated. The top college conference in the region, the Southwest Conference (SWC), was no different than the neighboring Southeastern Conference. No blacks wore the uniforms.

That didn't end until after Major League Baseball had come to Houston in 1962.

Jerry Levias became the first black scholarship athlete in the SWC in 1966. Other schools in the state had opened the doors for black students before then, but few were competing with whites. A circuit of black-only colleges in Texas and neighboring Louisiana, like Texas Southern, Prairie View A&M, Southern, and Grambling were where black students and athletes attended.

Texas Western in El Paso and The University of Houston (UH) were the ground-breaking exceptions to the segregation edicts still strong in many areas of the region. Neither school was a member of the SWC, and thus under no peer pressure to stay all white on the athletic field. At UH, under football coach Bill Yeoman and basketball coach Guy Lewis, an attempt was made by both to integrate their teams a year or two before they actually did. The coaches had met resistance from the administration and alumni. They eventually succeeded in 1964. The school gave the OK to use African American players in intercollegiate teams in November, 1963. To their credit, it was the pros that opened things up first. The American Football League Oilers and the MLB Colt 45s had been using players of mixed race since 1960 and 1962 respectively.

Warren McVea, the top high school running back in the country out of San Antonio came to UH as the school's first star black athlete. He signed a letter of intent on July 11, 1964. Basketball stars Elvin Hayes and Don Chaney from Louisiana both joined the basketball team one year later. Meanwhile at Texas Western (now University of Texas at El Paso—UTEP) basketball coach Don Haskins was working on it as well. He was going all out. He wanted to make his team the best it could be. He started with the freshman class of 1963, but it took a couple of years before he got his anchor in the middle. He found a big man in Houston in David Lattin. Lattin was a player Lewis had wanted for the University of Houston, but he could not get him admitted. Lattin actually first enrolled at Tennessee State in 1963, but left to play AAU basketball before signing to play at

Texas Western. The rest of Haskins's team would come from all over the country. Most of them were black.

Even though Major League Baseball had only been played in Houston since 1962, the Minor League Houston Buffs had featured black players since Bob Boyd joined the team on May 27, 1954. That, however, was not really something to be proud of. Major League Baseball had integrated seven years earlier. Houston was hardly a leader. When Boyd played his first game in Houston, black fans were still relegated to a section down the right field line and a special entrance into the park. That would not change for the Houston minor league team. The last season the team played— one year before the Houston Colt 45s joined Major League Baseball—it was segregation as usual at Buff Stadium. Baseball had integrated, even if some of the fans were not allowed to.

Even so, professional sports were still years ahead of some colleges— especially in the South. A team from Loyola of Chicago, which featured black stars and mostly African American teams, had won the NCAA Men's Basketball tournament in 1963. Black players had been integrated into most Northern or Western based college leagues for decades. Haskins's 1965-66 Texas Western basketball team would open the door much wider for racial integration in sports in Texas and ultimately in the South.

The integrated Texas Western Miners beat the all-white Kentucky Wildcats in the final game of the 1966 NCAA Tournament. Haskins had some white players on the team, but beat the Wildcats using only his black players. Kentucky represented the best of the past. Texas Western showed that times needed to change for the whole country. Cities in the Northern Midwest and East where baseball had existed on the major league level since the turn of the nineteenth century had learned that when Jackie Robinson broke the color line in 1947. Now it was the South's turn.

Major League Baseball had not had to deal with different racial laws or customs in the South until Robinson came on the scene. All the players before had been white. When Robinson broke the color line the restrictions against African Americans were something they had to deal with during spring training which had been focused in Florida for years.

At first, segregation laws were followed. Black players were separated from their white teammate with separate lodging and dining arrangements. Over time and with the pressure of communities possibly losing the profitable spring training, business things loosened.

With that history in mind, the people behind the move to get Houston into the major leagues had to lay some ground work. Segregation was the rule and not the exception all over the South when George Kirksey and Craig Cullinan started the campaign to bring the major leagues to the city that would, by the 1960 census, be seventh largest in the country. If Houston was going to join the great cities in the country, it couldn't just be due to population growth. The tradition of segregation had to be dealt with. The city, like most in the South even as far north as Dallas was still segregated in many ways. Houston joined the American Football League in 1960—two years before the Colt 45s would bring Major League Baseball to the city. As football Hall of Famer Ernie Ladd remembered from his 1961 rookie year with the San Diego Chargers, "We went into Houston my first year and the African Americans were still sitting only in the end zones. There was a black sportswriter, Lloyd Wells, who was calling us every name in the book because we went ahead and played with our brothers and sisters sitting in the end zone."

Jack Kemp was the star quarterback for the Los Angeles Chargers who played the Oilers in the first AFL Championship game played in Houston after the 1960 season. He remembered, "My father came to the 1960 championship game in Houston. My dad sat on the 45-yard line and the black families had to sit in the roped-off part. Black guys were sitting outside the stadium telling the black athletes not to play. My heart went out to those guys. They were going to play, but you know they had concerns having their parents sit in the roped off part of the end zone while my dad was sitting at the 45-yard line." The memories of both Ladd and Kemp were recorded in the book *Going Long* by Jeff Miller.

Houston did get some measure of respect when Bud Adams rescued the 1964 AFL All-Star game after racial restrictions and attitudes in New Orleans had caused the black players—with the support of their white teammates—to declare they would not play the game scheduled for Tulane Stadium. New Orleans was not a major sports city at that time, and the AFL had decided to play the game there as a possible prelude to putting a team in the city as an expansion or a relocation. The Oakland Raiders had been considering the possibility. When the players strike cancelled the game, Bud Adams accepted the challenge to host in Houston. Most players had returned home after the New Orleans game was cancelled, but all were tracked down and told to report to Houston the following weekend and the game would be played. Houston fans were not standing in line for tickets.

On January 16, 1964 only 15,446 fans were in the gathering at Jeppesen Stadium on the University of Houston campus to see the West beat the East 38-14. Houston, at least, had come a long way since the AFL started and Major League Baseball had come to town.

The racial situation in the South was apparently not a major concern of those in baseball that had sought to add Houston when expansion of MLB was considered. However, Houston leaders took care of a major possible problem themselves just in the nick of time. For the complete story, however, it must be pointed out the city was still a long way from being integrated. While the city administration had ended discrimination in all city-owned buildings about a month after the Colt 45s started playing—and almost two years after the Oilers had already started—it would be years before the schools were integrated and other walls were torn down. Less than a year before the Harris County Dome Stadium opened, Rice University finally was given the right to admit black students after the original charter set down by the school's founder was amended.

As reported in Robert Reed's book, *A Six-Gun Salute*, the franchise's opening game was less than two weeks away in 1962 when the major hotels in Houston dropped their whites-only policies. The move was started by TV-Radio executive Jack Harris, who asked Colt 45 owner Roy Hofheinz what would happen when teams with top black players would have to send those players to stay in separate hotels? Houston Chronicle publisher John T. Jones, whose Houston Endowment also owned three major hotels, jumped on board. On April 1, 1962 hotels in Houston were opened to all races. The first Opening Day was only ten days away. Such was the power of the Major Leagues. The American Football League had no such pull and for years Minor League Baseball had been played in Houston with a number of black players who had to deal with segregation. Their major league counterparts would not have to.

Houston Got the First Expansion Team since 1900

When major league baseball made its debut in Houston in 1962 with the expansion Colt 45s, it was a big deal, but attendance records were not in jeopardy. The first team had to play for three seasons in roofless open-air Colt Stadium adjacent to where the Harris County Domed Stadium (known eventually as the Astrodome) was being built. That meant it was very hot and humid during most games from June through early September. When it wasn't hot and humid, it was wet. Then there were the mosquitos! It was no joke that swatting mosquitos in the stands and on the field created more action than many games. The original Colt 45s set a standard Houston teams would follow for most of their first thirty-five years. Good pitching, but little hitting and thus less action than many fans would have preferred. The team hit only .246 with the league's fewest runs, homerun, and stolen base totals in the league while the pitchers' 3.83 earned run average was coupled with a league-best fewest homeruns allowed and second best 1047 strikeouts. Largely because of the lack of comfort, the excitement of being in the major leagues wore off quickly and only 924,456 fans actually saw the Colt 45s play during their 81 game home schedule. That was only seventh best in the ten-team league.

That first team actually performed better than prognosticators had guessed. They finished eighth in the ten-team National League, besting both the Cubs and fellow newcomers the New York Mets.

The two teams had been built in very different ways. The Colt 45s tried to go with as many young players as possible. The Mets, in the same market at the Yankees, went much more heavily with veterans. Former Dodgers like Gil Hodges, Don Zimmer, Roger Craig, Joe Pignatano, Clem Labine and Charlie Neal were on the roster at one time or another. Former National League stars from other teams like Vinegar Bend Mizell, Richie Ashburn, Gus Bell, Hobie Landrith, Frank Thomas, Ed Bouchee, and Felix Mantilla were also Mets that first year.

Most of those names are forgotten now, but in 1962 every baseball fan in New York knew who all of them were. The plan didn't pack the park. The old Polo Grounds drew only 922,530 fans from the country's largest city. The Mets won 40 and lost 120. The Mets couldn't hit or pitch.

Meanwhile the Colt 45s had a large number of "who's he's" on the field. Harry Craft managed a team with few former big stars, although a few players of note. Norm Larker had been a high average hitter in Los Angeles with the Dodgers. Joey Amalfitano had been a bonus baby signee of the New York Giants. Johnny Temple had been an all-star in Cincinnati. Hal Smith had hit a big homerun for the Pirates in their 1960 World Series win over the Yankees. Bob Lillis and Bob Aspromonte had been young Dodgers and top farm hands. There were no superstars in the making on either team. Still, the Astros were a lot better. They won 24 more games than the Mets.

Standing in a Swamp

The last two seasons playing at Colt 45 Stadium, the club regressed in support with the club not able to draw more than 725,773 in a season. The team was also not improving. They lost the same 96 games each year playing outdoors. There were a few highlights, though. On May 17, 1963, Don Nottebart pitched the franchise's first no-hitter when he beat the Philadelphia Phillies 4-1. The next season, 1964, pitcher Ken Johnson pitched the second no-hitter for Houston. His, however, is far more remembered because he lost the game! The Reds beat Ken 1-0 on April 23 when they scored a run thanks to two errors in the top of the ninth. Johnson made the first on a ball hit by Pete Rose. Then with two out, future Hall of Famer Nellie Fox made the second that allowed the run. The Colt 45s were retired in the last of the ninth as Joe Nuxhall got the complete game win. He gave up five hits, but no runs. Johnson gave up no hits and only one unearned run. He had pitched a no-hitter, but lost. Not many fans witnessed this historic game. The attendance at Colt Stadium was listed as only 5,426.

In 1964, the last season as the Colt 45s, the club had gone from a veteran somewhat-over-the-hill based team to a much younger group. Newcomers like Joe Morgan, Rusty Staub, Jimmy Wynn, and Jerry Grote were starting to get some playing time. The pitchers were generally much older, but seventeen-year-old Larry Dierker got into three games. Fellow youngsters who would spend several years in the majors like Chris Zachary, Dave Giusti, and Danny Coombs also got their first action.

Morgan, of course, was traded to the Reds on November 29, 1971, where he was a key part of the Big Red Machine and earned a Hall of Fame Induction. Had he been able to achieve the same in Houston, there is little doubt he would have been remembered as one of the Astros' top all time stars and first Hall of Famer. That nod would go to another second baseman who would join Houston nearly seventeen years after Morgan had moved to Cincinnati—Craig Biggio. Jimmy Wynn was the Houston all-time homerun leader for years until another familiar name broke and then shattered his mark. That man was Jeff Bagwell.

The Colt 45s developed some players that played major roles in Major League Baseball, but mostly for other clubs. Rusty Staub was a great Houston player, but when he was dealt to the Expos in 1969, he became an ever greater player the rest of his career. Jerry Grote caught the Mets outstanding World Series champion staff in 1969. Meanwhile the Houston franchise continued to struggle. In 1965 the focus left the team and to its new name and home. Good-bye Houston Colt 45s and Colt stadium. Hello eighth Wonder of the World as the Harris County Domed Stadium opened to host the newly re-named Houston Astros.

During the Colt 45 years, there is little doubt that "Mr. Colt 45" was third baseman Bob Aspromonte. After starting his career in the Brooklyn Dodger system, he was acquired in the expansion draft prior to the 1962 season. He was a fixture at third base from the first game through the 1968 season. Bob was a superb defensive third baseman, but only a middling hitter. He only hit 51 homeruns during seven seasons in Houston, but it was his homerun hitting feats that made him a Houston baseball legend.

The legend was born in the Colt 45s' first season when Aspromonte heard of a young boy from Arkansas who had been moved to a Houston hospital for treatment after being blinded in an accident that started after a lightning strike. The youngster, Billy Bradley, had listened to Colt 45 games on the radio and wanted to meet his hero. Billy had one of his parents call the team office and asked if Bob could visit him. Aspro picked up some souvenirs and headed to the hospital before he had to report to Colt Stadium for the game that night.

Upon preparing to leave for the park, Billy asked Bob to hit a homerun for him that night. That was a request normally reserved for people who might be able to do it like Willie Mays, Eddie Mathews or Mickey Mantle, but Bob hit one! He wasn't a homerun hitter at all, so being able to fulfill Billy's wish was amazing to Aspromonte.

But the story did not end there. Both Bob and Billy kept in touch through exchanges of letters. The next year, Billy was back in Houston for follow up treatment. Bob visited again and the same request was made. Aspromonte knew the odds against his being able to homer again after Billy's request were great. But he beat them. This time Bob Aspromonte hit a grand slam homerun. Billy Bradley's wishes had been answered two seasons in a row!

As a result of all the treatments, by July 26, 1964 Billy Bradley had regained some of his eye sight and was able to visit Colt Stadium to see Bob Aspromonte and the Colt 45s in person. Guess what Billy asked for when he renewed acquaintances with Bob before the game?

This time, Bob thought they may be stretching their luck too much. Not only was he currently in a slump, but homering in three games in a row after a request by Billy Bradley? "How about a couple of hits, Billy?" suggested Bob.

In the first inning with the bases loaded, Bob Aspromonte hit another grand slam homerun. Billy Bradley had his request honored for the third time!

By now everyone in Houston knew of the Bradley-Aspromonte relationship. After Aspro crossed the plate the game was actually stopped so he and Billy could embrace and Billy could be presented the ball. As Bob remembered in an article published by MLB.com in 2012, "As I'm crying and everyone is going crazy, I gave him the ball. You should have seen his reaction. What a spark of life came over that kid."

That wasn't the end of the story. A year or so later, after Billy had regained enough of his sight to resume playing baseball himself, Aspromonte received an envelope in the mail that contained a newspaper clipping. Attached was a note. The clipping told the story of Billy Bradley pitching a no-hitter in a Little League game. The note read, "This one's for you, Bob."

3 The Dome Starts a Change

Jet Lowe courtesy of the Library of Congress

"Not even Jules Verne or Walt Disney in their most fantastic moments of genius ever conceived anything like this unbelievable palace of baseball luxury."

– John Steadman, Baltimore News-American,
after seeing the Astrodome in 1965

In 1965 a man named Joseph Licklider saw an idea he conceived in 1962 become a reality when the Intergalactic Computer Network was established. It was the forerunner for the World Wide Web. CBS television dominated television viewership with six of the top ten shows aired on that network. *Gomer Pyle*, *The Lucy Show*, *Red Skelton*, *Andy Griffith*, *The Beverly Hillbillies* and *Hogan's Heroes* made up that number.

NBC had the top rated show, however, with *Bonanza*. It was the network's only top ten program. ABC had both Batman shows and *Bewitched*.

Most mid-sized and small cities were lucky to have three televisions stations. Cable television was in its infancy with its prime role to bring in stations to areas that could not pick up standard signals out of the air due to distance. No one had launched any broadcast satellites yet.

Baseball was limited to weekend games from all three networks. CBS showed Yankee games nation-wide on Saturdays in the last year of a Game of the Week around since 1955. CBS had purchased the Yankees in 1965, so those were the only games aired that year. On NBC, a true national game of the week featuring more teams was aired, and ABC even did a game of the week normally from the west coast. Few fans outside Major League markets could see their favorite team very often. Only Chicago and New York featured heavy television schedules. In Houston, only a relative handful of games were shown on KPRC-TV. The emphasis was still on radio.

The British invasion of pop music was strong with the Beatles, Rolling Stones, Dave Clark Five, and Herman's Hermits dominating.

In world news, the first U.S. combat troops entered Vietnam, more than 2,600 including Dr. Martin Luther King were arrested in Selma, Alabama, after demonstrating against voter registration rules, the unemployment levels were at 5.2%, and a postage stamp cost only 5¢!

But what happened in Houston was big news in its own right. The Harris County Domed Stadium was opened in April of 1965.

The Dome Was Truly a Wonder of the World

Although the Houston Colt 45s had finished their last season in Colt Stadium very unimpressively with a tenth place finish after a 66-96 record, an awful .229 team batting average and a league low in runs scored, hits, and homeruns, there was still excitement in Houston.

It had almost nothing to do with the team's actual prospects for 1965, but for the opening of their new home, The Harris County Domed Stadium. It was the dream of team owner Roy Hofheinz. Hofheinz had joined the drive to get the major leagues to Houston with big ideas. Without his big ideas, how soon Houston would have nailed down a big league slot would have been in doubt. When approached by Kirksey and Cullinan, the former Houston Mayor and judge knew nothing about baseball. So he started reading everything about it he could find. He also decided that if Major League Baseball was going to make it in Houston, a whole new concept for a stadium had to be considered. The city needed an indoor air-conditioned place. That was the beginning of the Astrodome, which was on display in model form when the Astros talked with Major League owners during their attempts to get a team in the city. If George Kirksey and

Craig Cullinan were the foot soldiers in getting the major leagues to Houston, it was Hofheinz and Bob Smith that brought the brains and money for getting it done. Hofheinz had the dream and plans for the Astrodome, which set his city apart from all of the other cities who wanted to join the Major League Baseball fraternity. Smith had the land and most of the private money behind the plan. In addition, it was hard to find a single city leader or politician that was not solidly behind making Houston a Major League Baseball city. Still the domed stadium was Hofheinz's baby. The vote to build the dome and thus assure Houston a major league franchise was no slam dunk. It passed 51% to 49% but would have not made it had the county had not gotten the black population behind the effort. They did it by promising the days of segregation in both Colt Stadium and, later, the Dome were over. Countless town meetings and a significant number of private meetings convinced a majority of the black community to support the building of the Dome, which assured MLB of coming to the city.

The Dome Would Sell 'Em First—Astros Would Not

Soon to be unofficially re-dubbed the Houston Astrodome for the team's new name, Houston Astros, the building truly was the eighth Wonder of the World. It was the first indoor sports facility in the world to be large enough to hold traditionally outdoor sports. (Pittsburgh's Civic Arena already had a retractable roof, but it was sized for traditional indoor sports like hockey and basketball.) Houston's stadium would not only be huge, with a seating capacity ranging from 45,000 to 62,000 depending on use, but it would have more features than any stadium, with a roof or not, had ever had. From luxury suites to moving seating sections with theatre style cushioned seats to changing the configuration from baseball to football in minutes, the Domed Stadium had them. Special restaurants and even the private quarters that Roy Hofheinz called home made the stadium something everyone just had to see. The pro football Oilers would not move into the Astrodome until 1968 as owner, Bud Adams, who had been on the original board of directors with the Colt 45s, had major disagreements with the Houston Sports Association over rental terms. He was quoted as saying, "The Astrodome is the eighth Wonder of the World and the lease terms are the ninth."

The stadium was built about six miles just to the south and west of downtown in an undeveloped area except for the temporary Colt Stadium. The area was actually swampy and did not drain well. When finished, it stood in the middle of a large parking lot looking not unlike a visiting air ship from outer space.

From the opening five-game exhibition series with the Yankees and Orioles when more than 200,000 fans were introduced to the Astrodome throughout the entire season, the building was the show, not the team. Joe Morgan hit the Dome's first homerun in an exhibition game against the team's Oklahoma City farm club. The first homerun hit in an exhibition game between two major league teams was hit by Mickey Mantle of the New York Yankees a day later. Philadelphia star Rich Allen hit the first homerun in a regular league game. As 2,151,470 fans passed through the Dome during games—second best in the NL—the club was losing one more game than had the last three teams that called Colt Stadium home. The Astrodome debuted with a 65-97 baseball team, ninth in the NL.

No one hit .300. Jim Wynn's .275 was the best, as were his twenty-two homeruns. Twenty-one-year old Joe Morgan became the regular at second base and hit .271 with 14 homers and a team-high 20 stolen bases. Fellow twenty-one-year old Rusty Staub also hit fourteen homeruns. The whole team only hit 97, which was ninth in the ten team league.

The Astrodome was cavernous with no wind, but air conditioning that made the place feel cold for many spectators and contributed to the dead air. The field was natural grass, but not for long. Both pitching and hitting marks were somewhat scarily similar to the numbers achieved with Colt Stadium. Even though playing in the air-conditioned building was far more comfortable, the Dome was not hurting or helping the team play better in comparison. At least more fans were in the seats. The field looked awful and fielders lost balls hit in the air during day games. The ceiling had skylights and the ball would get lost in the grid of the supports. So it was decided to paint over the sky lights in line with the normal path of batted balls. That lowered the amount of sunshine entering and the grass got worse. The grass growing problems were solved with the installation of what was called Astro-turf, and playing baseball indoors—especially in the parts of the country where the weather could be a problem---was being considered elsewhere. The Astrodome was simply the first stadium of its kind in the world!

Something happened after the 1965 season that would have major significance to Houston Astro baseball in the future. Craig Alan Biggio was born on December 14, 1965 in Smithtown, NY, the third child of Gordon Lee and Johnna Biggio. His father was a big Yankee fan. That would change twenty years later.

Star players on teams are somewhat relative. The best Colt 45 or Astro may have been the best on their teams, but not among the elite in the League. The Astros did have two future Hall of Famers in the lineup in 1967. One was thirty-five-year-old Eddie Mathews, who earned his Hall of Fame credentials during his career with the Braves. With the Astros he hit only .238 with ten homeruns and 38 RBIs that season. However, he did reach a career milestone as an Astro when he hit his 500th homerun off the Giants' Juan Marichal on July 14, 1967 at San Francisco's Candlestick Park. Mathews was a big name player, but no longer an all-star and near the end of his playing life. He would hit only twelve more homers in his career. The other future Hall of Famer, Joe Morgan, was in his third full season with the Astros. His fame would come later.

There were two bigger stories for the Astros in 1967. Jimmy Wynn battled Hank Aaron for the NL homerun title before being nipped by two long balls. Wynn, playing half his games in the cavernous dead -air Astrodome, hit 37. Aaron, in the launching pad that was Atlanta Fulton County Stadium, hit 39. Wynn hit 15 of his 37 homeruns at home. Aaron hit 23 of his 39 at home.

Midway through the 1967 season, Spec Richardson replaced Tal Smith as General Manager of the club. It was not a smooth run for Richardson. Hofheinz was running into financial troubles and there wasn't much cash to spend to improve the team. Attendance had dropped off. By 1975 General Electric and the Ford Motor Credit Companies took over. That would remain the case until John McMullen stepped in to buy the assets in 1979. When the credit companies took over Richardson was let go and Tal Smith returned from the New York Yankees where he had been serving under Gabe Paul who had brought him to Houston originally from Cincinnati when the Colt 45s were being formed. Smith's job would be to guide the franchise until a new owner could be found. Money was short, but Smith started to re-build the club. By the time McMullen bought the franchise, there finally was a light at the end of the tunnel.

Meanwhile, with all that going on in the background, the ball club did the best it could. In the early years of the Houston franchise, young players like Bob Aspromonte and Joe Morgan were good and so were Jimmy Wynn, Cesar Cedeno, Bob Watson, and Rusty Staub. Cedeno had Hall of

Fame raw potential, but while he lasted in the major leagues for seventeen years, his biggest years were over before he was twenty-four. Morgan was a future Hall of Famer, but he would not show it until he was traded to Cincinnati after the 1971 season.

You could include pitchers Don Wilson, who authored two no-hitters but died young in a carbon monoxide incident at his home, Dave Giusti, and young Larry Dierker, but none of those players were among the elite of major league baseball yet. They were good for Houston, but not great in the early to mid-1960s.

The Team Was Better before the '60's Were Over

It would not be until 1969 that Houston fans would have a team that lost fewer than 90 games. Harry Walker was brought on to manage midway through the previous season. He replaced Grady Hatton, who still was in charge on May 27, 1968. Perhaps it was an omen that better offense was coming that day as the Astros crushed the Dodgers 10-1. Jimmy Wynn, Rusty Staub, and Ron Davis had three hits each. Bob Watson had two. Wynn drove in three in the game at the Dome. The better offense promised would not come the next night since the Astros would only score one run at Atlanta.

However, it was also on May 27, 1968 when Jeffrey Robert Bagwell was born in Boston to Robert and Janice Bagwell. It would be Bagwell bringing the offense to Houston. Astro fans would just have to wait until 1991. The Bagwells in 1968 were big Boston Red Sox Fans. Ironic, isn't it, that families of two heated rivals—the Biggios in New York and the Bagwells in Boston—would raise sons later to become teammates, friends, leaders, and Hall of Famers for a somewhat unknown team way down in Texas called the Houston Astros.

Houston finally reached .500 for the first time in 1969, thanks in large part to the play of Jimmy Wynn. The "Toy Cannon" ripped 33 homeruns while accumulating 148 walks. That led him to a .436 on base percentage despite only a .269 batting average. That single season walk total is still among the top 20 all time. Future Astro Jeff Bagwell would break the Wynn team record with 149 walks in 1999. Larry Dierker won 20 games and Don Wilson added 16. Even so, it would still take more time for the club to show a real shot at pennant contention. The first seven years of the franchise never saw a team with a win-loss percentage of better than .444.

Astros Gained National Notice in 1970 Thanks to Jim Bouton

In 1969 the Astros acquired pitcher Jim Bouton from the Seattle Pilots in a late August trade. The Astros were in a pennant race. When they brought in Bouton, they were only 2 ½ games out of first place. As a pitcher, he didn't help the club that much. He did pitch a complete game in his only start, but overall was 0-2 in 16 games with a 4.11 ERA. The Astros would fade down the stretch, but still finish 81-81, reaching .500 for the first time in franchise history.

What Bouton did was make the team more well known. That season was the year he was writing his famous tell-all book about baseball, *Ball Four*. How much "inside" was the book about the Astros? Consider this excerpt from Bouton's first ride on the team bus after joining the team:

"I hadn't been on the bus two minutes when the players started warning me about manager Harry Walker, Harry the Hat. Before the day was over, half the club had whispered in my ear, 'Don't let Harry bother you.'

'Harry is really a beauty.'

'Harry's going to scream. He screams all the time. He's going to scream at you. Try to keep from laughing if you can.'

'Half a dozen guys have wanted to punch him.'

'When he starts shouting at you, restrain yourself and be patient. After a while you'll learn to understand him and live with him.'

'We've all adjusted to him, and you can too.'"

That memory was only part of the Astro-exposé portion of the book. It went far more inside the team than baseball preferred, but fans loved the book. And Astro stories were in the same volume as stories from Bouton's New York Yankee days. For a team that would reach only a .500 record for the first time that season, it was like hitting the big time.

It wouldn't be until 1972 that the Astros would finally break past the .500 point and win more than they lost. Walker had the team at 67-54, but nine games off the lead. He was fired and Leo Durocher came in to finish up, see the team finish at 84-69, and manage again in 1973. The 1973 Astros dropped back to 82-80, and Durocher parted. Preston Gomez managed the team in 1974 to a .500 record, then the wheels fell off in 1975.

Bill Virdon came in during the season with the Astros 38 games out of first place.

Virdon Gave Astros a Strong Manager

Things would start to get better after Bill Virdon was hired to manage the club at the end of 1975, just not immediately.

Virdon had a tough job when he arrived. The original owners of the Astros had either departed or had mismanaged the franchise. Judge Roy Hofheinz had lost interest as the team floundered and got more expensive to run. Always the showman, he even purchased the Ringling Brothers-Barnum and Bailey circus. In addition to his other interests, his health started to fail, starting with a stroke, and by the mid-70s—about when club President Tal Smith brought in Virdon to run the baseball team—the team had been turned over to its creditors. Improvements to the Astrodome were put on hold unless the landlord, Harris Country, could do them. Attendance dropped under 900-thousand a year in both 1975 and 1976. Smith had limited funds to work with so the plan was put in place to build a young team from players mostly developed in the farm system and, when ready, give them to Virdon for finishing school.

That process was underway when the team creditors finally found a buyer. No one in Houston, Texas or the whole region wanted to buy the team. But Dr. John McMullen, a resident of the New York/New Jersey area, did. The maritime businessman and trained naval engineer had been involved in baseball as a minority partner with George Steinbrenner's New York Yankees. That experience whetted his appetite for more input. As McMullan was widely quoted, "Nothing is more limited than being a limited partner of George Steinbrenner."

McMullen bought the team and lease to the Astrodome for $19-million on May 10, 1979. Thanks to the ground work laid during the poverty years by Smith and his staff, it wouldn't be long before McMullen would see his new team have its first ever success.

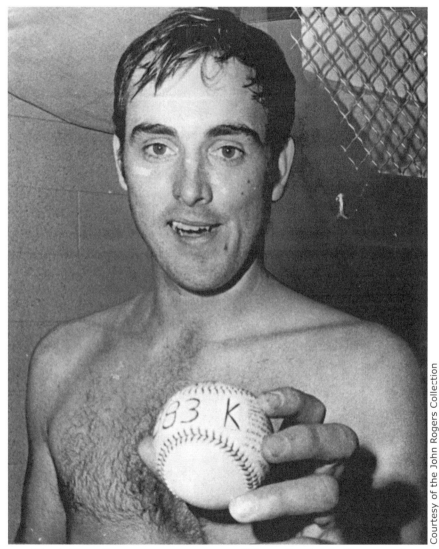

4 Astros Taste First Success in 1980

Courtesy of the John Rogers Collection

"Back then it was one power guy (Glenn Davis) built around a bunch of little scatter hitters and guys who made contact and run and hit and throw."

– Astro outfielder Kevin Bass on the Astro offensive style in the '80s, with Nolan Ryan pitching

In 1980 the big sports stories were the U.S. hockey team's win over the Soviet Union and ensuing gold medal win at the Winter Olympics in Lake Placid, then the decision to boycott the summer games in Moscow because of the Soviet Union's move into Afghanistan. The first true cell phone system was established in Tokyo the year before, but wouldn't hit the United States for three more years. Cable television had grown to 16-million subscribers and CNN was started.

In the news, 1980 was the year the world lost the first Beatle as John Lennon was shot and murdered in New York. It was also the year Mt. St. Helen's erupted in the Pacific Northwest, taking 57 lives and leaving ash over much of the Western United States.

It was also the year the Houston Astros would finally win a division title. An offseason decision by the team's owner went a long way toward making that happen.

Nolan Ryan Came Back home

Prior to the 1980 season with Bill Virdon in charge, and coming off an 89-73 record only one game off the NL West leader, team owner John McMullen decided to open the payroll and sign Houston area native, pitcher Nolan Ryan, as a free agent. Ryan had attended games at both Colt Stadium and the Astrodome while growing up in nearby Alvin. Signed by scout Red Murff for the New York Mets, Ryan appeared in the 1969 World Series before being sent to the California Angels after the 1971 season. In eight years with the Angels he won 138 and lost 121 without much offensive support. His earned run average during those eight seasons was a miserly 3.07 and he pitched four no hitters. Before leaving as a free agent to the Astros, he had seen his ERA jump to 3.72 and 3.60 his last two seasons and was now thirty-three years old. The Angels didn't want to meet Ryan's salary asking price at his age and with two subpar seasons behind him. McMullen took a chance and signed Ryan to a then record contract calling for more than one-million dollars a year. It turned out to be a wise move.

Astro Pitching Was Solid in 1980

Adding Ryan to a starting rotation that included fire-baller J.R. Richard, Joe Niekro, and Ken Forsch helped push the team into its first postseason. Ryan didn't get much offensive support in Houston either, but he led the NL in earned run average twice, threw his record breaking fifth no-hitter, and was 106-94, 3.13 in nine Astro years. The Astros finally won their first title—the National League West—by one game in a playoff over the Los Angeles Dodgers in 1980.

Art Howe was a key member of that team. "In '79 we had come real close. We had been leading most of the year, but let it get away at the end of the year. Nineteen-eighty was the year everything came together. Great teammates. It was the most fun I ever had as a player. It took us an extra day to do it, but we finally won our first division title which for me made it more special."

The playoff was needed after the Astros lost three straight games to the Dodgers in the final series of the season in Los Angeles. The Astros lost a three game lead in three days. In the playoff, Joe Niekro won his 20th game in pitching a complete game 7-1 victory. The extra game was extra special for Howe since he had three hits, and four runs batted in, half of them on a two-run homer in the third inning.

The Astros were able to win the pennant despite Richard suffering a career-ending stroke at mid-season. J.R. had a 10-4 record with a 1.90 earned run average before he was sidelined after 17 starts. "We all felt that if he hadn't had the stroke we'd be wearing several rings by now," remembered Howe. The club finished 93-70 and battled the Philadelphia Phillies on one of the best playoff series of all time. The Phillies won in five games. Four of the five went extra innings. Greg Luzinski of the Phillies hit the only homerun for either team in fifty innings of play.

During the 1980 season, the Astros had superb pitching, which was a Houston trait almost every year. In 1980 the team ERA was a major league best 3.10. The hitters were better than in the early years with a .261 average, but last in the NL with only 75 homeruns. The team had five players with double figure homers, but only Terry Puhl had as many as 13.

"We played small ball. We played the game right," continued Howe years later. "I remember Bill [Virdon] would have Craig Reynolds hitting second. If the lead-off guy got on in the first inning, he'd bunt 'em over. Cedeno would then drive him in and we'd be up 1-0 in the first. With our pitching we had lots of games we never lost that lead. If we got a 1-0 lead the other team was in trouble. With our rotation, it was tough to score at all, let alone the two runs needed to beat us. We had 'em behind the 8-ball right away. Especially playing in the Dome you had to play small ball. We worked on bunting. Everyone in the lineup knew how to bunt and to move runners. That's why it was such a special team because everybody sacrificed a little something for each other to win that year."

All was not happy, however. McMullen and the man who had been running the shop before his ownership, Tal Smith, had a falling out. Smith was fired. Former Cleveland Indian All-Star third baseman, successful businessman, and President of the New York Yankees, Al Rosen, came in to take over.

Player Union vs Ownership Battle Shortened 1981

The next season, 1981, the Astros were involved in a split season due to a player strike. They didn't play well at all in the first half. They lost eight of their first ten games. They finished 28-29. Then they won the second half with a 33-20 record, but despite being only third overall, made the postseason when a decision was made to match the two half season champions in the first round of the postseason. Ironically, the Cincinnati Reds had the best overall record of teams in the NL West, but didn't win either half and were not in the postseason.

The Astros were again lacking in power with only 45 homers in the 110 game season. That was 11th in the now 12 team NL. The team average was .257, good for fifth in the league, but runs scored were ninth. Again pitching made the Astros a winner. On September 26, Nolan Ryan pitched a record fifth no-hitter against the Los Angeles Dodgers in an NBC-TV national "Game of the Week" telecast. (Ryan would later pitch two more no-hitters for the Texas Rangers.) The team earned run average was an amazingly low 2.66.

The postseason was a major disappointment. Houston won the first two games in the best of five with the Dodgers, then lost three straight. Astro pitching held the Dodgers to a .198 mark, but Houston averaged only .175. Dodger pitching registered a 1.17 earned run average. The Astros' number was 2.45.

Astros Dump Winningest Manager after 1982

The Astros floundered in 1982, dropping to 77-85 and Bill Virdon was fired during the season and replaced by coach and former Colt 45 infielder Bob Lillis. Total lack of power on the team did in Virdon. The Astros hit only 74 homeruns. Phil Garner, with only 13 homeruns, led the team. Lillis guided the team to two winning seasons in the three he was on the job, but the club was not a contender. The club was 276-261 during his tenure.

During the years that John McMullen owned the Astros, a pattern seemed to evolve regarding his managerial hires. If he had a tough no-nonsense skipper and it was time to make a change, he tended to go to a more even-handed, players-type manager the next time. Virdon had been actually a little of both, but was perceived as a no-nonsense tough guy. He left with the most wins (544) in Houston history and a .510 winning percentage. He would hold that mark for many years. Lillis was softer. He had been an original Houston major league player with the Colt 45s in 1962.

The reality was that most players were able to adapt to whoever was in charge. Sometimes teams just didn't get the job done and the owner thought some changes were needed. Changing all the players couldn't be done. It was much easier to change managers. McMullen and his general managers did.

Lillis was originally named "interim" manager and remained that way till the end of the season. He was not owner John McMullen's first choice to be the head man in 1983. First offered the job was Joe Morgan. McMullen offered the future Hall of Famer the job for the 1983 season, but he wanted to sleep on it. "I gave the offer a great deal of thought," Morgan remembered in *Joe Morgan: A Life in Baseball*. "I asked my father, my wife, and Sparky (Anderson) what they thought. They all advised to take the job."

But he didn't accept the offer after conferring with Billy Williams, who asked him to only accept it if playing was out of his blood. When Morgan decided it wasn't yet, he told McMullen the next morning he would have to pass on the offer.

The Astros then removed "interim" from Bob Lillis's job description. He was the man for 1983.

Then Lillis took the team to an 83-79 record in 1985 in his fourth full season, but owner McMullan was not satisfied and decided that wasn't good enough for the talent on hand. He made another change. In came the fiery and very demanding Hal Lanier for 1986.

Astros in 1986—Houston's Best for Franchise's First Thirty-Five Years

The 1986 Astros turned out to be the strongest Houston team to that point, and the best the team would put on the field for the next twelve years. It would also be the last postseason team until the Biggio-Bagwell era would take over.

Although on a pitch count limit to preserve his thirty-nine-year old elbow, which was hanging on almost literally by the thread of a ligament, Nolan Ryan went 12-8 with a 3.34 ERA in only 178 innings—the fewest he had thrown in a full non-strike season since his last year with the Mets in 1971.

Ryan wasn't the top gun in 1986. Mike Scott won eighteen games, led the National League in earned run average, innings pitched, shutouts, and strikeouts. He also pitched a no-hitter in the game at the Astrodome that clinched the National League West title. He was named the Cy Young Award winner—the first of only three in Houston history. Roger Clemens would win in the NL in 2004. Dallas Keuchel would later win the award in 2015 for the Astros, who were then an American League franchise.

The 1986 Astros won 96 and lost 66. They won the NL West by ten games. The Mets would keep them from the World Series, but like the series with the Phillies in 1980 it would be remembered as one of the best and most exciting in baseball history. While none of the players on the 1986 Astros would still be around when the real "Golden Era" would start in 1994, many would still be around when both Craig Biggio and Jeff Bagwell broke in with the team.

In 1986 Craig Biggio was playing his sophomore season at Seton Hall University. He had developed from "the worst defensive catcher I have ever seen," as his coach Mike Sheppard remembered, into All-Big East during that year. He was not yet considered a significant major league prospect, but if he ever was, his dreams were with the Yankees.

In the meantime, Jeff Bagwell, only eighteen years old, was about to start his first year as a baseball scholarship athlete at the University of Hartford. He went to school as a shortstop, but was converted to third base by coach Bill Denehy. Jeff thought of being on his favored Red Sox someday. As a hitter, he copied many mannerisms of his favorite player, Carl Yasztremski, including altering his stance at times. Bagwell was also an outstanding soccer player and had offers to play that sport in college. "It was not really a viable option for me to play soccer. I was good because I was aggressive, but there was no future in that, although I probably did get more offers to play soccer than baseball. It was fun, but that was not where I was going with myself," Bagwell told Bill Brown in 2010.

Meanwhile, the Astros were looking good in 1986, even if they again failed to make it all the way to the Series. But the next season the wheels fell off. The 96-win team of 1986 dropped from 30 games over .500 to 76 wins and ten games under .500. Age may have made it happen.

1987 Was Not as Much Fun, but the Draft Was Memorable

The pitching was the primary culprit. Scott and Ryan were fine. But the other three starters and much of the bullpen, was pedestrian or worse. The team ERA ballooned from 3.15 to 3.84. Offensively first baseman Glenn Davis dropped from 31 homeruns while hitting .265 to 27 homers and a .251 average. Outfielder Kevin Bass dropped from 20 homers and a .311 batting average to 19 homeruns and a .284 mark. In most cases, the drops were not large, but added up to fewer runs being scored while more were being surrendered by the pitchers. One player, catcher Alan Ashby, was having perhaps the best offensive season of his career in 1987 with a .288 batting average to go with 14 homeruns and 63 runs batted in for 125 games. But Ashby was thirty-five years old, and there was soon to be a new name in contention for his job.

Craig Biggio Opened Eyes at Seton Hall

Craig Biggio played his junior season in 1987 at Seton Hall, and then declared for the Major League draft. He was now twenty-one years old and eligible to start his professional career. His credentials were solid. Even if scouts were still somewhat in question about his arm as a catcher they all saw he was a true baseball athlete. The also saw a potentially good hitter. As a junior Biggio, while toiling behind the plate, still hit .417. He was named first team All-Big East again. On June 2 1987, the Astros would be clobbered by the Chicago Cubs 13-2. However, something good did happen for the team that day. Craig Biggio was drafted. He was chosen by the Astros as the 22nd pick in the first round of the Major League draft. Alan Ashby's time was ticking away. Biggio's clock had just started.

5 Craig Biggio Arrives in the Major Leagues

Courtesy of Scott Anderson / Dreamstime.com

"When we first approached him about it he was not tuned
into the idea at all. But it was not from a personal standpoint.
Our second baseman at the time was Billy Doran. Billy was
a guy Craig really looked up to and he didn't want to do
anything to disrupt that. So we traded Billy."

– Former Astros GM Bill Wood on Biggio's move
from catcher to second base in 1992

Craig Biggio had attracted attention for more than just his own talent
and potential. His team at Seton Hall had been one of the strongest college
teams in the country, and certainly the best in the East during his three
seasons. Under no-nonsense head coach Mike Sheppard, a team of rare
distinction had been built. During Biggio's time as a Pirate, he had many
future major leaguers as teammates including Mo Vaughn and John Valentin, plus several others who were drafted and played professionally with a
few spending at least some time in the majors.

College Team Had Major League Talent

A book was written about that Seton Hall team. Titled, *The Hit Men and the Kid Who Batted Ninth*, it told the stories of the main men on that club—including Marteese Robinson who was the best college hitter of them all. Robinson led the NCAA with an astounding .529 average in 1987. Vaughn, Valentin, and Biggio all made the majors as players of course. And so did Robinson, but not on the field. He spent four seasons in the minors, but didn't reach the major leagues until he worked as a scouting executive in the St. Louis and Washington organizations.

Biggio Was Just an All-American Kid

Craig Biggio was on the right track well before his college exploits made him a pro prospect. Born in Smithtown, NY, on December 14, 1965, he was the third child of Gordon Lee Biggio and Johnna Biggio. Siblings were Terry and Gwen. All grew up in Kings Park, Long Island. A pretty normal kid, his life included delivering newspapers, playing every sport available, and getting extra instruction from his dad. Academics were not always a high priority.

Craig's father was an air-traffic controller who had played catcher in high school. Already thinking ahead, Gordon taught Craig all he could about his old position with the thought being that catching would be the quickest way to the major leagues. That would turn out to be true in Craig's case for sure. Craig once said that he loved the position because it allowed him to control the game. From his early baseball days, Craig Biggio was a team leader. So was Thurman Munson during his career with the Yankees. There were a number of similarities between the high school Biggio and the Yankee mainstay until the latter's tragic death in a plane crash in 1979. Munson was the major leaguer Craig most respected. Both were good hitting catchers who knew how to run a pitching staff and lead a team, even if their throwing arms may not have been the strongest.

Father's Words Were Received and Followed

Biggio, despite his small size as a youth, was also a talented football player. He actually preferred football so much that, at one point, he was considering giving up baseball as a high school freshman in the middle of the season. Gordon would not allow it to happen with another parental message, "You finish what you start." Biggio followed that order and later attributed it greatly to his never leaving the Astros when he was a free agent.

Of course, Gordon also recognized his son's best chance for long term success in sports was baseball, knowing of the talent being shown on the baseball field when Craig was 14 and he was playing on a Connie Mack League team with 15-18 year olds.

Even so, the football potential shined through during his high school years. He had scholarship inquiries from several colleges including Boston College, Syracuse, Penn State, and South Carolina. He had been an honorable mention All-American at tailback for King's Park (New York) High School was a strong defensive back.

In high school Biggio was first a catcher, then shifted to shortstop as a junior, and back to catcher as a senior. He was very raw defensively, but could hit and had outstanding running speed.

Biggio: An Amazing High School Footballer

With football still in his blood, Biggio played the sport in season and was very good. As a running back he won the Hansen Award as Suffolk County's best football player. Craig accepted the award in honor of former neighbor Chris Alben, who had died of leukemia. Biggio had been close to both Chris and his younger brother Charlie during Chris's long illness. Craig helped Charlie get through the shock of losing his big brother. The future would see Biggio taking an ever larger role in helping youngsters and their families deal with serious illness.

Biggio was a superb high school football player sometimes compared to Doug Flutie for his size and ability to both throw and run the ball. He was a quarterback for almost three seasons when passing for over 100 yards and rushing for over 100 yards in the same game was not uncommon. Even so, his head coach Doc Holliday felt Craig should be a tailback. During his senior year, the switch was made and Holliday looked like a genius when in one game Biggio rushed for 224 yards, threw an 80 yard option pass for a touchdown, and caught a nine yard touchdown pass as well.

In another game in which Kings Park was crushing its opponent, Coach Holliday took Biggio out of the backfield after he had rushed for 200 yards in the first half. He let him play in the defensive backfield and all he did was intercept a pass for a touchdown, run a punt for a touchdown, and do the same with a kickoff.

Biggio was very much a top-level football prospect, but for some schools, his academic achievements may have caused some concern.

But his school year wasn't over. He still had baseball. Up to his junior year, he had not gotten a lot of attention for pro scouts, partly because of his football talent and partly because physically he didn't fit the usual mold for a catcher.

But one spring day, Major League Scouting Bureau representatives Larry Izzo and Bryan Lambe were on hand to take another look at shortstop Tony Pellegrino of Commack South. The other team that day was King's Park.

As Kings Park took infield practice, Lambe decided the Bureau needed a scouting card on the Kings Park catcher. Just watching him work during practice showed Lambe something about Craig Biggio.

Football Opened Up Eyes First but Baseball Caught Up

Biggio was only a junior and far more noted for his football talent. His catching skills were noted, but Lambe was most interested in something more. As he was quoted in David Siroty's book, *The Hit Men and the Kid Who Batted Ninth*, "When a scout goes to see a team play, without knowing who the kid is, you can tell when they get off the bus just by the way they carry themselves. He had 'that look.' I thought he could be a catcher like [Thurman] Munson at the time. He didn't have a really strong arm, but he had a tremendous quickness, got rid of the ball quickly, and no ball was going to get by him behind home plate. I thought he would eventually shift to second base."

Football could have resulted in a full ride to college. Baseball then, as now, more often involved partial scholarships for most if not all players. The reason was simple. Football at the big schools generated a lot of revenue and had full scholarship limits for more than one hundred athletes at that time. Baseball may have had room for up to 15 full rides. But a baseball team needed more than 15 players.

Two things worked against Biggio as a football player. His height and his weight. Betting on a 5'10 (maybe) 165-pound football player from a football program that didn't always face the top competition was a risk. Even so, Boston University wanted to sign Biggio to a scholarship to play as a defensive back. They never got to submit Biggio's name for academic qualification because Craig and his family decided to accept an offer from Seton Hall to play baseball first.

Fortunately, "normal" sized athletes are the rule rather than exception in baseball. Biggio's senior season on the diamond in high school was the clincher. He was dominant. Returning to catcher, the increased responsibility did not harm his offense. He hit .417 and ran the show during a tough summer league that opened a lot of eyes.

Near the end of his high school senior season, scout Ralph DiLullo visited with Craig and his family to see if he would have interest in signing a minor league contract if the Tigers drafted him. But he also let it be known it probably would not be a wise move since Biggio had been accepted by Seton Hall. DiLullo told the Biggios Craig's draft spot would be so low that the signing dollars could never come close to matching the value of a college education.

So Biggio was going to go to Seton Hall as a catcher something his father was very happy to hear. Gordon Biggio had been a catcher in high school but could never advance due to the Korean War. He was in the Air Force during that conflict. It may have cost him a chance to continue his education and baseball playing, but gave him a leg up on his lifetime career as an air traffic controller.

"My dad was an awesome dad. Whenever we wanted to play ball, or whenever we wanted to do anything, when he had time on his schedule, he would do it. He was the bread winner. He'd work 7 AM to 3 PM, 3PM to 11PM or the midnight shift. He would never say anything. If we said, 'Hey dad, do you want to hit some ground balls to us?' He would just say, 'Ok, let's do it.' He was a hard disciplinarian. His big thing in life was respect and values. That is one of the things that stays with me today. I'm what I am today because of the respect and values that he made sure I had," Biggio remembered.

Witness to Death on the Diamond

During the summer before he began his college career at Seton Hall, something happened on a baseball field that Biggio will never forget and it was tragic. He was playing for the same Connie Mack League team that he had joined originally under-aged at fourteen years old. He was now eighteen. He was playing second base only because the regular at the position was missing. He usually had played catcher or shortstop. Today the shortstop would be eighteen-year old Adriano Martinez.

During the game, the weather started to change. With clouds rolling in, the air was still until lightning hit the field. Biggio remembered a very loud noise and he being on the ground thinking he had just been hit by lightning. He felt a burning sensation down the back of his legs and into his back. For an instant he was unconscious. The lightning had hit somewhere near the field and knocked everyone down except the left fielder who witnessed everything in front of him.

When Biggio came to, he found himself in a fetal position. He looked over to Martinez. What he saw was that the bolt had killed him.

Later it was surmised the lightning bolt had hit the backstop, radiated though the field and then was carried into Martinez body because he was wearing metal cleats. All of the rest of the players had been wearing rubber cleats since they had been transitioning away from metal to rubber in high school.

Biggio was the first to reach Martinez. What he saw is burned into his memory forever. Smoke was coming from his chest. His baseball shoes were burned off his feet.

The tragedy affected Craig heavily. He had seen death firsthand. He had seen a fellow ballplayer lose his life just trying to play the game he loved. Biggio became more and more withdrawn and his mother noticed right away.

After a few days, Johnna and Gordon Biggio thought it might be a good idea to ask neighbor Charlie Alben if he might be able to help them bring the real Craig back.

It was Charlie Alben's youngest son Chuck that Biggio had helped overcome the grief of the loss of his older brother Chris years before. Biggio served as a surrogate older brother for Chuck. Charlie and Chuck both reached out to Craig in his time of need. Soon the real Craig Biggio was back.

Seton Hall Was a Good Fit

How Biggio wound up at a school that did not even have a football team, was a direct result of a decision Craig made during his final high school baseball season. Baseball was the sport his size and abilities best fit—the sport he might have a chance of playing professionally after college. Odds of the same success at his 5'11" 165 pound size weren't as good in football.

Craig's success in college did not come early. As a freshman in 1985 he hit just .262 as the starting catcher. That is really not so bad for a first year player, but in addition to learning how to deal with college, life things were not perfect at home. Gordon and Johnna Biggio were getting divorced after more than twenty years together. It was an amicable parting, but still an adjustment for Craig and his two older siblings.

Playing in the Atlantic Collegiate Baseball League back home for the Long Island Nationals during the summer after his freshman year, he moved to the infield. Larry Izzo, who had first seen Biggio in high school, was still following him. The report filed on June 21, 1985 called him a marginal prospect as a second baseman, not a catcher. Biggio's hard-nosed attitude scored more points with Izzo than any of his talents.

The summer was a good one for Biggio, though. He made the league All-Star team and played a game in Boston's famed Fenway Park.

Back at Seton Hall for his sophomore year, he went back behind the plate, hit .351, and was All-Big East. Then the next summer he moved up to the Cape Cod League, still as a catcher, and hit 5 homers, and stole 21 bases in 39 games. Now the interest in Biggio by scouts was getting much stronger.

By the time Biggio had finished his junior year at Seton Hall, most of the holes in his game from two years before were gone. He hit .417 with 14 homeruns and 68 runs batted in. He also showed a much better arm behind the plate. It wasn't that much, if any, stronger, but very accurate with that "Munson-like" quick release. A catcher who could hit? You bet the scouts were noticing.

Welcome to the Astros System

On Tuesday, June 2, 1987 Craig Biggio began his Astro career. The Major League Baseball Amateur draft was held that day. Biggio, having completed his junior year at Seton Hall and past his twenty-first birthday, was eligible. If things went well, he would turn pro. If not, he could return to Seton Hall for his senior year and a degree.

It went well, although Biggio was so nervous waiting to find out that he spent time at girlfriend (and future wife) Patty Egan's family's summer home on the Jersey shore that day.

Shortly past 2 PM, the phone rang at the Biggio home in Kings Park. It was Houston Astro scout Clary Anderson. Clary informed Johnna Biggio her son had been selected by the Astros as the 22nd pick in the first round.

Mom then quickly called Son. "When I found out, a lot of tension was released," remembered Biggio. A quick call to father Gordon, who was at work, was next. Craig's sister found out from their mom. Only one left out was older brother Terry who was working in Minneapolis. He found out while watching a Cubs telecast on WGN-TV. The Cubs were playing the Astros, and after the Cub announcers mentioned their pick, fourth overall pitcher Mike Harkey, they gave note to the first choice of their opponent that day. That is how Terry Biggio found his brother was on the way to professional baseball and ultimately to the major leagues.

Harkey was nationally known after pitching for college powerhouse Cal State Fullerton and coach Augie Garrido. Biggio was nationally unknown. Harkey made it to the major leagues and was around for all or part of ten seasons going 36-36 with a 4.49 earned run average. Biggio taken 18 choices later became a Hall of Famer.

Harkey signed for a $160-thousand bonus. Biggio signed for $110-thousand. The Astros weren't being cheap at all. Harkey was number four overall. Biggio was number 22. Houston won in the long run.

Off to Asheville and Becoming a Pro

There was very little time for Biggio to celebrate being a first round pick, or even $110-thousand wealthier. Before June was over, he was on his way to start his professional career with the Asheville Tourists of the South Atlantic League. Biggio arrived the same day the Tourists clinched the first half championship. Even so, manager Keith Bodie told Craig he would be playing every day, and hit third in the lineup. No doubt Bodie was only making that decision on orders from Houston, but it was good for Craig to hear. In his debut the next day, he collected two doubles and an RBI. He also threw out a runner that tried to steal second.

Biggio's first professional homerun hit a few days later was self described as "a high fly ball that was hit to right field over a short fence."

When his rookie pro season was over, Biggio had played in 64 games, hit .375 with 9 homeruns and 49 runs batted in. He also stole 31 bases in 41 tries. His manager, Keith Bodie, as quoted in *The Hit Men and the Kid Who Batted Ninth*, said, "It didn't take long to know he was going to the major leagues. A couple of days watching him play and you knew he was special. He was head and shoulders above everybody else. Not only his performance, but in his approach to the game."

Astro owner John McMullen wondered if Biggio might be able to make the jump to the major leagues with only minimal minor league experience. This was before teams started to worry about "player control" "arbitration" and even free agency as much as now. Free agency options existed but the dollar figures were nowhere near as great as now. The thinking was much more about whether a young player was ready to handle the pressure, much tougher competition and periods of failure.

McMullen was concerned about the psychological effect of failure on a young player. Biggio's college coach Mike Sheppard told the owner he didn't think that would ever be a problem with Biggio. If he went 0-10 he would just work harder. He was the same player when things were going well as when not.

After his short season with Asheville, Biggio didn't immediately go to Houston, but was put on the fast track. He was invited to play on the Astros Instructional League team in Arizona. While his statistics did not stand out during the short run of the league, everything else about Biggio did. Asheville manager Keith Bodie urged the club to think about promoting Craig all the way to the majors. He didn't get a major league roster spot for Biggio, but did get him an invite as a non-roster player to Houston's 1988 spring training in Florida.

That sounds a little better than it really was. All clubs add minor league catchers to the spring roster to have more of them available to catch the dozens of pitchers who will be getting their arms in shape. Still it was a great honor for Biggio who had only 64 games of minor league action under his belt.

Then, when Yogi Berra started to take an interest in Biggio, something had to be up.

Two Astro coaches, Matt Galante and Hall of Fame catcher Yogi Berra both lived in the New York/New Jersey area. Since both were from nearby, they made plans to meet with Biggio while he was working out with his old teammates at the Seton Hall batting cages.

If his college coach Mike Sheppard had the most influence in making Biggio a professional prospect it would be Berra and Galante that would have the most influence in making him a Hall of Fame major leaguer.

Sheppard knew Berra well from working clinics with him in the area. So when he was told by Craig that Yogi and Matt would be coming over, he decided to play a trick on the former Yankee star. Knowing that Yogi and Craig had not yet met, he conspired to put an Astros shirt and cap on his 5'7' 250 pound student manager Mike Cocco and pass him off as Biggio.

The story, as related in *The Hit Men and the Kid Who Batted Ninth*, when Galante and Berra arrived the manager was involved in some drills with the catchers. Biggio was away from the action and laughing. Sheppard pointed over toward the rotund manager when the Houston coaches wanted to see Biggio. Galante had seen some photos of Biggio and knew something was not right, but Berra had no idea anything was up.

When he first saw the big guy trying to look like a catcher Yogi was surprised but simply said, "We'll make a player out of him. We'll make a player out of him."

When Yogi moved closer Sheppard introduced him to "Craig Biggio." Yogi then looked at the rotund student manager, and then at Galante, and then back at Sheppard and simply said, "He must be some phenom!"

Once he was introduced to the real Craig Biggio, Yogi was impressed. "I saw him hitting the ball, working in the cage. Craig was a good worker, he worked hard to get where he's at."

From that first meeting at Seton Hall, Biggio and Yogi Berra were very close. Berra passed on his experience and knowledge about catching and hitting to his protégé. When Craig was elected to the Baseball Hall of Fame in 2015, among the proudest were Yogi Berra and Matt Galante. Yogi, in ill health, could not be on hand, but Matt had a prime seat. Galante's major role in Biggio's Hall of Fame entrance came a few years after than the Seton Hall meeting.

Biggio Made an Impression in the Spring of 1988

Even though Alan Ashby was coming off his best offensive season in his career in 1987, he was thirty-five-years old and the team looked to Biggio as his future replacement. How soon was the question. Most felt it would not happen until 1989 or 1990, after Biggio had gained more professional experience. But what he showed them during spring training in 1988 changed that timeline.

He had an RBI single in his first exhibition game on March 8 against the Milwaukee Brewers, but what was most impressive was his work with his pitchers. Both ace closer Dave Smith and long reliever Larry Andersen had high praise. In comments relayed by Houston's daily newspapers Smith said, "He handles the glove well and I like his attitude. He's going to be a major league catcher." Andersen added, "He learns quickly. He caught me once before and knew today exactly what I wanted."

Biggio drew the attention of Nolan Ryan who even suggested a catching platoon with the switch hitting Ashby sharing time with young Biggio.

With Biggio hitting .385 during the early days of spring training, even his manager Hal Lanier was thinking Craig might be a major leaguer quicker than most expected. Some writers were already thinking of Biggio going one step further and moving Ashby out of the picture already, either as trade bait or relegation to a back-up role.

Biggio took the high road. With every story printed about his replacing the veteran, Craig had to be tactful and recognize that it was still Ashby's job.

Ultimately the Astros decided that while Biggio might be their catcher of the future, Ashby was still their catcher now, and it would do Biggio better to be playing every day in the minor leagues than only a couple days a week giving Ashby a rest. In baseball most teams prefer veterans to hold back up roles and have their top prospects play every day in the minors until they are ready to take over a full time job with the big club. Biggio, despite carrying a spring average of .333 through March 25, was assigned to the minor league camp the next day and reported to the Triple A Tucson Toros. That was still a big jump after less than a full season on the A level to be moved within one stop of the major leagues.

It was at Tucson that the thoughts his old college coach Mike Sheppard offered to Astro owner John McMullen were tested. Biggio got off to a horrible start with the bat. He was hitting only .167 for his first 36 at-bats. He was un-fazed. He just worked harder, learned what the much more veteran pitchers were trying to do and made adjustments.

Biggio got things straightened, out and within two weeks had raised his average to .309 and racked up 13 runs batted in during the stretch. He also stole seven bases.

While he was a very good receiver who knew how to work with pitchers, Biggio still did not have a classic catcher's gun for an arm. To throw out baserunners with any regularity, he had to make sure his throws got away quickly. Few runners can outrun a throw if it leaves the catchers hand quickly enough, the pitcher has kept the runner from an excessive lead, has a quick move to the plate, and the catcher's throw is on target.

Catchers like Johnny Bench, and later Pudge Rodriguez, had arms so strong they could overcome most of the advantages that the average catcher had to have in order to throw out runners. Biggio could not. But with his hitting, speed and ability to handle all the other aspects of catching, there was little concern. And Biggio worked hard. His Triple A manager Bob Didier put it this way, "He was very coachable. He was a good receiver. He didn't have a really strong arm, but we kept working on a quicker release. That was one of the knocks, he didn't have a really strong arm. There are guys like that. Craig learned how to get rid of the ball. You make adjustments. And when you hit well…"

Baseball has a number of catchers from the past that didn't throw the ball well, but could hit way better than the average catcher make All-Star teams and maybe even the Hall of Fame. Ted Simmons, Tim McCarver, Mike Piazza, and Thurman Munson were on the short list of some of the best hitting catchers of all time. None had arms even close to Bench or Rodriguez.

What would ultimately set Biggio apart was his running speed. That was what would ultimately result in his switch from behind the plate to second base. However, in 1988 that was still a few years in the future. Biggio was the future regular catcher for the Houston Astros. There was no doubt about that.

There was doubt about how soon Biggio would get his shot with Houston. In 1988 veteran Ashby was off to a good start at the plate, but on June 25, he had to go on the disabled list when he suffered a dislocated vertebrae. The Astros had Alex Trevino, but would need another catcher. Biggio was the man who would get the call. He wouldn't be backing up the veteran Trevino. He would be playing almost every day in the major leagues.

As a hitter, Biggio's introduction to the major leagues was rough. In 50 games and 123 at-bats, he hit only .211 with only three homeruns and five runs batted in.

However, his debut as a catcher was memorable. In his first start, he teamed with lefty Jim Deshaies in a six hit shutout of the San Francisco Giants. Biggio got his first hit June 29 off Dodger pitcher Orel Hershiser. On July 9 he caught Nolan Ryan for the first time. It was a 6-3 win for Ryan his hundredth win as an Astro. The game was not without incident.

Astros Strength and Conditioning Coach Dr. Gene Coleman remembered that Biggio tried to execute a move he learned in the minor leagues that was not appreciated in the majors. "In the minors they instructed the catchers that if your pitcher makes the third out in the previous half inning that after the throw to second to end the warm up pitches you are supposed to go out to the mound and talk to the pitcher to give him more time to catch his breath. So Nolan makes the last out of the inning and finished his warm ups. Biggio, following what was taught, starts heading out. Third baseman Buddy Bell cuts him off. 'Where the bleep are you going?' Biggio said, 'Going to give my pitcher a breather.' Bell jumped on him. 'Your pitcher's been pitching longer than you've been alive. He's in better shape that all of us. When he needs to take a breather, he'll take a breather. Now get your skinny ass back behind the plate and never come out here again.' Bidge later said, 'I caught Nolan a few more times, but I never went out to the mound again.'"

Biggio was impressing his teammate, however. On August 22, Biggio led the Astros to a 9-7 win at Chicago in the first Astro night game at Wrigley Field. He hit a 10th inning two-run homer off future Hall of Famer Goose Gossage.

Hitting woes soon put Biggio on the bench backing up Trevino, and when Ashby was ready to return from the disabled list, Craig was sent back to Tucson. That was a short stay. He was sent down on August 30, but returned to Houston on September 6 after rosters were expanded. Biggio never played in the minor leagues again.

As a hitter, Biggio was always learning. He once told Astro television play-by-play announcer Bill Brown, "I look back at video clips and my stance probably changed at least three times during my career. One constant which never really changed was where I stood at the plate. I wasn't really a fan of the outside pitch, but I could hit the inside pitch. It didn't matter where you threw it, I could hit it. I could get to it. So my theory was always that I wanted to stand near the inside point of the plate. So obviously if the pitcher wants to come in and if it's too far in you are probably going to hit me. But yet again, I can hit anything inside that doesn't hit me. The weakness for most hitters is usually the outside pitch. So, not only would I stand very close to the plate, but also up in the front of the batter's box because I wanted to catch breaking balls before they got to their nastiest point. Where they should break is right where home plate is. I tried to catch them before they were breaking."

After an 82-80 season in 1988, the Astros let manager Hal Lanier go and brought in former Astro favorite and, at the time a coach with the Texas Rangers, Art Howe, to replace him. Art was excited when he got the job, but not quite attuned to what was coming. One of his first statements after being hired was that signing Nolan Ryan to a new contract would be one of his priorities. However, owner John McMullen, who had made Ryan baseball's first $1-milllion per year player for the 1980 season, thought Big Tex's time was about up. The contract offer to Ryan called for a significant pay cut. Ryan rejected the offer so McMullen let the Texas Rangers hand out the big money to bring Ryan north. As for a chagrined Howe, "Yeah, it turned out like a trade…me for him. One of the worst trades the Astros ever made. When I came to Houston I thought I was going to have Nolan as my workhorse…him and Mike Scott. We would have had a nice 1-2 combination."

In 1989 the Astros started the season with Ashby and Biggio splitting the job at catcher. The first few games of the season, with neither catcher having a strong start at the plate, it was almost a different catcher every game. Alex Trevino was also still around, but used sparingly. It was Biggio on opening day, Ashby in game two, then back to Biggio, etc.

By early May, Ashby was still not hitting. His average was below .200. Biggio was not tearing the cover off the ball, but he was the future. Ashby was the past. At one point Ashby was getting a few starts in a row because he was on display. The team itself was hovering around the bottom of the National League West. So, looking ahead to the future, the club had put him on the trading block. The decision had been made to go with Biggio every day and start re-building.

A deal was worked out with the Pirates that would have brought Houston area native Glenn Wilson to Houston for Ashby. But Ashby, who had been in the major leagues for ten or more years and five or more with his present team, had the right to decline. With a large family and roots in Houston the thirty-six-year old catcher told owner John McMullen he wouldn't accept the deal.

That move would end Ashby's playing career and open the door for Biggio to really start making his mark on the major leagues.

A short time later while already on the team bus for a ride to the airport for a flight to Chicago, Ashby and his luggage was pulled off the bus and he was told he had been put on irrevocable waivers. His major league career was over. (He would resurface in Houston after McMullen had sold the team, as Larry Dierker's first bullpen coach in 1997 before moving in to the radio-TV booth the next season.)

When the Astros next played, on Friday afternoon at Wrigley Field, Biggio would be the number one everyday catcher for the team for the first time. He caught Jim Deshaies again, with whom he had worked in his first major league game a season earlier. Deshaies didn't pitch a shutout this time, but he won 3-1 with another complete game. Biggio, batting eighth, was 1-3 at the plate with a run scored. He did experience the Cubs stealing two bases in two tries. One was a theft of home by Darrin Jackson in the sixth. It was the only run Chicago would score.

On June 3 the Astros met the Dodgers in a game that will live long in Astro lore. The game started on the evening of the third and ended the morning of June 4. It lasted 22 innings and took seven hours and 14 minutes to play. Astro shortstop Rafael Ramirez singled off Dodger stop-gap pitcher, infielder Jeff Hamilton past stop-gap first baseman, Fernando Valenzuela to drive home Bill Doran with the winning run at 2:50 AM. Craig Biggio started behind the plate but was part of a double-switch in the top of the seventh. He was 2-3 at the plate. His replacement, Alex Trevino caught the last 15 innings and was 1-7. The Astros didn't have to use any pitchers playing positions or position players pitching, but Manager Howe did use pitcher Jim Deshaies as a pinch hitter. Deshaies had a lifetime .088 batting average. He was struck out in the 17th inning by Orel Hershiser.

That game was only the first to have extra play in that series. The next day the Astros and Dodgers played 13 more innings. Biggio homered in the last of the ninth to send it to extra frames. As the ball was sailing toward the wall, famed Dodger announcer Vin Scully was heard to say, "Don't tell me!" Scully had worked solo for 19 of the 22 innings the night before after working a TV network game in the afternoon. He worked most of the 13 inning game as well. Houston won the second game on a sacrifice fly by Astro pitcher Mike Scott.

On July 27 Biggio had a day off from starting, but came off the bench in the eighth to pinch hit with the Astros trailing the Giants 5-3. He hit his first career pinch hit homer off Steve Bedrosian. The Astros won 7-5. The team had climbed back into the pennant race since Biggio had taken over behind the plate. When he got the job full time on May 12, the club was 14-19 and in last place in the division. They finished 86-76. Once Biggio became the regular catcher, the team was 72-57.

History was made on July 29, 1989 when Manager Art Howe installed Biggio in the leadoff spot. Craig became the first Houston catcher to bat leadoff since Ron Brand did it for the club more than twenty years before. In the game, Biggio hit a homer and had a single in an 8-1 win over San Francisco.

Biggio had a big day for two reasons on September 14 in Los Angeles. He caught his first twenty-game winner as Mike Scott achieved the honored level with an 8-1 whipping of the Dodgers. Biggio hit two homers and drove in six of those runs. While the Astros wound up third in the National League West they were only six games off the top spot won by the Giants.

For the 1989 season Biggio played in 134 games hit .257 with 13 homeruns and 60 runs batted in. He also was successful on 21 of 24 stolen base attempts. That percentage of .875 was better than Vince Coleman, Ricky Henderson, or Tim Raines. Trying to stop runners from behind the plate was another story. Eighty-three percent of the stolen bases attempted with Biggio behind the plate were successful. That was the highest percentage against any catcher in the major leagues. The Astro brass was noticing. They had a player in Craig Biggio, but how long would he be a catcher? He was less effective the last couple of months in that 1989 season when his average and on base percentages dropped off considerably from earlier in the season. He also was less likely to steal bases. All catchers wear down as a season progresses. The twenty-four-year old Biggio was no exception. But he could do more than catch. He could hit. He could run. Wearing down from catching helped neither the team nor Craig.

In 1990 the biggest thing in Craig Biggio's life happened. There is no question or debate. That was when he married longtime girlfriend Patty Egan. They had met while Craig was at Seton Hall. The Biggio-Egan marriage passed the twenty-five year mark in 2015 and has included the birth of three children. Son Conor was first on January 1, 1993. Then came Cavan (4/11/95) and daughter Quin (9/27/99). The Biggio's were one of the sports world's most envied families. The marriage also made Craig leave the stereotypical "jock life" for family. Patti had trained as a nurse, but worked as a "mom-in-chief" during all of Craig's active years as a ball player and his many absences from the home.

This had also been the case at home when he was growing up. Sadly, his mom and dad parted ways after Craig had left for college. It was during his time at the Catholic-sponsored university that he converted to Catholicism in part to help him get over the pain. Father and son rarely communicated during his major league years due to ill will on his father Gordon's part. He had blamed his children for supporting their mother more in the divorce. Craig opened up to *Sports Illustrated*'s Michael Bamberger in 1996. Gordon Lee Biggio died on September 7, 2007. He lived long enough for Craig to achieve his 3,000[th] hit. The Astros were in New York playing the Mets when he died, but he was then living in North Carolina. His obituary called for donations to be made to the Sunshine Kid's Foundation, Craig Biggio's top charity. Craig missed just one game in the series.

Only Off-Field Blemish for Biggio Came Very Early

Early in his Astro career during the 1989 season, Biggio had been arrested for a DWI which made the papers. Admitting he had a few beers with teammates celebrating a win over the Padres the night of June 7, Biggio had been pulled aside and ticketed for drunk driving. The arresting officer said Craig registered a 1.3 on a roadside test which was just above the 1.0 limit. Teammate Ken Caminiti testified Biggio was not impaired although an officer said that he made the stop after Biggio had been clocked at 50 in a 35 mph zone and seemed to be driving erratically.

After the misdemeanor matter was settled, Biggio made an apology to Astro fans. His quote as reported by United Press: "I made a serious error in judgement in choosing to drive after drinking. I have a responsibility to the community and I did not live up to it last night."

Biggio's attorney pointed out Craig's apology was for drinking and driving and that his client was not legally intoxicated on the night he was arrested.

That incident—a year before his marriage to Patty—was the ONLY blemish on Craig's very public life. The only one.

In 1990 with Biggio having established himself with the Astros the question was how long should he remain a catcher? He got off to a decent start at the plate despite not hitting the long ball while the Astros were struggling as well. By the time the season was over Biggio had boosted his batting average to .276 with four homers and 42 RBI's. He improved slightly in throwing out 25% of those who tried to steal with him behind the plate. And he was still stealing bases. He stole 25. He also dabbled at another position playing in 50 games in the outfield to go with 100 behind the plate. The Astros wanted his bat and speed in the lineup even when he was not catching. When would catching be in the past was the question.

How Long Would Biggio Catch?

It wouldn't happen in 1991. He would play some more at other positions but would wind up his full time catching career as an All Star first. The Astros had another position conversion to deal with first. They had a minor league third baseman they had acquired near the end of the 1990 season in a trade with Boston who showed promise. They already had a third baseman in Ken Caminiti and since they had traded their power hitting first baseman Glenn Davis to Baltimore in the offseason, that spot was open. Mike Sims, from the team's Tucson farm would get the first shot, but he would have to win it in the spring. The Astros would have a problem if Sims didn't have a strong spring.

6 Bagwell Joins The Astros—at First Base

Courtesy of John Sutter

"There's two opposing players I fell in love with
—Jeff Bagwell and Craig Biggio."

– Hall of Famer and former Atlanta Brave manager Bobby Cox

The 1990 season had not been a good one for the Astros. After finishing third in the National League West in 1989 with an 86-76 record, the club dropped a spot in the standings with eleven fewer wins. "The next year [1990] we got a little old," remembered manager Art Howe. "That's when [GM] Bill Wood and I realized we should go with rebuilding the club."

The 1990 team only hit 94 homeruns with leading power man Glenn Davis dropping off from 34 to 22 homeruns. Injured part of the season, Davis was traded during the offseason to Baltimore in a multi-player deal that brought outfielder Steve Finley and pitchers Pete Harnisch and Curt Schilling to the Astros. "We had some very good players in the organization at the Double A and Triple A level and we realized with all the guys getting older, getting hurt, and their performance dropping off we felt it was time to go with the youth movement," recalled Howe. "We had quite a few of them. We had Luis Gonzalez, Andujar Cedeno, and Biggio was in only his second full season when I came over. So we had a lot of young players. We had older pitchers. Our staff was pretty old. That's when we made that trade with Baltimore."

Best Trade in Houston Baseball History

Late in the 1990 season the Astros had parted with Larry Andersen to Boston for a Double A minor league third baseman named Jeff Bagwell. Andersen had been a popular player with the Astros both on and off the field. He had been a major contributor to the Sunshine Kids after being brought in by former pitcher Joe Sambito. The Sunshine Kids was a charity that supported the kids and families that were having to deal with major medical battles, most notably cancer treatment. Andersen's participation would be missed. But it wouldn't be long before Craig Biggio would do far more than just fill his shoes. And the player the Astros acquired for Larry would grow into one of the two biggest Astro heroes of all time.

Bagwell Had the Genes

Jeff Bagwell came from a baseball family. Born on May 27, 1968 in Boston, his dad, Robert, had pitched in college at Northeastern University and later on some semi-pro teams. His mother, Janice, played softball into her late twenties.

Jeff, however, while at Xavier High School in Middletown, Connecticut, played soccer originally as his primary sport. He had some colleges interested in him for his soccer skills, but he also played shortstop and was good enough to be offered a partial scholarship to attend the University of Hartford. Bagwell was considered a good but not great player during most of his high school and college years. He did hit over .400 each of his three years in college, but the overall level of pitching he faced made it hard for scouts to fully judge him until he started playing summer ball after his sophomore season. Hartford did have some games against Maine, which in those days frequently made it to the College World Series. As Jeff remembered, "It wasn't like playing Oklahoma State all the time, but it was Division I. We had a bunch of good guys at Hartford. What did it for me was when I played at Cape Cod."

The Bagwell family were big Boston Red Sox fans, but Jeff actually being good enough to play for them, or anyone in the major leagues for that matter, was not much more than an idle thought until then.

However, after a season playing college ball for coach Bill Denehy, a former major league pitcher, those thoughts of the major leagues started to get stronger. Denehy moved Bagwell from shortstop to third base and helped him gain a spot on a summer league team in the famed Cape Cod League. There he was playing with some of the top names in college baseball and future major leaguers like Albert Belle and Frank Thomas. Bagwell didn't put up the kind of numbers players like that were registering. The first year in the league Bagwell said he didn't think he hit more than .205, but he didn't feel over matched. "I was scared to death when I first went to that league. Then I saw Robin Ventura play. He had just had that 58 game hitting streak at Oklahoma State, but I thought myself that he wasn't that much better than me. He is just on TV a lot. That was where I really got going as far as my belief I could play," Bagwell recalled in a conversation with Bill Brown years later.

The next season when he returned, Bagwell was a new player. He hit over .300 and was now a real prospect. He would be eligible for the major league draft.

Telling Brown, "I played in an All-Star game at Fenway Park and I called my dad and asked him if I had been drafted yet. He said, 'I haven't had a phone call yet.' I was kind of depressed and got in the car with one of my buddies and started driving back. Two and a half hours later I get to my house. Our whole driveway is filled with cars and my dad comes out and throws me a Red Sox shirt. Pretty happy for my whole family and me, having been a Red Sox fan all my life."

Not a first round prospect yet, Bagwell was drafted in the fourth round by his beloved Red Sox. While he could have returned to school for his senior year and perhaps a better draft slot and more money, he couldn't pass up the chance to play for the Red Sox. As a third baseman, he was playing behind future Hall of Famer Wade Boggs in Boston. But Boggs wouldn't be there forever. It was calculated that when Bagwell was ready, Boggs's career would either be over or very close to it. What Jeff did not figure was that there were other third basemen higher in the Red Sox system that might be highly regarded. There were. Scott Cooper was the expected heir apparent by Red Sox officials. He was already at Triple A Pawtuckett. Tim Naehring was also ahead of him on the depth chart at the time at Double A. Bagwell was assigned to Winter Haven in the Class A Florida State League after he agreed to a low dollar signing bonus. In 69 games between Winter Haven and the Red Sox rookie league team in the Gulf Coast League, he compiled a .310 batting average with a .386 on base percentage. He only hit two homers and drove in just 22 runs, but he showed a good eye with more walks than strikeouts. The next season, 1990, he was promoted to double A New Britain in the Eastern League. That was really great. He could live at home during the season. He was outstanding except as a power hitter. He hit just four homeruns in 136 games, but registered an outstanding .333 batting average to win the Eastern League batting championship. He also had an on base percentage of .422 and slugging percentage of .457. Bagwell may have hit only four homers, but had a total of 45 extra base hits including 34 doubles, seven triples, and the four homers. He was also selected the Eastern League MVP. He was on the radar of scouts all over baseball.

If there were any dreams of Bagwell being on a fast track to Boston, they were quashed just as his season was ending at New Britain. On August 30, 1990 he was traded to the Houston Astros for thirty-seven-year old veteran relief pitcher Larry Andersen. The folks around the Red Sox were excited. They were in a tight pennant race. They needed Andersen. Bagwell was a still unproven minor leaguer plus they still had Wade Boggs, Scott Cooper, and Tim Naehring ahead of him.

In Houston, the attitude was "Why do we need a minor league third baseman? We have Caminiti." And Andersen was a popular Astro.

The biggest reaction was likely in the Bagwell household. Jeff wasn't going to be on the Red Sox? "I was devastated. I was living at home that season and we were three games from going to the playoffs. I was having a good year."

As quoted in a Leigh Montville *Sports Illustrated* article from 1993, Bagwell remembered, "I was one of the saddest guys you'll ever see. All my life everything had been Boston. I was born in Boston. My father was from Watertown. My mother was from Newton, just outside Boston. Our house was one of those places where you couldn't mention the word Yankees. My grandmother was huge Red Sox fan. She knew everything about the team. I called to tell her the news and she started crying. My dad and I were in the car a day or so after the deal was made and he said this might turn out to be the best thing that could have happened. He had researched and knew the Astros had had a bad year in 1990 and Ken Caminiti had had a bad year so I might have a chance."

Although Jeff would never be a Red Sox player, he would turn out to be a major leaguer much quicker than anyone thought.

"When I went to spring training with the Astros in 1991, I figured I would wind up playing at Tucson," Bagwell recalled. Again his father saw the bright side, "You know what? Tucson's not bad." He said that after Caminiti got off to a hot spring. As Bagwell remembered, "He was like ten for ten. But I just kept playing and I hit well. I was just a kid. I didn't know any better. Then with less than two weeks left in camp I got called in to the manager's office. I figured I was being sent down."

He never saw Tucson. During camp he impressed Astro manager Art Howe, his coaches, and the front office with his bat. He was hitting very well against some major league pitchers. With only two weeks left before the regular season began and the club still unsettled at first base after the offseason Davis trade, it was decided to give Bagwell a first baseman's glove and move him across the diamond. The decision was made because the player expected to play first base was not hitting at all. As Art Howe remembers, "Mike Sims was the guy we felt would be our first baseman in 1991. He had come up at the end of 1990 and hit .308 with a homer and two RBIs in 13 at-bats. He had worked his way through the farm system. We—and he—felt it was his job to lose, really."

During the 1990 season at Tucson, Sims had shown promise. He had hit .274 with 13 homers and 72 runs batted in. Not exactly "can't miss" numbers in his first year on the Triple A level, but he had hit 39 homeruns and driven in 100 three seasons earlier on the Class A level.

"Several things happened in the spring of 1991," said Howe. "I had three guys who played third base. I had Ken Caminiti, the incumbent, plus Jeff Bagwell and Luis Gonzalez. I was trying to work all three of them in games, get them playing time, whatever. Sims was getting almost all the time at first base. As the spring went on, Mike was really struggling. I mean he was really having a bad spring. In the meantime, the three guys at third base were wearing the ball out. Every time they played they got at least two hits and it's pretty obvious all three were ready to play at the big league level. Caminiti already was, of course. And Mike is striking out three of every four times up. He wasn't even putting the ball in play. So toward the latter part of spring training, I went to Bill Wood and I said that Caminiti is going to be our third baseman. He's the best defensively of the three. He's got a cannon for an arm. Luis has less arm strength, but he runs well. Why don't we try him in left field? At the time I'm looking at first base and I know Bags isn't the tallest guy in the world, but we need his bat in the lineup."

At this point Gene Coleman, the Astros strength and conditioning coach, entered the scene. According to Coleman, "Art told me I want you to take Baggy inside and measure him because we are thinking of moving him to first base, but he's kind of short so he needs to be six feet tall to play first base. So I went and got him and when we were walking in he asked me, 'Where are we going?' I said we were going to measure you. 'Why?' Artie said you have to be six feet tall to play first base. 'I'm six feet tall.' You're what? 'I'm six feet tall when I stand on first base.' We never made it to the clubhouse. I went back and told Art, he's six feet tall. 'You sure?' He's six feet tall."

Jeff's height was always listed officially at six feet tall during his career, although teammate Casey Candaele once posted a chart on the wall of the clubhouse—he called it the "Bagwell Growth Chart"—and it topped out at five feet, ten inches.

Once Howe was convinced Bagwell was tall enough for the position, he approached GM Wood and asked him what he thought of moving Bagwell across the diamond. Wood pointed out the season was only two weeks away, but he gave Art his blessing to give it a shot.

"I remember I called Jeff in," said Howe, "And I asked him if he would rather be playing every day at first base in the big leagues or every day at third base at Tucson? He said, 'Where's my first baseman's mitt?'"

Jeff later remembered his thinking at the time, "I went to Hartford and not Harvard, but I could figure that one out."

Art had someone on the Astros minor league staff that he knew could be a great teacher. "I had Bob Robertson coaching in the system. I had played with Bob in Pittsburgh and I knew he was an outstanding first baseman. I called Bob and I said you gotta take this kid every day and work with him. You think you can get him ready?"

Both Robertson and Bagwell were on a back field both early and late working at first base. In addition, Jeff was still in the lineup every day and kept hitting. "I still gave Mike Sims some playing time, but now he really felt the pressure since he knew what was going on," remembered Howe. "You want a nice target for your infielders to throw to. That's why the height thing came up, but I really liked Baggie's strong hands. He was scooping up all the short hopped throws. He had a strong arm and would make all the plays and more than many first basemen."

Bagwell had a lot going for him with the switch. His own manager, Art Howe, had played both sides of the infield during his career. Bagwell had played both shortstop and third base during his amateur career. He could handle first. About the only problem was his lack of height. Most teams had been reluctant to station anyone less than six feet—and preferably taller—at the spot to give fielders larger targets and give the first sacker a longer reach on stretches for throws.

Bagwell was officially listed as being six feet tall. That may have been a basketball-like stretch. But it really didn't matter. Steve Garvey had manned the post for the Dodgers for years. He was listed at only 5'10" tall. Jeff was quicker than most first basemen. He had a stronger arm than most first basemen and would use it. "I think playing third base made him that way," believes Howe. "He was aggressive. You remember Garvey was a highly regarded hitter but not overly tall, and he never made any throws. Bags was aggressive. I mean on a bunt play, he'd be down that hitter's throat and he'd field a bunt and go to second base to get the lead runner. He was very accurate with his throwing. The fact that he had come from third base and had to throw. It was a piece of cake for him. He loved making plays."

Bagwell's first manager, Art Howe, happened to have Jeff's last manager Phil Garner on his coaching staff. Like Art, Garner remembered how good Bagwell was with both the bat and glove. "What many don't consider about Jeff was there was a stretch before his shoulder was hurt he was the best first baseman in the league. When I was managing in Milwaukee, we tried to bunt at times, and when we played Houston, Bagwell was a terror. He'd field the ball on the third base side and make the play for the force at second. He did it several times against us. You had to actually build a bunt scheme against Bagwell because he was so good. He was very quick. He was daring. He'd come right in your face and he didn't care if you swung the bat or not. If you're going to put Ozzie Smith in the Hall of Fame for his defense you should have put Jeff Bagwell in the Hall years before just for his glove. That is not a slight on Ozzie, but to emphasize how good Jeff really was before his shoulder went out."

Gene Coleman remembered one play Bags made on a bunt attempt by future Hall of Famer Ryne Sandberg of the Cubs. "Sandberg was trying to sacrifice. He popped it in foul territory to the third base side. And Jeff caught it."

When the Astros opened the 1991 season, Bagwell was at first base. It was a position he would hold for the next 14 seasons before continuing shoulder problems would force him into a pinch hitting and designated hitter role to close out his career.

Bagwell's Debut Came in a Down Season for the Astros

The Astros season was a washout in 1991. It marked the end of Mike Scott's career after two bad starts. Jim Deshaies from the 1986 team would also be gone from the staff after the season. Nolan Ryan was in his third year playing for the Rangers in Arlington. He pitched his seventh career no hitter that season for Texas at age 43. The Astros won only 65 of 162 but it was a success for the team's rookie first baseman. Bagwell hit .294 with 15 homeruns and 82 runs batted in. The homers were the surprise. Not only had Jeff not shown much homerun punch in the minors, but in the majors his home games were played in the Astrodome where many fly balls went to die. Bagwell hit six homers at home and nine on the road. Was his manager Art Howe surprised? "I wouldn't say it was a surprise, but we were happy with it. And then he started getting stronger and I felt even more power might be coming. He had a nice stroke. He could hit the ball to all fields better than most young players. Someone told me along the way during my playing days that you learn how to pull the ball from experience, and I knew that was still coming from him."

Bagwell Showed His Potential with His Third Major League Homerun

If hopes for Jeff Bagwell were to have a first baseman adept with the glove who could also hit for average with some doubles and an occasional homerun were all that was expected at first, he made folks wonder if that may be short changing him in a game at Pittsburgh's Three Rivers Stadium on May 5, 1991. In the seventh inning of that game, he hit a pitch by the Pirates' Bob Kipper into the upper deck in left field. The ball was only the ninth one hit into the upper deck in the twenty-two-year old stadium. It was measured at 456 feet and most observers felt it was the longest of the nine to reach that level.

Only his third major league homerun, Bagwell was modest following the game. "I never saw it. You hit three homers a year like I do and the pitchers don't like it if you start watching them. That doesn't look so good. I asked somebody when I got back in the dugout and he told me where it went."

National League Rookie of the Year

In that 1991 season Jeff led all major league rookies in batting average, on-base average, hits, RBIs, walks, games, game starts, and plate appearances. He was named National League Rookie of the Year. Bagwell took 23 of 24 first place votes. Orlando Merced of Pittsburgh got the other

Rudy Jaramillo was the Astros hitting coach during Bagwell's first three years. Jeff always gave him great credit for his early development in the major leagues. So did manager Howe. "Rudy was a workaholic. He gave this guys all the swings they could handle and more. Bags had a funky stance. (Some said it looked like a man sitting in a chair without the actual chair. Teammate Ken Caminiti was more graphic, "It looks like he is sitting on the john. He's the one guy who can work on his stance in the bathroom."

Actually Bagwell didn't always look that way at the plate. He used a wide stance back from his college days, but would tinker with it at times—just like his idol Yasztremski. However, early during his super 1994 season with the Astros, he got some advice from future Hall of Famer and eight time National League batting champ Tony Gwynn who told him, as reported in a 1999 *Sports Illustrated* article by Tom Verducci, "When you change your stance so many times, you have no foundation to get back to when you struggle." Enter the "sitting on the john" stance- permanently. As Art Howe remembered, "The key to that stance was he hardly had any stride at all. In fact, it often looked like he even stepped backward before his swing. The main thing Rudy really taught him was to get his front foot down early, because you can't swing until that front foot is on the ground. And I think he really took to that. He would get his foot down with the wide stance and generate his weight shift on the swing from a solid strong base."

Bagwell's First Game Impressed

Jeff also showed his manager something in the season's opening game against Cincinnati. But Jeff admitted he was a bit nervous before the game. "The Reds had won the 1990 World Series and the ballpark was jumping. It was literally shaking. The fans were going crazy. I was nervous. We had planks on the floor of the bench to walk on and when I was standing on them they were shaking. My dad was there and it was a big day for me because I finally knew I had actually made it to the big leagues."

The Reds were the defending World Champions after sweeping the Oakland A's. Their big three in the bullpen were known as the "Nasty Boys" with right-hander Rob Dibble, the nastiest. His fast ball could touch 100 MPH and sometimes he would use it to loosen up the hitters. The at-bat Howe never has forgotten was an opening day matchup between Dibble and this new kid playing first base for Houston. The Reds were leading 6-1 into the ninth, but Houston was putting something together. Eric Yelding tripled to open the inning. Steve Finley scorched a line drive to center field that was caught, but was deep enough to drive Yelding in. Then Craig Biggio singled, resulting in Reds manager Lou Piniella removing starter Tom Browning for Randy Myers. But Myers walked both Luis Gonzalez and Ken Caminiti. Piniella had seen enough. With rookie right-handed hitter Jeff Bagwell coming up, he lifted Myers for Dibble. The bases were loaded with one out. The Reds lead was 6-2. Howe remembers, "Bags is batting the top of the ninth. I remember the first pitch. I don't know how he got out of the way. It went between his helmet and his head. He undressed him. He went down in a heap. I'm thinking oh man, this is pretty serious here. Let's see how Jeff reacts to this. Well, Jeff worked the count and on the 3-2 pitch he hits a line drive right up the middle that almost took Dibble off the mound. I thought to myself…we've got a player here." Unfortunately for the Astros, the line shot was caught by shortstop Barry Larkin, who tossed to second baseman Mariano Duncan to retire Luis Gonzalez off the bag for a game ending double play.

The other bright spot from the 1991 season was having Pete Harnisch and Craig Biggio being named to the National League All Star Game. Biggio made it as a catcher in the last season that would be his primary position.

Biggio hit .295 in 1991, one point higher than Bagwell. Craig had been ripping the ball at the time NL skipper Joe Torre named him to the team. Biggio hit .359 in April, .311 in May, and .309 in June. As had been the case in his previous two seasons he tailed off as the season wore on but not as much as before. Even so, the wear and tear on his body, outstanding hitting and base stealing skills, and his continuing below average ability to throw and contain the opposition running game, meant a change needed to be made. During the offseason after the 1991 campaign and into the spring, it would be done. Craig Biggio would start his journey to becoming a Gold Glove winning All-Star and later Hall of Fame second baseman.

From All Star Catcher to All Star Second Baseman

The conversion from catcher to second base was another project headed by manager Art Howe, but handled on a daily basis by coach Matt Galante.

Galante, who had seen Biggio work out with Yogi Berra almost five years before, had been an Astro coach since 1985. He had coached both bases and as bench coach. His primary teaching role was with infielders.

His job was to convert Biggio's catcher's hands into infielder's hands, plus ingrain the footwork and positioning that needed to be second nature with middle infielders. Handling the pivot on double plays would be very important since Biggio had played shortstop in his high school days, but rarely saw infield duty from the other side of the bag.

So what went into making Biggio a second baseman?

As reported in an article written by Jose de Jesus Ortiz for the Houston Chronicle in 2015 prior to Biggio's Hall of Fame induction, the move was suggested by Manager Howe and Coach Galante before the 1991 season was over. Bill Doran had been traded to Cincinnati prior to the 1991 season, and that year Mark McLemore and Casey Candaele had played the position. Biggio—who had made the All Star team as a catcher earlier that very season—was not in favor of the idea. He knew there had been talk about his moving even before Doran had moved to Cincinnati. He obeyed his bosses request to give it a try late in 1991 and then had a ball go right through his legs on the first chance hit his way. For the record, it happened at Candlestick Park in San Francisco on September 30, 1991. Galante was concerned that error might keep Biggio from wanting to learn the position. In fact right after the miscue, Galante turned to Howe and said, "He's not going to want to make a switch now." But he played second for the final two games of the season against Atlanta and then got down to work in the offseason.

Art Howe said the switch was a necessity for a number of reasons, "He was such a great athlete. He could really run, but as the season would progress, he would start limiting his stolen bases. He always had the green light to run when I managed him, but sometimes I'd have to give him the steal sign and he still wouldn't go. I called him into the office after a game and I told him I really needed him to steal. You've got the speed to do it. But he told me his legs were heavy from squatting and he didn't want to run into outs. I appreciated that, but there is a lot his talent is leaving on the table that he could bring to the team. And there was another factor and that was his size. His lack of size for collisions at the plate, which were legal in those days, was scary. Dave Parker in those days was putting big catchers in the hospital on almost a weekly basis. I could just imagine Craig being run over by one of those big guys and ending his career. I had also seen him taking ground balls before games with his catcher's mitt. He looked pretty smooth."

A year before Howe had called for the moving of Jeff Bagwell from third base to first. This change was more radical, but there was plenty of time to get it done.

"Bags had only two weeks. We had the offseason and all spring with Biggio," said Howe. "Matt Galante certainly deserves all the credit. He was out there early, late. I mean there were days with Bidge's hands were swollen from taking so many ground balls. He and Andujar Cedeno were working on feeding each other on the double play. Every day he had something and Matty worked with him. He turned him into a heck of a second baseman almost over-night. Obviously they both deserve a ton of credit.

The bottom line is Bidge. He did it. He put his mind to it and gave it all he had and became a Gold Glove winning All-Star."

"At the time it was a nervous decision," Biggio told the Chronicle, "but once we made our decision to do it, we zipped up our catcher's gear and never looked back."

To learn the position Biggio requested his former team-mate Billy Doran, who had been the Astros second baseman when Biggio broke in and was now playing for the Reds, fly into Houston to help him. Doran accepted and the pair got together at the Astrodome, which was undergoing the change from an astro-turfed baseball and football stadium to the site for the annual Houston Livestock Show and Rodeo. With the turf removed Biggio and Bagwell found a plot of dirt to work on. Doran and Biggio worked on the thinking part of playing the position as much as fielding ground balls or making throws. It gave Biggio a basic foundation to take to Kissimmee, Florida, for Astros Spring Training.

Then came Galante. One of the first things Biggio told Galante let him know he now had a strong pupil. "He said, 'If we're going to do this thing we're gonna do it right. I want to win a Gold Glove.' And he won four of them. He never really played the position before, but that was good. He didn't have any bad habits."

Biggio had done some research and found the move was somewhat unprecedented in baseball history. In fact, only one player played at least 100 games at both catcher and second base in baseball history. It was a player named Tom Daly who played from 1887 to 1903. Historians say Daly was a weak-armed catcher who, after his transition to second base, became known for making throws to first underhand. Biggio was determined not to be a liability at the new spot, but one of the best.

To help Biggio (and his agent Barry Axelrod) feel better about the switch of an All-Star catcher to a new position, the Astros agreed to a two-year contract extension.

The extra work needed to make the transition resulted in some angered exchanges between Galante and his pupil at times. As Craig later said learning the mental part of the game, from where to be on relays and cut off plays to communicating with his middle infield partner to knowing what pitch his pitcher was going to throw and being positioned properly, was all new. Learning scouting reports from a second baseman's standpoint was also new.

But one of Galante's innovations in getting Biggio to physically use his hands correctly put Craig off at first. Instead of a glove, Matt wanted Biggio to use a paddle type device with a small layer of foam on one side. The object made Biggio use both hands in fielding balls for a quicker release on the throw. Biggio would stop the ball with the paddle device on his glove hand and quickly make the exchange to this throwing hand. At first he hated using the thing. Too many errors resulted. But eventually as he got the hang of it, Craig realized its purpose.

Former Astro and future Hall of Famer Joe Morgan had not used the paddle device in his day, but instead he used a very small fielder's glove. The object was the same. Use the glove to stop the ball and get it into the throwing hand as quickly as possible.

While the extra work with and without the paddle added hours (and often swollen hands) to Biggio's normal spring training day, that year it was worth it. Now similar devices are made and sold by sporting goods companies as training aides. Galante and his wife made his, and Gold Glove Hall of Fame second baseman Craig Biggio resulted.

Bagwell at First and Biggio at Second in 1992

When the 1992 season began, it was Jeff Bagwell at first base and Craig Biggio at second. The right side of the Houston infield would remain the same through the 2004 season. Art Howe says you can't think of the Astros without thinking of Biggio and Bagwell. "For me they are both worthy of Hall of Fame honors. Those two guys for fifteen years were the right side of the Astros infield. When you thought of the Houston Astros you thought of those guys. They made the Houston Astros. They were quality human beings on and off the field. They did a great job in the community. Bags is a low key guy, always kind of quiet, but really respected by everybody in the league and especially his teammates. Biggio is more outgoing but has every bit of the same respect."

That pairing would be immortalized in statuary in the Houston memory garden built beyond left field off Crawford Street outside Minute Maid Park and before Cooperstown induction and in both the Texas Baseball Hall of Fame and Texas Sports Hall of Fame.

In 1992, of course, the Astros were playing home games at the Astrodome. The team pattern of good pitching and weaker hitting that had mostly existed since the club was founded as the Colt 45s in 1962 was still very much in play. Consequently, baseball was always running second to football. It wasn't that the Houston Oilers, Houston Cougars, or Rice Owls had captured the city due to consistent excellence. It was that Astros baseball had never captured enough fans because it paled in comparison to football in action. The team had not drawn more than two million fans at home since 1980 and had done it only two times in thirty years. The 1991 club had attracted only 1,196,152 fans—an average of fewer than 15,000 per game. That was last in the National League. That club had also lost 97 games.

The 1992 Astros, with Bagwell and Biggio manning their new positions, was sixteen games better than the 1991 unit. They reached .500 at 81-81 with a very young team. And they did it the hard way. The season featured a 25 game road trip!

Republican Convention Forced Astros on the Road

George H. W. Bush was the President of the United States and was planning on a second term in 1992. However, to make it officially on the ballot, the Republicans needed to have a nominating convention. George was a long time resident of Houston and he thought bringing the convention to his hometown would be a good thing. It did cause a problem. National Political Conventions are held in the summer. That is when baseball teams have their seasons. At one time arenas like the Summit—home of the NBA Houston Rockets—were large enough. But by 1992 they weren't and something larger was available. The Houston Astrodome was much larger and would be perfect.

So from July 27 through August 23, the Astros would be on the longest scheduled road trip in modern major league history. In 1899, the Cleveland Spiders had a 50 game trip with the team trying to stave off dissolution. The Montreal Expos had played 26 straight games on the road in 1991 after a beam collapsed at Olympic Stadium. Neither of those road trips were scheduled in advance. Houston's was. The Astros would play 26 games in 28 days during that period and all of them out of town. When they started, they were 45-54 and 13 ½ games out of first place. What was worse was they had been awful on the road up to that point. They lost 27 of their first 40 games away from the Astrodome prior to the trip. But they were only two under .500 at 12-14 on the long trip. When they came home, they were 56-68 and 19 games off the lead. The trip took them to Atlanta, Cincinnati, Los Angeles, San Diego, San Francisco, Chicago, St. Louis, and Philadelphia. After the Chicago series, the team and staff spent a quick off day in Houston, but that was the only visit during the nearly month long grind.

Owner John McMullen claimed he had been forced into vacating the Dome because hosting the convention was what city officials wanted. "I was under a lot of pressure to this this. It wasn't my idea. Looking back," he said years later, "I wish I had told them to go to hell."

One of his reasons was that McMullen had to pay out money to settle a Major League Baseball Players Association (MLBPA) grievance that was filed because McMullen had not consulted the union before the fact. Much of the money McMullen had to fork out went to additional perks for the players on the trip and donations to amateur baseball programs as directed by the MLBPA.

The Astros survived the trip, and many felt the extra closeness even improved team unity. Maybe so, because the club went from 13 games under .500 when they returned home, to .500 at 81-81 at the end of the season. Houston was 25-13 in all games after the trip ended. Something else happened during the 1992 season that was noteworthy. About the time the Astros long road trip was beginning, John McMullen sold the Astros to Drayton McLane Jr. of Temple, Texas. McLane would not take over until the season was over and the sale could be approved by Major League Baseball. The purchase price for the team and lease at the Astrodome was announced at $115 million. The hotels and HSE cable television network the Astros also owned were of no interest to McLane and were retained by McMullen. McLane remembered, "After I bought the team and the resulting publicity, all of a sudden people came wanting my autograph and to pose for pictures. That was quite a change for a mostly unknown grocery distributor from Temple, Texas."

Meanwhile, back on the field the Astros were young enough to handle the rigors of the road. No starting everyday player was older than twenty-nine (Ken Caminiti), while five of the eight regulars were younger than twenty-five. The club was still not a good hitting team, as their .246 team average and puny 96 homerun totals would attest, but they were fourth in the National League with 139 stolen bases.

The pitching was much improved in the bullpen, but starters were sub-par. Only Mark Portugal among the regular starters carried an ERA under 3.70 and the team total 3.72 was 11th in the now twelve team National League.

Thirty-five-year old closer Doug Jones was the overall star of the staff. He had 36 saves, won eleven games, and compiled a 1.85 earned run average in 80 games. Three Astro pen men pitched more than 100 innings: Jones (111.2), Joe Boever (111.1) and Xavier Hernandez (111.0).

While both Biggio and Bagwell had OK seasons, they were nothing special. After his Rookie of the Year season in 1991, Bagwell never felt he had it made.

"No it probably took longer than that. I was just having fun that first year, hanging out with Casey [Candaele] and Cammy [Ken Caminiti], getting some hits," said Jeff. "I had a pretty big year. I probably felt after that whole year I could play. And then, of course, immediately I started struggling a little bit in '92."

Bagwell hit .273 with 18 homers, 96 runs batted in, and a .368 on base percentage.

Still Bagwell and Biggio played in every one of the 162 games. Biggio hit .277 with six homers, 39 runs batted in, 38 stolen bases, and an on base percentage of .378. While those total numbers may not have stood out, the season will be remembered as Biggio's second as an All Star. He became the first and only player in major league history to be an All-Star at both catcher and second base. And he did it in successive seasons! Defensively, he committed only 12 errors and only three in the last 74 games after the All-Star break.

Team Was Stronger in 1993 but Howe Was Still Axed

While still not a contender really, but with so many young players who could be projected to be improved with experience, a decision was made after the 1993 season to do two somewhat contradictory things: bring in the fences at the Astrodome, and sign some big dollar starting pitchers. Drayton McLane's new ownership wanted to achieve two goals: get into real contention, and thus boost the interest and attendance at the Astrodome.

Drayton McLane Jr. did not know much about baseball. He was trying to learn on the job and often frustrated coaches and his manager Art Howe with some of the things he said. As Art recently recalled, "I remember we lost the first three games of the year and he came into my office and asked, 'What's wrong?'. He was used to football. You lose two or three in a row in football and your season's done. I just said, we've got 159 more to go and I think we're gonna lose three in a row a few times." (For the record, the Astros would have ten more streaks of three or more straight losses including three five game stretches of consecutive defeats.)

McLane was all in favor of one idea his rookie ownership year and had the right idea. It just didn't work as well as hoped. Previous owner John McMullen did something similar in 1979 when he went for a big name local pitcher. For the 1980 season it was Nolan Ryan. This time McLane went for two. Former NL Cy Young Award winner Doug Drabek, a former University of Houston star, and former Texas Longhorn star Greg Swindell were paid substantially to anchor the Astro starting rotation, which had been uncharacteristically weak in 1992 even with an improved record from the season before.

The left-handed Swindell was only twenty-eight years old when he joined the Astros. He was coming off a 12-8 2.70 year in Cincinnati after starting his career as the second pick in the free agent draft out of Texas by the Cleveland Indians. At twenty-three he had won 18 games in Cleveland. On December 4, 1992, Swindell signed a four-year $16.4 million contract with the Astros.

Drabek, a native of Victoria, Texas, had been an eleventh round pick by the Chicago White Sox in 1983. As a minor leaguer, he was traded to the New York Yankees where he made his major league debut in 1986. Doug won 8 of 15 decisions in 21 starts. After the season, he was traded to the Pittsburgh Pirates where he had some great seasons. He was the 1990 NL Cy Young Award winner after winning 22 of 28 decisions with a 2.61 earned run average. The last five of his years in Pittsburgh, he never won fewer than fourteen games and had no ERA above 3.08. In 1992, he had won 15 with an ERA of 2.77 for the Pirates. At only thirty years old, there was no reason to expect anything less than that, especially when one added his home field would be the notoriously "dead air" Astrodome. Even with the fences coming in ten feet and a plan to raise the indoor temperature a few degrees, no one thought that would negatively affect Drabek. That was why on December 1, 1992, the Astros and Drabek agreed on a four-year $20-million deal.

In 1993 instead of leading the Astros rotation, Drabek and Swindell were no better than the fourth and fifth starters. Mark Portugal was tops with an 18-4 record and 2.98 earned run average. Then came Pete Harnisch at 16-9 and 2.98. Number three was twenty-four-year old Darryl

Kile, a product from the Astros own farm system. The right-hander with a big overhand curve went 15-8 and a 3.51 ERA.

Drabek was only 9-18 with a 3.79 earned run average and Swindell, the other big money free agent was just 12-13 with a 4.16 ERA. The club still improved to 85-77.

Even with the Drabek and Swindell disappointments in 1993, the club was getting much better. With the Dome fences about ten feet closer all around and a warmer atmosphere, more power resulted. Craig Biggio led the team with 21 homers—the first time he had really shown homerun punch. Bagwell added 20 and five more players hit homers in double figures. Biggio had a great overall year. He hit .287 with 21 homers, 64 RBIs, and 15 stolen bases, although he was caught 17 times. Craig had a .373 on base percentage aided by his being hit by pitches ten times. It was the first time Biggio had been hit that much during a season. He would get pretty good at "taking one for the team" before his career was over, with a modern record of 285 hit by pitches all his when he retired. Bagwell posted a .320 batting average to go with his 20 homers, 88 RBIs, 13 of 14 stolen bases, and a .388 on base percentage. Jeff's season ended early and he did miss the last 20 games in 1993. He was hit by a pitch from the Phillies Ben Rivera on September 10th that broke the fifth metacarpal bone in his left hand—something that would happen to him in each of the next two seasons as well.

The club still improved to 85-77. That was good enough for third in the division, six games off the lead. It was not good enough for Art Howe to retain his job. Much more had been expected out of the Astros with their new big dollar pitchers, but the improvement was only four games. Owner McLane, who had changed few personnel on the Astro staff since buying the team, made two big changes after 1992. He fired manager Art Howe and General Manager Bill Wood. They were replaced by young fiery Terry Collins as manager and Bob Watson as General Manager. Collins had been a coach with the Pirates under esteemed manager Jim Leyland. He had also served as manager in the Los Angeles Dodgers farm system. He had far less experience than Howe, but was a personality more in line with the new owner. McLane wanted a manager more exciting. As he put it, "Bill Wood as GM and Art Howe had been there, but there wasn't a lot of excitement on the team. It just wasn't their personalities. Art was a traditional baseball man. He did it by the numbers. I wanted a little more personality. I wanted someone who interacted with the players so that is why we selected Terry Collins to replace him and then as you remember, made Bob Watson the General Manager."

Watson had been a star Astro player who had moved into management, and with his hiring, would become the first full time black GM in baseball. Both would benefit from the ground work set in place by the Howe/Wood regime.

Courtesy of Jim Ellwanger

"Nineteen ninety-four was the beginning of a time
we changed the culture. We were able to make Houston
a baseball town again."

– Craig Biggio on the importance of what happened in 1994

The 1994 Houston Astro baseball season will be remembered as being bitter-sweet for several reasons. One reason is the season was interrupted and ultimately ended early due to a labor dispute between the player's union and the owners. The Astros, under new rookie manager Terry Collins, were only a half game off the new Central Division-leading Cincinnati Reds when play was shut down with almost fifty games left on the schedule. Jeff Bagwell was having the best season he would ever have. One of baseball's best ever in the modern era.

The season was the first in which the two leagues had split from two divisions to three. The Astros left the geographically challenged National League West which had the Atlanta Braves, Cincinnati Reds and Astros competing with teams really in the western portion of the country. Now they were in the National League Central with the Reds, Cubs, Cards, and Pirates. Only the Pirates were not located in the Central Time Zone, but at least were only one time zone away.

Had there not been a labor shutdown, Jeff would not have been playing anyway down the stretch in 1994. He had been hit on his left hand while batting and suffered the second break of a bone in the hand. On August 10, just before the work stoppage was to begin, a pitch from Andy Benes came in high and tight and broke the fourth metacarpal bone in his hand. The strike actually kept Jeff from pacing the floor the rest of the season. He hated to be out of the lineup.

As he told Bill Brown years after he had retired, "We had times when I played one hundred sixty-two games and I thought, you never know this might be the night I do something big. Looking back on it, I was more selfish because I later learned what it was like to be a pinch-hitter in 2005 and I've watched these guys. Getting those extra guys in games means a lot to a ball club. I didn't think I was selfish when I was playing every game at first base, but now I understand. I just thought we were probably a better team with me out there even if I didn't get any hits. Just draw a walk. Play defense, something like that. But that being said, looking back at it now if somebody told me more to understand the extra guys need some at-bats because in the long scheme of things, when they are coming up in the eighth and ninth innings as key pinch-hitters, those four at-bats they may have gotten a couple days back can go a long way."

Just how good were things going for Bagwell prior to the injury and shut down of play in 1994? He hit .368 with 39 homeruns and league leading 116 runs batted in. He would lead the league with a .750 slugging percentage while also stealing 15 of 19 bases. He also won a Gold Glove for his work at first base. That was all in 110 games. If one enjoys projecting what those numbers might have been had Jeff played in 160 of the 162 game schedule, he would have hit 56 homeruns and driven in 169 runs! Of course, projections are fun but don't mean anything except to emphasize what kind of season Jeff was having. Bagwell's 39 homeruns were the most ever hit by a Houston player, besting Jimmy Wynn's franchise record by two. Astonishingly Bagwell was able to hit 23 of them in the Astrodome. After the season, Bagwell won the National League MVP Award in a unanimous vote. To that point, only Orlando Cepeda in 1967 and Mike Schmidt in 1970 had ever been unanimous winners in the NL.

A number of Bagwell's achievements during 1994 were truly amazing. On June 24 vs the Dodgers in the Astrodome, he hit two homeruns in one inning and then a third in his next at-bat. He finished very strong in the shortened season. Over his last 64 games, Bagwell hit .397 with 28 homeruns and 74 RBIs. After the All-Star break he hit .432! The greatest season in Jeff Bagwell's career came two seasons before he took the field with the extra muscle and size he would have after extensive offseason work following 1995. Bagwell credited his work with hitting guru Rudy Jaramillo, who had worked for the Astros from 1990 through 1993, for letting his power come out. "He helped me understand my swing and I actually learned how to hit and I was like, 'I don't need anything more. I'm good.' When I walked on the field, I thought I was the best player on the field, and I didn't need anything more than that. It was never an ego thing with me, and I think at some point it became ego to some people." Bagwell made those comments to Jerry Crasnick of ESPN in 2004.

Craig Biggio was having a pretty good year himself in 1994. He hit .318 to go with 6 homers, 39 RBIs, and 39 for 43 in stolen base attempts. While Bagwell's on base percentage was a superb .451, Biggio's number was nearly as sparkling at .411. Biggio and Bagwell were both NL All-Stars and both were Gold Glove winners. It was the first for Biggio, just two seasons after his switch from being a catcher. The Astros right side of the infield were both ranked #1 at their positions by the Elias Sports Bureau and many others in the game.

For really the first time in Houston baseball history, the offense was much stronger than the pitching, although Doug Drabek did bounce back. When play ended, Doug was 12-6 with a solid 2.84 ERA. He was the only

Astro starting pitcher with an ERA under the 4.37 of Greg Swindell. Another University of Texas alumni Shane Reynolds was up and coming, but Darryl Kyle had an offseason. The bullpen was solid. It included a twenty-one-year old lefty, Mike Hampton, who appeared in 44 games.

For the first time the Houston offense's batting average at .278 and second in the National League ranked higher than the team's pitching earned run average on league stat charts. The ERA was fifth in the NL at 3.97.

New manager Terry Collins liked to play aggressive baseball and the Astros were second in the National League with 124 stolen bases and tenth toughest to throw out.

Five players stole more than thirteen bags with Biggio's league leading 39 tops. James Mouton had 24.

While the shortened season saw the Astros finish second in their division by a half game, interest in the club was growing. Two of the largest crowds ever to see the team at home were on hand during 1994. 50,016 saw the Astros host the Cardinals on April 30 and 48,945 saw the Astros take on the Giants on August 6. The team averaged 26,460 per game. That was in the bottom half of the NL averages, but would have gotten the club over 2.1 million had the whole season been played out. It would have been the highest total since 1980.

The Astros were moving into the consciousness of fans both nationally and locally. And it was Craig Biggio and Jeff Bagwell that were leading the way.

Baseball Strike Fouled-Up End of '94 and Start of '95

The 1995 season could not build on the momentum from 1994 for one very good reason. The baseball work stoppage was still not over. It had cost the cancellation of the 1994 World Series and the members of the MLB Player's Association remained on strike through the winter. But Major League Baseball was determined to play in 1995 no matter who was on rosters. When spring training began, teams had been filled with anyone who could play a little and was not afraid to buck the union. It reminded some longtimers of the years during World War II. Rosters were filled with veterans near the end of the line, career minor leaguers who felt this might be their only chance to play in a major league uniform, and some who did not agree with the union-management conflict.

Fans at the Astros camp saw no Jeff Bagwell or Craig Biggio. Instead manager Terry Collins and his staff were working with players named Donovan Mitchell at second base and Jeff Ball at first. Chad White was in center field, Dave Rohde at shortstop. Others in the starting lineup for the last two pre-season exhibition games, which were played in the Astrodome on March 30 against the Yankees and March 31 in Arlington against the Texas Rangers respectively, included Juan Guerrero, Lance Madsen, Tim Evans, Tony Gilmore, Craig McMurtry, Ken Gillum, Mark Skeels, and Tyrone Narcisse, among a few others. Because the umpires were honoring the player's union strike, the officiating of the games was handled by college and high school umps.

The game in the Dome marked the 30th anniversary of the first Astrodome game—the meeting with the Yankees in 1965. This one was hardly memorable. Only 9,525 fans bothered to see the faux major leaguers. Houston beat the Yanks 10-1 thanks to a seven run fifth inning. The pseudo-Yankees made three errors in that inning.

The last game with replacement players was won by the Rangers 3-2 before 14, 398 at The Ballpark in Arlington. The Astros fill-ins finished the spring with a 19-8 record. Then the strike ended.

The real Astros held a mini spring camp (most of the players had been working out on their own) and the official National League season opened on Wednesday, April 26 in San Diego. Doug Drabek got the start and the win. Jeff Bagwell started as he has finished in the 1994 season with a two-run homer in the third. The homer was off Andy Benes, who had ended Bagwell's season the previous August when he had hit him with the pitch that had broken a bone in his hand. He also drew two walks and scored three of the Astros' ten runs in the 10-1 win.

Nineteen ninety-five was not going to be able to mirror 1994 for anyone. The team was able to play only a 144 game schedule thanks to the late start. They won 76 of them, good for a .528 winning percentage and second place in the division in Collins's second season as a major league skipper. This time, however, they finished nine games behind the first place team. The Astros were in first place on three occasions, but only by a half game each time and the last was on May 11th when Greg Swindell, with a save from Billy Wagner, beat the Pirates in Pittsburgh 12-4. Biggio was 2-4 with an RBI and two runs scored. He also stole a base. Bagwell was 2-6 with both hits homers off Paul Wagner. He drove in three runs.

After the win the Astros were 9-5, but would lose their next four and never see first place again. Most of the season they were locked into second place behind the Reds in the NL Central Division while dropping a few games under .500 or going a few games above. They were close enough, but never really in the race; double figures off the first place team from Cincinnati until the very end.

Attendance showed the non-competitive season and fall-out from the strike. Many casual fans all around baseball got used to not having the game starting at the end of 1994 and into the spring of 1995, and they had found other things to do. It may have cost Montreal more than anywhere else. The Expos had been built into a contender and solid team by 1994 and may have been on their way to having as strong chance to win a World Series. They were 74-40 and leading the NL East by six games when the strike hit. They had drawn almost 1.3 million fans to the Olympic Stadium in only 52 home games. Moises Alou, the star left fielder for that team, remembered, "We were so good that when we were stretching on the road, it was like we knew we were going to kick that team's ass. And the other team knew it, too." By the next spring, Alou was disillusioned. The Expos started dismantling the team to make up for lost revenue during the strike. Lost from the team was their ace starter, top closer, their leadoff hitter and their cleanup hitter. Alou still said he understood, "Once you become a free agent or command a high salary, you don't belong on this club anymore. People are just waiting here." It was the beginning of the end for Major League baseball in Montreal.

Even when the strike hit in 1994, the players were told by management it wouldn't be lengthy. General Manager Kevin Malone, quoted in Howard Bryant's book, *Juicing the Game*, said, "Stick around fellas, this isn't going to last long." He was wrong and both the fans and players in Montreal knew a golden opportunity to win a championship was lost. The franchise never was able to overcome the heart break and neither were the fans. In 1995, the combination of strike fall-out, questionable ownership decisions, and a less successful team started the slide that resulted in a good baseball city losing its team to Washington a few years later.

The Astros were harmed as well. In 72 home games played in 1995, they drew just over 200,000 fans fewer than they had in 59 home games in 1994.

Craig Biggio and Jeff Bagwell didn't match 1994 either. Craig was actually better! Not so for Bagwell, but he had a physical excuse.

Biggio's batting average dropped from .318 to .302, but he had a better year. He hit a then-career record 22 homeruns after only hitting six in 1994. He drove in a new career high 77 runs while leading the National League for the first time by scoring 123. While his league-lead-tying 44 doubles from 1994 were reduced to 30, his extra base totals for 1995 of 54 were only one less than his 1994 number. Biggio's total bases count rose from 127 to 154.

Bagwell had a good year for an average player. However, after what he did in 1994, no one felt Bagwell should play like an average player. Jeff got off to a very slow start in 1995 and was hitting only .183 with just four homeruns and 14 RBIs through the end of May. Then he got hot in June and July. He hit .339 with five homers and 21 runs batted in during June, and in 28 games in July he hit .330 with seven homers and 31 runs batted in. His average had climbed to .283 with 16 homeruns and 66 runs batted in.

At that point, his left hand got in the way of an errant pitch and for the third straight season, he suffered a broken metacarpal. It was his fourth metacarpal that was broken for the second time. This time it was a pitch from former teammate Brian Williams, then with the San Diego Padres.

Bagwell was out of action for the whole month of August. When he was sidelined, the Astros were in second place within 3 ½ games of first place. When he returned on September 1 the team was still in second, but 13 ½ games out of first. If the Astros were going to contend in 1995, they needed a hot Bagwell. He had heated up before the injury, but then he was gone.

After the third broken bone in his left hand in three seasons, Bagwell consulted with management and employees of the Houston-based Douglas Protective Equipment Company. It was decided that adding a protective pad to the back of his left hand batting glove could work to protect the back of his hand by redistributing the force of a pitched ball should he be hit in the hand again. The protection consisted of a padded plastic shell sewn on as a flap to the back of his glove. The company that designed the piece was most famed for his work with football rib protectors and shoulder pads and umpire chest protectors. While it wouldn't help Bagwell get back on the field any sooner, when he did he would have protection. He never had another broken hand bone for the last ten years of his career.

As for the rest of 1995, by the time "Baggie" returned, the team was out of the race. However, on his return he started hot. He hit .339 with five homers and 21 runs batted in during 28 games after coming off the disabled list.

When the season was over, his totals paled by comparison with 1994, but still solid for the 114 games he played. A .290 average with 21 homers, 29 doubles, 88 runs scored, and 87 runs batted in. After the season, Bagwell was determined to do better in 1996. He hired a body builder named Herschel Johnson. Johnson suggested that Bagwell concentrate on "baseball muscles" and not go for a lot of bulk. Bagwell wasn't worried about that. He wanted to be as big and as strong as he could be. The result of a winter of his intense weight-lifting and a high protein diet was 20-25 more pounds of muscle. Jeff is adamant that at no time did he use any illegal supplements—either steroids or human growth hormone, but he did use creatine and androstenedione—which were legal at the time—to allow him to work out longer. "I tried it [Andro] and it didn't work for me," said Jeff in a 1999 *Baseball Weekly* story. "My homeruns went down." He admitted the temptation to use performance enhancing drugs (PEDs) was there, but he resisted. In an interview from 2001 in the *Florida Sun Sentinel*, he said, "One thing I know is I can go home after my career is over and say I did it myself."

The loss of Bagwell for a month hurt the club, but there were other reasons the team took a step back as well. The team batting average (.275) and runs scored (747) were both second in the 14 team National League, even without much homerun punch. The Astros were 12th in the league with just 109 homers. The team pitching earned run average jumped to 4.06 and the hurlers allowed the 11th most runs in the league. The club was lacking a sure fire closer. With only 32 saves, the Astros ranked 12th in that category. Todd Jones was OK, but had only 15 saves to lead the team. Both Doug Drabek and Greg Swindell gave up way more hits than innings pitched and saw their earned run averages zoom to 4.77 and 4.47 respectively.

Shane Reynolds moved into the starting rotation along with Mike Hampton. Both showed promise. Darryl Kile was still a work in progress, but his numbers were puzzling. He was 4-12 with a 4.96 earned run average, yet in 127 innings pitched, he allowed only 114 hits. He was a much better pitcher than his numbers. His time would come.

Collins' Run as Skipper Ended after 1996

The 1996 season would be the last for Terry Collins as skipper of the Astros, despite yet another second place finish. The main reason for the change was simply that the club had not improved during his three years. However, there were more rumblings that Collins autocratic style of managing was starting to wear thin. Before the season, team leaders Biggio and Bagwell were made unofficial team captains and encouraged to take leadership roles on the club. They had shown that they were the best players on the team and both knew what was needed to get the most of their abilities and had a strong desire to win. As related in Larry Dierker's book, *This Ain't Brain Surgery*, "This seemed like a good idea, but it didn't work out. Bagwell cared deeply about the team, but his leadership talents are mostly non-vocal. Biggio was a team guy too and he liked to talk, but he was a driven man, a perfectionist. It worked well for him, but left him intolerant of those less motivated." When Dierker had those thoughts, he was still a broadcaster for the team. The inference from Dierker's feeling was that players started to come to Biggio and Bagwell with their complaints. One or both often agreed with their teammate, and at that point the manager started to lose the clubhouse. It was a concern of both club President Tal Smith and General Manager Gerry Hunsicker before they made the managerial change.

What that means is that the manager's authority was usurped. Some orders were either ignored or only followed partially. Players would openly question some decisions made by Collins and his staff. Sometimes those complaints would find their way into print or on the air. Other comments might be made "off the record," but inferences were clear. Collins was at times a micro-manager and was often impatient with pitchers and made more changes than the hurlers liked. Of course, the pitchers caused a great deal of that with inconsistencies and ineffectiveness so it really wasn't all on the skipper. The season included a nine game losing streak. They were deceptively a contender, but not a real one. They finished second six games behind despite finishing only two games over .500 at 82-80.

Collins's last club dropped off offensively from second in runs scored to eighth. From a .275 team batting average to .262. They did hit more homers from 109 to 129 but that was still only 14th in the NL with the per-formance enhancing drug era growing in some circles of the major leagues.

Biggio and Bagwell Did All They Could on the Field

Playing a full 162 game season for the first time since 1993, both Craig Biggio and Jeff Bagwell saw no reason to ever sit. Both played in all the games. Biggio set a team record with 723 plate appearances and 605 official at-bats. Bagwell appeared at the plate 719 times.

The duo walked 210 times as the opposition knew who they had to be most careful with. Craig had a .386 on base percentage while Baggy was on base at a .451 clip. Both combined for 46 stolen bases. Biggio pilfered 25 and was tossed out only seven times. Bagwell was 21 for 28. Biggio's main numbers were a .288 average with 15 homers and 75 runs batted in. Bagwell hit .315 with 31 homers and 120 runs batted in. Those numbers were better than his totals for 1995 before he added the extra weight and muscles, but not that much more when you factor in that Jeff played 48 more games in 1996. The biggest change had nothing to do with muscles. Jeff walked nearly twice as much in 1996, and his on base percentage jumped from a good .399 to an outstanding .451 in '96.

Derek Bell in right field and Sean Berry at third base had nice seasons. Bell hit 17 homeruns and drove in 113. Berry also knocked out 17 homers and drove in 95. But the Astros pitching dropped even further with a 4.37 earned run average while also surrendering 154 homeruns and more hits than innings pitched.

Only thirty-three-year old Doug Drabek was over thirty in the rotation, and younger hurlers like Sean Reynolds, Darryl Kile, and Mike Hampton showed promise. Greg Swindell was jettisoned early in the season. Don-nie Wall took most of Swindell's starts, but a youngster who debuted late in the season, Chris Holt, had shown some promise in the minors. Todd Jones with 17 saves was still the top closer, but twenty-two-year old Billy Wagner was prepping to take over. It would be very soon.

The Astros made the managerial switch after the season, feeling Col-lins had gone as far as he could and the team was not getting better. The new manager would create some shockwaves in baseball, but another move in the previous offseason—or lack of one—could have been even greater.

Biggio Was a Free Agent and Heavily Wooed

Between the 1995 and 1996 season prior to Terry Collins's last season as manager, Astro second baseman Craig Biggio was in a position to cash out on his National League All-Star status. He was a free agent. The St. Louis Cardinals, San Diego Padres, and Colorado Rockies all made strong bids. On an almost daily basis, Craig's mind was swirling. As he told Denver baseball writer Tracy Ringolsby a few years later, "One day I was going to stay [in Houston]. The next day would be a bad day [in talks] and a good day with the other team. At the end I was either going to the Colorado Rockies or stay in Houston. Finally we got something done with Houston in the last minute." Reports were the Rockies offer was for $20-million over four seasons with a fifth year option. The Astros offered $22-million. The Rockies would not guarantee the fifth year so Biggio stayed home. Drayton McLane remembered he was keeping touch from long distance. "I had businesses internationally in Europe and Asia and so I would call Craig every day. I'd be in Poland, Spain, Germany, or China from all over and he'd ask me where I was today. He didn't even know where some of the countries were that I was doing business. So he and I got very close. I told his agent, Barry Axelrod, who was also Bagwell's agent, how much we valued Craig as both a player and a human being and I sold them on the idea that both Craig and Jeff would someday have a great chance to make the Hall of Fame and I wanted to make them a commitment to keep them here to help their chances after playing for only one team."

All that was well and good, but as agent Axelrod remembers, "That negotiation was grueling. Everybody thinks free agency is kind of the gold ring. That once you get to free agency, that's the greatest thing ever. But you've got all these people courting you and recruiting you and telling you how wonderful you are and how they're going to win all those World Series rings and all that stuff. In Craig's case, it was more than just the Rockies most of the way. The Cardinals were very aggressive and so were the Padres. It's funny how things stick with you," Axelrod remembered. "I'll see Tony LaRussa periodically and he will always get off, you know, 'If you'd let Biggio sign with St. Louis he'd have two more rings.' And Bob Gebhardt who I later worked with in Arizona and was the GM of Colorado…every time I see him—it's good natured—but one regret he has is he didn't step up quite enough to get Craig. Bob is sure he would have been a force in Colorado."

Once Biggio made the decision to stay in Houston, Axelrod had to tell the other suitors they would not be getting Craig. "I will still say that, without question, some of the hardest phone calls I had to make in my career were to teams we had to say no to. It was very difficult for Craig to say no to the Padres, Cardinals, and Rockies in order to stay in Houston. But he did it and he could have made more money. There were a couple of times he even apologized to me saying, 'I know I could be making more and I don't want to make you look bad (as an agent) by not getting enough money.' I told him my job was to help put you in the place you are most comfortable. That is where you are going to be the most productive. I don't think there is one ounce of regret with Craig about how things turned out."

Reflecting more, "I'm very proud of it (that Biggio and Bagwell played their whole careers in one place) to tell you the truth. It gets mentioned a lot that I had something to do with it. Drayton McLane has talked about it. Some other executives…Craig talks about it. I am proud they got to spend their whole careers with the same team. At one time we tried to count 'em up…how many active star players with ten or more years were still with one team. We came up with only about five or six. Craig and Jeff, Cal Ripken, Tony Gwynn, Tom Glavine at the time, and maybe one or two others."

"Craig was one of two players I represented that brought up how cool it was as a kid to look at the back of the baseball card and see a player who had been with one team their whole career. Used to be a lot of them, Ernie Banks, Stan Musial, Ted Williams, Mickey Mantle or whoever. The other player that thought that was great was Mark Grace. He never wanted to leave the Cubs, but they forced him to become a free agent. While he went to Arizona and was on a World Series winner, he has never forgiven the Cubs."

The commitment from McLane was they would never be traded as long as they were under an Astro contract.

The next time Craig had a free agency chance in 2000, the issue was settled quickly as he and the Astros inked a three-year extension. He also got some contract consideration when the Astros asked him to move to the outfield to make room for Jeff Kent at second base prior to the 2003 season. He would sign one more contact extension to get him through his 3,000[th] hit season to the end of his playing career. Craig made no secret that his involvement with the youngsters in the Sunshine Kids program in

Houston had a bearing in his decision to stay home. That—and perhaps something planted in his mind by his father years before, "Finish what you start."

After the decision to replace Terry Collins was made following the 1996 season, who team president Tal Smith, general manager Gerry Hunsicker, and owner Drayton McLane chose to take over caused shockwaves throughout baseball. It would lead to the best period in Houston baseball history. Biggio and Bagwell were right in the middle leading the way on the field.

8 Dierker Takes Over in the Final Days of the Dome

"A team is only as good as it thinks it is. Confidence is crucial."

– Larry Dierker to Tal Smith and Gerry Hunsicker when
being surprisingly interviewed for the manager's job.

Courtesy of Lambda Chi Alpha Fraternity

In 1997, a glass ceiling in U.S. government was broken when Madeleine Albright became the first female Secretary of State. Islamic extremists conducted a major act of terrorism when 70 people, including 60 foreign tourists, were gunned down while visiting Egypt's Valley of the Kings. Hong Kong was returned to Chinese rule. Gas averaged $1.22 a gallon. "The Lion King" debuted on Broadway.

And the Houston Astros had a new manager.

Larry Dierker came up as a pitcher through the Houston system after being signed following his high school graduation at 17 in 1964. The native of Southern California was in the major leagues with the Colt 45s after pitching in only nine minor league games the same year. He had reached his 18th birthday when he made his first major league start. During eleven full and three partial seasons Dierker won 139 games. He won 20 games in 1969 had wins in double figures nine times. He even pitched a no-hitter in 1976. Although arm troubles ended his career after eleven games with the St. Louis Cardinals in 1977, the only other franchise he spent any time working for, Dierker returned to Houston working in sales for the club before moving into the radio-television booth full time.

He had been working as a partner with Gene Elston, DeWayne Staats, Milo Hamilton, and Bill Brown primarily since the late 1970s. In 1996, he had spent nearly twenty years in the booth.

When Smith, Hunsicker, and McLane decided Dierker might be a strong managerial candidate it caught Dierker and the rest of baseball by total surprise.

Astro fans were excited to have longtime player and broadcaster in the managerial chair. Not everyone was of course, especially his old broadcast partner Milo Hamilton.

Hamilton and Dierker had been paired on radio for years. Maybe it was a case of familiarity breeds contempt, but neither were exactly best buddies. Dierker, a former player, was not afraid to question the very professional announcer Hamilton if he said something Dierker did not agree with. Hamilton did not like to be questioned. He was, after all, a Ford Frick honoree by the Hall of Fame and had been in the game since the early 1950s! For all his popularity with fans Hamilton was less popular with many of the people he worked with. A very large ego was the center of the problem. Milo was not a bad man. He volunteered to MC any charity fund raiser in which he was asked, but his ego caused a lot of internal problems (and jokes made behind his back). So when the Astros announced the hiring of Larry Dierker to be the new manager of the Astros, many were watching what Milo Hamilton's reaction would be at the introductory news conference. That included club owner Drayton McLane.

"We had the announcement scheduled and no one knew who the new manager was going to be. We kept Larry in the next room and Tal Smith, Gerry Hunsicker, and I took our places. Then we brought in Larry. I looked at Milo's face. It's a good thing he wasn't carrying a concealed weapon!" laughed McLane.

While all the players liked "Dierk" as a broadcaster—unless he had said something uncomplimentary about their play on the air—having him become their new manager caught them by surprise. Sure he had been a very successful major league player, but that had ended twenty years before and he had never coached or managed on any level. How could he make the Astros a winner?

The managerial replacement most of the veteran players, including Craig Biggio and Jeff Bagwell, would most liked to have seen in the job was Matt Galante. He was an Astro-lifer like Dierker, and he had actually managed in the minor leagues and coached for years with the big club. He lived, breathed, and ate baseball. He had made Biggio into a Gold Glove winning second baseman and helped in the conversion of Jeff Bagwell from third base to first where he, too, had become a Gold Glove winner. Even so, public comments by the players about Dierker once he had taken over were positive. Darryl Kile said, "I think it's a lot more relaxed in here. He's given us the freedom to do things and play our game. It's just a different clubhouse than before." Bagwell added, "During the games Larry's been laid-back, smiling and having a good time. That helps."

Dierker had impressed the Astro brass with his knowledge and insights provided during his years on the air particularly during the disappointing Astros 1996 season. He was old school, but was not averse to incorporating some of the new statistical information made available thanks to the use of computers: where to position players on defense thanks to hitting charts, how players hit some pitchers and the reverse. The actual numbers for pitcher-batter matchups was another of the features Dierker had often used on the air. He also wanted to temper their use in some situations by keeping his best pitchers on the mound longer than Terry Collins had. He wanted to train his pitchers both mentally and physically to try to go deeper into games when they started. His thinking was that his start-ing pitchers are supposed to be the best pitchers on the staff. Why use a number of mid-level early or middle relievers any more than absolutely necessary just because of a pitch count?

As for his regulars, he wanted to preach and have his coaches teach basic fundamentals, but would let his players play the game. He would not over-manage every aspect of a game. He would never call pitches. Keep-ing runners close would be between the pitcher and catcher. There would be almost no "take" signs for hitters. They were expected to think for themselves. He would also rely on the veterans like Biggio, Bagwell, and Luis Gonzalez to keep the clubhouse loose, happy, and on the right track.

Astros Were Only Slightly Better but the Postseason Beckoned

Most Astro fans would be very surprised to learn that Larry Dierker's first Astro team in 1997 won only two more games than Terry Collins's last team the year before. What they may not know is that shows the power of winning championships. In 1997 an 84-78 record was good enough to win the National League Central. 82-80 in 1996 was only good for sec-ond place.

Dierker had been very popular for years as one of baseball's most astute observers from the broadcast booth. And with the coaching staff led by Houston's all-time winningest manager, Bill Virdon, as his right hand man, things were in good hands.

The Astrodome saw 2,046,781 fans come through the gates. That was eighth best in the 14 team National League. Getting off to a good start helped too. The Astros opened at home, taking two of three from the Braves, then sweeping the Cardinals, and were 5-1 before hitting the road for the first time.

Shane Reynolds beat John Smoltz in the opener 2-1 with Billy Wagner getting the save. Craig Biggio had two hits and scored a run. Jeff Bagwell drove in a run on a ground out. New catcher Brad Ausmus, acquired from the Tigers in an offseason trade, ran the show behind the plate and contrib-uted two hits.

In the second game against Atlanta's Mike Hampton, now put into the starting rotation fulltime, out dueled Greg Maddux as the Astros won 4-3. Billy Wagner got his second save.

The Astros first loss came in game three. Tom Glavine bested Darryl Kile 3-2. Kile pitched a strong eight innings, but while Biggio had his third straight 2-4 game, the Astro offense managed only eight hits. Bagwell was 1-4.

When the Cardinals came to town, both Biggio and Bagwell had three hits in the first game. Bagwell's third in the bottom of the 11th scored Ray Montgomery providing the Astros with a walk off 3-2 win. Manager Dierker had gotten six and a third innings from his starter Chris Holt then saw six pitchers from his bullpen hold the Cards scoreless the rest of the way.

The second game of the Cardinal series demonstrated the Dierker managerial style. Veteran starting pitcher Sid Fernandez was struggling but got through five innings having allowed four hits including a lead-off homerun by DeLino DeShields and two walks. When the Astros batted in the last of the fifth, Ray Montgomery was sent up to hit for Fernandez. Montgomery struck out, but two hitters later James Mouton homered and the Astros took the lead they would never relinquish. In the sixth, Dierker sent Ramon Garcia to pitch. He never was relieved. He threw four shut-out innings for the save. While it appeared to be what many thought was something only "Dierker thinking" would do, he had a basic explanation following the game. "We had used six pitchers yesterday. Garcia was one of them, but he had only faced one batter and thrown one pitch. We had to save arms. He was doing great so why make a change?"

The Astros walk off win and the win by the duo of Fernandez and Garcia started to get fans thinking. Maybe this club might be special. Maybe Larry Dierker as manager can get us over the hump.

As noted earlier the opening home-stand was not exactly an omen of things to come. The Astros would not be able to average winning five of every six. In fact, after those first six games, the team would be 79-77 the rest of the way. It would be good enough to win, but certainly not easily.

Both Craig Biggio and Jeff Bagwell did their parts as usual. Like Terry Collins before him Larry Dierker put their names in the lineup every day and let them play. Both were in all 162 games for the second straight season. Bagwell was extremely productive. He broke his own Astro single season homerun mark with 43 while also driving in 135 runs. His batting average was .286 while his slugging percentage was .592 and his on base average .425. If that wasn't enough, he walked 127 times, hit 40 doubles, and stole 31 bases. The thirty-one-year-old Biggio was right behind. Craig hit 22 homers, drove in 81 runs, had a .309 average to go with a .415 on base percentage, and .501 slugging percentage. He led the major leagues by scoring 146 runs, the most in a single season in the National League since Chuck Klein's 152 in 1932. He also had 37 doubles, eight triples, and stole 47 bases! As a side-note, Biggio went the entire season without grounding into a double play. That had only been done two other times in Major League history by players who were in at least 150 games. Augie Galan of the Cubs did it in 154 games in 1935 and Dick McAuliffe of the Tigers did it in 151 games in 1968. Biggio played in 162 games with 619 at-bats. It could have been Craig's best overall season as he looked back, "In '97 we went to the playoffs the first time. This is what I remember. I remember they both [1997 and 1998] were crazy for me numbers wise, but in '97 we got to the playoffs for the first time and we really didn't have a team to compete with the Braves the way they were at the time, but we were happy. It was the first time we got there, but we got there."

The team pitching dropped off from what it was able to do in that first home stand, but was still an improvement from 1996. Three starters pitched more than 200 innings, led by Darryl Kile in his breakout year, and 19-7 record. He had six of the Astros 16 complete games, which ranked third in the league. Mike Hampton won 15, but the other starters were sub .500. The fifth spot in the rotation had been a problem all year. Billy Wagner was the anchor in the pen with 23 saves. One of 1997's fill-in utility pitchers, Jose Lima, was mediocre in 1997 with a 1-6 record and an earned run average of 5.28 in 52 games. He would be very important the next two seasons however.

While the 1997 Astros started the season winning two of three against the Braves and finished strong with seven wins in their last nine games, including the division clincher in the Astrodome on September 21 against the Chicago Cubs, they were no match for the National League East champion Braves in the postseason. Atlanta ousted the Astros in three straight.

Jeff Bagwell's memories from 1997 don't dwell on what happened against the Braves, but that the young Astros had won a postseason spot. "If you remember we had come in second place a bunch of times. When we finally clinched in '97, the day with Hambone [Mike Hampton] pitching, that was pretty special for us as a group. The Astros hadn't made the playoffs since 1986, eleven years and it was a nice feeling. And we went on a nice run after that, making the playoffs several times."

In the division clinching game on September 21 against the Chicago Cubs, both Biggio and Bagwell were keys as usual. From his lead-off spot in the batting order, Craig walked three times, scored twice, stole a base and had an RBI double. Bagwell had a double and triple, scored one, and drove in one. Mike Hampton threw a complete game four hitter. The Astrodome had 35,623 fans on hand to celebrate the team's first postseason berth since 1986.

The playoff matchup would put the Astros against the Atlanta Braves. They had beaten the Braves two of three to open the season, but were only 4-7 against them for the full season. It would be 4-10 once the playoff series was over. Atlanta had too much riding on sweeping the best of five Division Series 3-0. Greg Maddux held both Biggio and Bagwell hitless in the opening game as the Astros collected only seven hits in the 2-1 Atlanta win. In the second game, it was Astro pitching that failed primarily as the Braves took a 13-3 win. Hampton and most of the bullpen was ineffective. The Astros had only six hits. Biggio had one of them.

The third game and only one played in Houston was played before a record crowd of 53,688. The Astros were held to just three hits—one of them by Bagwell—as John Smoltz kept the Astros in check. Chuckie Carr's homerun was the only Astro run in the game.

As the stars and leaders of the team, both Biggio and Bagwell were criticized for not coming through in such big games. The reality was no one was hitting for Houston. Derek Bell and Billy Spiers, for example, didn't have any hits at all in the three games. While the team pitching staff had a very solid 3.00 earned run average, the Braves allowed only one earned run per nine innings. The fact that the Braves top three starting pitchers were all Hall of Fame quality can't be under-estimated either.

The 1998 Team Was Built into Astros' Best

In 1998 with a division championship under their belt and two major stars, Craig Biggio and Jeff Bagwell to anchor the offense, the goal was to take the next step. Make the team stronger in all phases of the game. Certainly winning only 84 games again would make it very difficult to even get into the postseason, let alone get far.

During the offseason, the Astros rebuilt their outfield by signing free agent Moises Alou to play left field. He replaced long-time favorite Luis Gonzalez. In center field Carl Everett was brought in. Everett not always had been an easy player to deal with on other clubs, but he toed the line with the Astros. Word was that the Astros three leaders, Biggio, Bagwell, and catcher Brad Ausmus got to him early and told him how the Astros worked—including how to work with the media which had been an Everett problem in the past.

Sean Berry and Bill Spiers shared third base. Berry, as in 1997, was considered the regular, but only because Spiers was versatile enough to fill in all over the field and often was in the lineup at another spot.

To get more offense in the infield, Ricky Gutierrez was elevated to the starting shortstop job, supplanting Tim Bogar. The latter may have had more range than Gutierrez, but Ricky had a solid 1998 with a fielding percentage of .976 and only 15 errors over 141 games. He also hit .261 with 13 stolen bases.

The rest of the Astro lineup was Biggio at second base, Bagwell at first base, and Ausmus behind the plate.

The Astros hit .280 as a team with 166 homeruns. The average was second best in the National League. Their on base percentage of .356 was first. The homerun total was sixth. And they were still playing home games in the Astrodome. They led the league in runs scored with 874 and were second in stolen bases. And that stolen base total was a full team effort. Eight players stole ten or more bases.

Craig Biggio had 50 stolen bases and also hit 51 doubles. He joined Tris Speaker as the only two players in the 20th century to hit fifty in both categories in a single season. That was only part of his tremendous season. Biggio also had a .325 batting average and a .403 on base percentage. He homered 20 times, drove in 88 runs, and totaled 210 hits. That was the first 200 hit season in Houston history.

His highlights during the year were many. When he hit his 49th double on Sept. 14 against the Mets, he broke teammate Jeff Bagwell's club record. When he recorded his 196th hit, he set a new Astro record, besting the old one held by Enos Cabell since 1978. He had two two-homer games, the eighth and ninth of his career during the season. Biggio was on his fifth straight NL All Star team and seventh overall. It was a year never to forget for Biggio. His achievements were not the only highlights.

Jeff Bagwell played in 147 games and hit .304 while reaching base at an amazing .424 clip. He hit 34 homers and drove in 111 while also stealing 19 bases. Astro fans were used to heroics from Biggio and Bagwell. The difference in 1998 was General Manager Gerry Hunsicker's additions. Moises Alou was amazing and Carl Everett more than just solid.

Alou hit .314, but he also led the team in homeruns with 38 and RBIs with 124. The nephew of former Astro outfielder Jesus Alou, Moises fit right in. He and Bagwell developed a close friendship that lasted long after their years playing together ended. His professionalism and ability made him a great fit with the Biggio-Bagwell-Ausmus core of the team. Everett started 113 games in the outfield and hit .296 with 15 homeruns, 76 runs batted in, and 14 stolen bases. It was quite an offensive unit. Throw in the Berry/Spiers combo at third base, which added 20 more homers (13 by Berry), and the club was loaded.

From the start of the season the Astros were the class of the National League Central. Then Gerry Hunsicker made a traded at the deadline that turned the Astros from a super team to a powerhouse.

For three minor leaguers, Hunsicker pried lefthander Randy Johnson away from the Seattle Mariners. Johnson had been having a bad season with Seattle, but much of that stemmed from contract talks. The Mariners had neither the funds nor inclination to sign their star pitcher to a new long term deal at the end of the season when he could become a free agent. So they put him on the market to try and salvage something before losing him. The Astros made the best bid.

When the Astros acquired Johnson, and once he proved his weak start in Seattle was a fluke, Houston became the team to beat in many pundit's eyes. Jeff Bagwell told Bill Brown he was more cautious, "I didn't feel like that. I was just so excited for something like that to happen. He shows up the first day in Pittsburgh and just dominates. He just dominated the whole time here. One thing I do remember about that team is that I noticed sitting in the back of the bus and looking over at all the players we had that my golly we could do this! The Yankees were having a great year, but I thought we had two lefty pitchers in Hampton and Johnson who were really, really special. They (Yankees) had some lefty hitters like Paul O'Neill and Tino Martinez. So we might get some outs there. Of course, I NEVER expected to lose to San Diego. But I never expected to face the same pitcher twice in three games (Kevin Brown). It was game, off-day, game, off-day." Biggio concurred with Bagwell, "We had the team the Yankees didn't want to play. We just weren't able to play them."

Moises Alou knew that team was special, but maybe not the best he had played with. As he told Brown, "I was on a World Series champion in Florida and in 1994 I was on probably the best team in the game that year," Montreal had a large lead in the NL East before the work stoppage, "and the Cubs in 2004 were also very good." The more he reflected however, "We had Everett, Lima, Hampton, Johnson, Bell, Baggy, Biggio, and myself. Wow, that was a good team!"

In three active seasons with the Astros Alou hit .331 with 95 homeruns and 346 RBIs. He also made long lasting friends with both Brad Ausmus and Jeff Bagwell. Both became fast friends and both called the other their closest friends in baseball.

The team was good before Randy, but the big left-hander made it great. Johnson only made eleven starts for Houston. But anytime he made one at home it was a sellout. And when he made one anywhere else it was almost a guaranteed Astro win. In those eleven starts, Johnson was 10-1 with an earned run average of 1.28. He pitched 84.1 innings and struck out 116 batters. He had four complete game shutouts in those ten wins.

Johnson was the best, but the Astro pitching rotation was as deep and effective as at any time in club history. Even though Darryl Kile and his 19 wins in 1997 had moved on to Colorado as a free agent, the remaining starters were very good. Shane Reynolds moved into the number one role most of the year and was 19-8. Jose Lima came out of nowhere to move into the rotation and won 16 and lost eight. Mike Hampton was 11-7. Sean Bergman was 12-9. The team earned run average of 3.50 was second best in the NL. Out of the bullpen, Billy Wagner was the shutdown man in the ninth inning. He had 30 saves and 97 strikeouts in only 60 innings of work.

The 1998 Houston Astros won 102 games and lost only 60. No club accumulated a better record in Houston history. In the first round of the playoffs, they wouldn't even have to face the Braves. As the team in the league with the second best record they would meet the San Diego Padres. That turned out not to be an advantage. The Braves had won even more games than the Astros, 106, but the Padres had won only four fewer, 98. They were strong in one area that would turn out to be too much even for the powerful Astros. The Padres could pitch, especially Kevin Brown.

Brown out-dueled Johnson in the opener allowing Astro hitters only four base hits in a 2-1 Padre victory. Greg Vaughn's homer off Johnson in the eighth was the difference in the game. Seventeen Astros struck out with Brown getting 16 of them in eight innings. Trevor Hoffman gave up an unearned run in the ninth, but got the other strikeout and the save. Biggio and Bagwell were both hitless.

In the second game, the Astros evened the series and both Craig and Jeff were keys. Biggio was 1-3 with two walks and two runs scored. Bagwell had one hit, but drove in three. Houston had to rally in the bottom of the ninth to win after blowing a two-run lead in the top of the inning. Bill Spiers's third hit of the game drove in the game winner.

The Padres were able to come back with Brown on short rest for game three. Again he was unhittable. This time he went 6 and ⅔ innings allowing only three hits and one run and the Padre bullpen kept the Astros in check with Trevor Hoffman picking up his second save to close out the 2-1 win. Mike Hampton was the Astro pitcher with no support in this one. Houston had only four hits with Biggio and Bagwell 0-3 each. Both reached base once each and Biggio drove in the only Astro run with a base loaded walk in the seventh inning. The Padres took the lead and won it on a homerun by Jim Leyritz off Scott Elarton in the bottom of the seventh.

Game four wasn't close. Randy Johnson started for the Astros. He was OK. He pitched six innings and allowed only one earned run. A second run was un-earned. But the Astros offense couldn't handle Sterling Hitchcock and three relievers at all. The Astros had only three hits. Biggio had a double. Bagwell had a single and run batted in. But that was it.

For the second straight season, the Astros had made the postseason. For the second straight time, they couldn't hit a lick and they were ousted.

In their two first round playoff losses to the Braves in 1997 and the Padres in 1998, they had hit just .167 and .182 respectively with two homers and 12 RBIs in seven games. Biggio and Bagwell were certainly culpable. Biggio was 3-23 in seven games for .130 and Bagwell was just 3-26 for .115. They weren't the only ones with problems hitting. In 1998, with a much bolstered line up, Moises Alou was only 3-16 (.188) and Derek Bell only 2-16 (.183). What happened to Houston's best team ever was evident, but it was still unexplainable. As owner Drayton McLane put it, "I thought we'd win the World Series going away. I haven't figured out yet what happened that year."

During the off-season, the Astros made a bid to sign Randy Johnson to a long term contract, but his plan all along was to try and return to his off-season home in the Phoenix area. The Diamondbacks came up with the deal that Randy and his wife most liked and the Astros could not bring him back and had lost three players in the July trade they could have now used. It was a gamble that did not work out in the long term. But while Johnson was an Astro it worked. When Johnson was inducted into the Baseball Hall of Fame in the same class as Craig Biggio in 2015, he admitted he thought the 1998 Astros was the best team he ever was part of and while with the team he pitched the best of any point in his career. They just couldn't make it all the way.

Caminiti Returned and the Astros Won Again

In 1999, the club still had a strong offense with Biggio, Bagwell, Derek Bell, Carl Everett, and Moises Alou expected to lead the way. Plus Ken Caminiti had been re-acquired to man third base. There were concerns. Steady Brad Ausmus was gone. He was traded to Detroit in a five player deal shortly after the first of the year during the offseason. Then word got to Houston that Alou had seriously hurt a knee when being thrown off a treadmill. He would require surgery and miss the entire season.

The loss of Ausmus was partially for financial reasons and partially the club looking ahead. They had good hitting Tony Eusebio available to take the bulk of the catching load, and a young player in their system named Mitch Melusky only about a year away from making the club.

The loss of Alou hurt, but not as much as it might have. Another young player, Richard Hidalgo, who had spent some time with the Astros in 1998, had great potential as a power hitting outfielder. He would get his chance in 1999.

As for Biggio and Bagwell, they were both still in their prime. The hitting would still be solid and the pitching staff had at least three very solid starters even with Johnson gone. Those three would get a lot of work from manager Larry Dierker, but would get the job done.

Nineteen ninety-nine would be the year the Astros would play their last games in the Astrodome. It would be replaced by a new retractable roof stadium downtown originally named Enron Field in 2000. The new facility would change baseball in Houston in many ways, but that was still months away. The upcoming season would be memorable for more than the end of the Astros in the Dome. It would be a year of milestones for the team's greatest two players, and a season with yet another postseason chance.

Craig Biggio, now thirty-three years old, was not showing his age. He hit .294 with an on base percentage of .386. His numbers showed 16 homeruns, 73 runs batted in, 56 doubles, 123 runs scored, and 28 stolen bases. Defensively, the man who once was a catcher led all NL second basemen in putouts, assists, total chances, and double plays turned. On May 4, with his 344th career double, he became the franchise leader surpassing the mark set by Cesar Cedeno in 1981.

As for Jeff Bagwell, he set the Houston franchise record for homeruns during a career, passing Jimmy Wynn. The milestone was passed in Chicago on April 21 when he blasted his 224th career homer. After a season with 42 homers, Bagwell had hit a career total of 263. Bagwell also passed Wynn in career walks and most walks in a single season and Cesar Cedeno in total extra base hits. The rest of the season for the thirty-one-year old Bagwell was typical of Jeff in his prime. In addition to the 42 homers, he stole 30 bases, the second time in his career he had been 40-30. He and Barry Bonds were the only two in baseball history to do it twice.

Bagwell was a monster—again. He hit .304 with those 42 homers, 126 RBIs, 35 doubles, 30 stolen bases, and 149 walks. The walk total bested Jimmy Wynn's team record set thirty years before by one and ranks among the top 20 for a single season in baseball history. He set a new Houston record, breaking another of Jimmy Wynn's when he hit his 22nd homerun on the road in a single season. He finished the season with 30 of his 42 homeruns on the road. His on base percentage for the whole season was .454.

Without Alou, Carl Everett was even better than in 1998. He hit .325 with 25 homers and 108 runs batted in. He also stole 27 bases. Caminiti, signed as a free agent in the offseason, hit 13 homers and batted .286 in only 78 games. He missed nearly three months with a strained right calf muscle. Although he had been an All-Star and NL MVP with San Diego, he had begun using performance enhancing drugs (PEDs) while with the Padres and acquired an addiction to alcohol and hard drugs that concerned his close friends Jeff Bagwell and Craig Biggio when he returned. He had never been reluctant to take a drink after games and both Biggio and Bagwell knew that, but now he was caught into something more serious than even a return to alcoholism. They had been concerned about his alcohol use as early as 1993 when both Biggio and Bagwell urged him to check into John Lucas's substance-abuse treatment center in Houston. He didn't stay long, but claimed sobriety for more than two years. By the time he returned to the Astros on a two-year contract for 1999, his problems had resurfaced.

The Final Successes and Fall of Ken Caminiti

Cammy was only few years older than both of them, but he had preceded them into Houston and all three had been long time friends. Biggio and Caminiti even shared ownership in a ranch in south Texas called the Cambo Ranch. They used it mostly as a hunting refuge. When Caminiti died of a heart attack suspected to have been caused by a drug over-dose in New York in 2004, his body was brought back to Texas and buried on the ranch.

In 1999, it was just good to have Caminiti back. He was playing well until he was shelved with the injury, and the Astros were good again. However as Gene Coleman remembered, "When he came back from San Diego he told me he had used steroids, and his normal testosterone levels were a fraction of what someone his age should have. He was really having trouble maintaining body mass and recovering from injuries and games played. But he was committed to doing it right and legally. Toward the end of his time here he got involved again. I remember we had a meeting with Gerry Hunsicker after one of the games and he told us Cammy was going to rehab again and we really never saw him again."

Caminiti played only 137 games over both 1999 and 2000 for the Astros with only 59 of them in 2000 before he was gone. He signed with Texas as a free agent for 2001 but was released on July 2. He then signed on with Atlanta to finish the season, but that was the end of his career.

While Caminiti had made himself an MVP with San Diego in 1996, his battle with alcohol both before and after that were what did him in. That, and the later inclusion of the use of cocaine and heroin. One of the more poignant and sad stories of the hold alcohol had on him during his career was relayed by Coleman. "One time when we were in Atlanta after he had undergone an earlier rehab for alcohol addiction, he told me the best thing was now he got to go home from road trips with meal money." Presently each player on the road is paid over $100 per day above their regular salary. In Caminiti's day the total was less, but still at least $75 per day. With the Astros, the travelling secretary, Barry Waters, would go down the aisle of the plane handing out packets of cash to cover the entire trip. Players would sign a receipt. The money was to cover meals, clubhouse fees, and any other incidentals such as laundry service in hotels, and tips. The team would pay for hotel room and tax, but the players were responsible for all incidentals. Some frugal players could pocket a large portion of their meal money. Caminiti was not one of those.

As Cammy told Coleman, "I've never been able to go home with meal money. It went for alcohol. Because I'm not drinking now, I can figure tips. When I was drunk I could never figure them so I'd give 'em $100 tips. Now I can figure them out."

"Kenny was a real warrior on the field," remembered Coleman. "He was the kind of guy you wanted to go out there on the field with, and I can't tell you the number of times he made a play that fired the team up. The problem was he had an addictive personality. First he had a problem with alcohol. He used the weight room to build himself up partially because he wanted to cover up a missing pectoral on one side of his chest. He had a little divot there. He was self-conscious when not wearing a shirt. So, the steroid period in San Diego may have been almost as important to him to cover that as what it did for him on the field."

Even with the injuries and falling off the wagon in 2000, Caminiti produced on the field when he returned in 1999. He hit 13 homers in 1999 and 15 more in 2000, but he was now thirty-seven-years old and his body was starting to fail.

No Johnson but Still Good Pitching for Astros in Dome's Final Season

Certainly the Astros 1999 pitching staff missed having a dominant starter like Randy Johnson, but for the first time in franchise history two pitchers won 20 games. Lefty Mike Hampton was 22-4 with a 2.90 earned run average. Jose Lima was 21-10 with a 3.58 ERA. Shane Reynolds was the third big winner. He went 16-14 with a 3.85 ERA. Chris Holt and Sean Bergman rounded out the rotation most of the year with Scott Elarton getting 15 starts. The team ERA of 3.83 was not especially good, but in the era of the hitter in MLB, it was still third best in the National League.

Billy Wagner collected 39 saves while striking out 124 in only 74⅔ innings pitched. The staff led the league in fewest homeruns allowed, fewest walks and most strikeouts and second in fewest runs allowed.

Meanwhile, the offense's best number was being third in on base percentage. The runs scored and batting average was only eighth in the league and they were only 11th in homeruns hit with 168.

No complaints though. The Astros finished 97-65 to win the NL Central again. Coach Matt Galante got credit for 13 of those victories while Manager Larry Dierker was sidelined after suffering a grand mal seizure during a game played at the Astrodome during the season. The Astros needed all 97 wins to take the prize in the division. They had to hold off the 96-game-winning Cincinnati Reds by clinching the pennant in the Astrodome's last regular season game. They had won only five of their last eleven games heading into the finale.

On Sunday, October 3, the Astros beat the visiting Los Angeles Dodgers 9-4 to clinch. Biggio and Bagwell were both 1-3, but Bagwell scored three runs and drove in one. Ken Caminiti back in the lineup after his calf injury, hit the last homerun in a regular season game at the Dome when he crushed one batting left-handed into the right field seats in the third inning. Bagwell got to his second 40/30 season when he stole second base. Mike Hampton went seven innings on the mound allowing only one run. Fans had jammed the Dome to say good-bye and also hope for a clinching win. A crowd of 52,033 got both.

Following the game, the image burned in fans memories was of Craig Biggio and Mike Hampton tooling around the Dome warning track on motorcycles, puffing on cigars while confetti fell from the ceiling in celebration.

The Astros had made the postseason for a third straight season under manager Larry Dieker. They had still not gotten past the first round. Now the Atlanta Braves would be the foe again.

The Braves Did It Again!

Again the results were very disappointing. They didn't start that way, though. Houston beat the 102 game winning NL East champs in the opener in Atlanta 6-1. Shane Reynolds got the win over Greg Maddux as both Caminiti and young Daryle Ward hit homers. Biggio was 1-5 and Bagwell 1-4 with a run scored. Things were looking good. It was only a tease.

Kevin Millwood held the Astros to a single hit in game two as the Braves won 5-1 to even the series. Jose Lima was ineffective, but it didn't matter with the offense doing nothing. Caminiti homered for the second game in a row for the only Houston run. Bagwell and Biggio were 0-7 combined. The whole team was 1-29!

The series shifted to Houston but the Braves didn't care. It was tougher with the game lasting 12 innings at the Astrodome, but the Braves won 5-3. Brian Jordan's two-run double in the top of the 12th broke the tie. Caminiti was 3-5 for the Astros with an RBI. Biggio was 1-5 and Bagwell 0-2 with three walks and a run scored. The Braves were not giving Bagwell anything to hit, but not enough teammates were able to take up the slack.

The Astros had a chance to even the series in game five, but fell again. The final score was 7-5. This time the pitching did them in. The Braves had 15 hits off Shane Reynolds, Chris Holt, and three other relievers. The Astros got to John Smoltz, scoring four runs in seven innings, some of them part of a four-run eighth inning. But they already trailed 7-1 before that rally started.

Tony Eusebio and Caminiti homered in the seventh. It was Caminiti's third homer in five games. Cammy with his heroics would boost his overall postseason average, including play in San Diego, to .471 when the game was over. Meanwhile, Biggio, after an 0-5, had a postseason average of just .105 while Bagwell was only a bit better at .154. It was obvious the opposition knew Bagwell had to be controlled. He had an amazing on base percentage in postseason play of .421. With such a discrepancy between his batting average and on base percentage, the game plan was that walking Bagwell was a far better option than giving him pitches to hit.

With the three wins to one loss to the Braves, the Astros were now 0-3 in the Dierker era in the postseason. Almost un-noticed was the Astrodome era was over, too. The postseason loss before 48,553 on October 9, 1999 marked the last major league baseball game ever to be played in the eighth Wonder of the World. Disappointing? Certainly, but something new was coming to Houston in 2000 and the postseason loss was mostly forgotten by the next spring.

After rumblings in the mid-90s that the Astros might be put up for sale or moved to Washington, D.C. if something couldn't be done to boost interest and attendance—namely a new stadium—city father's decided to figure out how to work out a deal with club owner Drayton McLane to build a new home for the Astros. McLane was tired of the dollars in upkeep needed for the Astrodome, especially after his main tenant, the

Houston Oilers of the NFL, packed up and moved to Tennessee. He saw what new venues had done around baseball in other cities. And he wanted to be able to play outdoors on real grass when possible. "Baseball is an outdoor sport," he would often emphasize when pitching for a new home. City leaders thought they could help with the development of downtown if they put a ballpark in place there. In somewhat of an irony, the owner of the Houston Oilers, Bud Adams, had come up with a downtown plan in the early 90s. Bud Adams proposed a stadium that could hold both the Oilers and the NBA Houston Rockets who felt their home at the Summit was now a bit cramped and out of date.

Adams biggest mistake was his timing. While tired of paying what he felt was exorbitant rent to the Astros, who controlled the Astrodome lease, for a facility with too low a capacity for the modern NFL, in 1987 he had convinced Harris County, which actually owned the building, to tear out the unique Astrodome scoreboard to add more seats for football. However, his club still couldn't win in the postseason. They had ripped the hearts out of Oiler fans when they lost a 35-3 lead in the AFC Wild Card game in 1993 and lost 41-38. The team had only been 10-6 during the regular season, but losing that large of a lead left a bitter taste in fan's mouths. The team was still good after that debacle. In fact, they were even better in the 1993 season with a 12-4 record, but they lost in the first round of the playoffs again. This time Kansas City, led by Joe Montana, ousted the Oilers 28-20. Coaching heads rolled and the club fell to 2-14. By the end of the 1995 season, when efforts to build a new stadium died, Adams announced his team would leave Houston. In 1996, the lame-duck Oilers drew few fans. They averaged 31,825 fans per game, more than 25,000 under the league average. On December 15, they drew only 15,131 for a game against Cincinnati. It was their final home game ever. The club was let out of its lease for 1997. The franchise moved to Tennessee and took the team nickname with it, even though the name would be re-branded as the Tennessee Titans once they were fully located in Nashville.

During this period, Drayton McLane, who had taken over the Astros in 1993, was selling the Astrodome to the media and public as a fine place. He had even done some cleaning up and refurbishing. It wasn't long, however, after he learned the full cost of running a major league franchise and saw what was happening in baseball with all the new stadiums being constructed that he changed his tune. He used the tried and true formula of intimating, if not directly making threats, that the Dome was not any longer state of the art. Houston needed something better to generate more revenue or maybe the club might need to look at a new home. His timing was also perfect. The Astros were good and the football team was leaving town already.

While Adams had used Jacksonville as a "threat city" before he got the county to make changes to the Astrodome for his football team, and ultimately did move his team to Tennessee less than a decade later, McLane and his team was linked to a desire by Washington, D.C. to get back in the major leagues. The nation's capital had been without major league baseball since the second coming of the Washington Senators were moved to Arlington, Texas in 1972. McLane's business was based in Central Texas, but he had a significant presence in Washington where his international branch was based.

With a desire to help bring more people to downtown Houston and the loss of the Oilers looming, officials pushed the idea of a new downtown home for the baseball team. Seeing that new downtown ball parks had helped revive inner cities in Baltimore and Cleveland, similar plans were in the works for Detroit and San Francisco. The ballpark proposed and later built would be designed for baseball—unlike the Dome—which was built to hold all sorts of events by its creator Judge Roy Hofheinz. The new park would be air conditioned but not exclusively an indoor park. It would have a retractable roof like the Skydome in Toronto. And it would have natural grass. The seating capacity would be only about 41,000, but the ballpark would also have a personality and character. It would not have a symmetrical playing area. The outfield distances would vary. The heights of the outfield walls would also vary. The fans would love the place. All seats would be much closer to the playing field than at the Astrodome—or any of the other circular all-purpose stadiums commonly built starting in the late 1960s.

What would first be called Enron Field was built over an old Union Pacific railyard on the southeast side of Houston's downtown. It was decided to incorporate the area's railroad past in the design. The former station, Union Station, was retained and upgraded to provide office space and serve as one of the main entrances to the park. A train-like vehicle was placed on a short bed of rails above the left field wall.

The playing field included a very short 315 foot left field line, but with a 20 foot high scoreboard in front, a 436 foot deep centerfield fronted by an incline starting about 400 feet from home plate with the flag pole inside the fence, a low wall in right field and little room from home plate to the backstop. It was a throwback to the early days of baseball.

Until it opened, no one knew for sure how it would play, but they had an idea since the most common prevailing wind pattern came in from the Gulf of Mexico inland. That meant the wind would blow out toward left center field more often than anything else.

With the configuration of the ballpark and wind patterns, it might have been better had home plate been located closer to what was the left field corner. Right field would have been a sun field in that configuration and the fans down the first base line would have been more comfortable than they are now with the roof open, but the prevailing winds would have been coming in instead of out. One reasons the architects couldn't design the park that way was the train station area could not be used as the main entrance to the park if the Astros wanted to sell alcohol. What professional sports franchise can afford to pass on that option? That entrance was too close to The Church of the Annunciation Catholic Church. So the main entrance was located behind home plate which was several hundred yards from the church entrance and thus out of no man's land.

Many Astro fans-and hitters- were looking forward to a new style of Astro baseball. For most of the history of the franchise Astros baseball was not always very exciting. The club had a large number of good pitchers and that was a main feature, but the home games in the Dome were, more often than not, low scoring and featuring a number of what seemed like well hit fly balls that died once they reached the outfield. Even moving in the fences ten or more feet couldn't change that. The enclosed building simply had dead air. In addition, the place was kept quite cool. Wearing sweaters or jackets to games was not uncommon for fans, and players not in the game would be sure to have extra coverage on the bench and bull-pen. The ball did not carry in the dead cool air. It was a wonder that players like Jimmy Wynn, Glenn Davis, and Jeff Bagwell had produced as many homeruns as they had. There were getting absolutely no help from their home field. In later years, the fences would be moved in some and the air conditioning set for a higher temperature and things were better, but the Astrodome was always a pitcher's park.

At Enron Field, that would change in 2000.

9 A New Ballpark Starts a New Astros Era

Courtesy of Malingering

"It's like Wrigley Field when the wind is blowing out...I just have to make some adjustments to my pitching style."

– Jose Lima before the opening of Enron Field

Enron Field Was a Record Setting Hitter's Park in 2000

For Jose Lima, the adjustment would not come. After winning 16 and 21 games in his last two seasons while pitching home games at the pitcher-friendly Astrodome, in 2000 Lima dropped off to a 7-16 record with a whopping 6.65 earned run average and was gone before the next season reached the mid-point. After surrendering 30 homeruns in 1999, he led the league and threatened the major league single season record of 49 when he was touched for 48 homers in 2000. Lima had always been a fly ball pitcher and Enron Field just did not fit. Fly balls that were hauled in on the warning track at the Dome were now several feet or yards in the seats. His worst outing was on April 27, when Eric Young and Ricky Gutierrez hit back to back homers leading off the first inning for the Cubs before 42,271 Enron Field Fans. Before the inning was done, he would give up two more long balls. Hector Rodriguez hit a two-run homer and Damon Buford hit another solo shot.

That set a franchise record: one pitcher surrendering four homeruns in a single inning. If Lima was not shell-shocked in seeing the new ballpark that game certainly did it. It may have finished him off as a consistently dependable pitcher. For the rest of his major league career he had some moments, but never approached his success in Houston in 1998 and 1999.

Lima wasn't the only pitcher victimized. The Astros pitching staff gave up 234 homers in 2000. The team earned run average zoomed from 3.83 to a franchise worst at 5.42. To say the pitchers didn't adapt to their new home was an understatement. Only one regular starting pitcher finished over .500. Scott Elarton was 17-7 but his earned run average—best of the starters—was 4.81.

The new home was nice for the hitters, but not enough to counter act what it did to the pitchers. And it carried over on the road. The Astros in 2000 were 39-42 at home and only 33-48 on the road. It made the two-time division champs no better than a fourth place team at 72-90 for the season

Record Setting Homerun Production Helped Pack the New Park

While not being in a pennant race was a downer, fans still packed the new ballpark. The Astros drew 3,056,139 people, fifth best in the National League. They may have lost more than they won, but they were both frustrating and fun. Offense is fun for fans and there was plenty of that. Houston hit a team and National League record 249 homeruns. This was the same franchise that for many years in its history couldn't hit as many as 100 homers in a 162 game season.

Craig Biggio and Jeff Bagwell were only among many leaders. They had lots of help in the most powerful lineup in Houston history. In 26 games, the Astros scored ten or more runs. Unfortunately, they had 27 games in which the opposition scored ten or more.

Biggio didn't take much advantage of the ballpark, but he also only played 101 games. During a game played in Florida on August 1, he was taken out on a slide at second base by Preston Wilson of the Marlins that resulted in torn knee ligaments. His season was finished early. He would go on the Disabled List for the first time in his career. Team Strength and Conditioning Coach Dr. Gene Coleman remembers that day.

"It happened in the middle of the game. We had a getaway day game on August third and Craig comes to me on crutches and said, 'Hey I need to go over to the Marlins weight room and work out.' So I took him over there at eleven o'clock on crutches and we had to walk through where the Marlins were having breakfast. Everyone is looking at Craig, like your season's over, why is he doing this? Craig told me he was doing it because he wanted to be comeback player of the year the next year."

During his years with the Astros, Biggio was always driven to be the best. Dirty in the first inning, he was always grinding. Teammates and opponents noticed.

While he was able to play, Biggio hit .268 with 8 homeruns and 35 runs batted in. His on base percentage was an outstanding .388 and he had been 12 of 14 on stolen base attempts before going down. Biggio was the most notable but the club suffered other injuries that helped foul up the season. Original starting center fielder Roger Cedeno missed time, Moises Alou sustained a calf muscle pull, and closer Billy Wagner had elbow surgery.

Bagwell hit a career high 47 homers to go with 132 runs batted in and a .310 batting average. His on base percentage was .424. The difference in 2000 was that many other Astros were having superb offensive seasons as well. Twenty-five-year-old outfielder Richard Hidalgo broke through with 44 homeruns to go with 122 RBIs and a .314 average. Moises Alou returned from injury in 1999 back to his old form by hitting .355 with 30 homers and 114 runs batted in, even after missing some time with his calf problem. Veteran catcher Brad Ausmus had moved on after the 1998 season. That was unfortunate, even with rookie Mitch Meluskey hitting .300 with 14 homers and 69 runs batted in. Ausmus might have had more effect keeping his shell-shocked pitchers relaxed. Young Daryle Ward moved to left field playing 119 games and hitting 20 homeruns with 47 RBIs and a .258 average.

The Astros had three non-regulars hit homers in double figures led by Lance Berkman, who hit 21 while hitting .297. Ken Caminiti was again very effective in less than a full season with 15 homers, 45 RBIs, and a .303 batting average in only 59 games.

The Astros led the National League in homers, slugging percentage and total bases. They were second in runs scored, hits, and batting average (.278).

Unfortunately, the pitching staff was last in earned run average, hits allowed, runs allowed, and homeruns allowed.

The season wasn't exactly one to forget with the wildly high scoring games, the homers, and the new ballpark, but it wasn't something fans would support for long. GM Jerry Hunsicker knew that, and certainly manager Larry Dierker did too. After all, in all sports it is "What did you do today" that matters most. There were even those questioning in the offseason whether Dierker would even be back as manager in 2001. Post-season spots for the three previous seasons were old news.

Pressure Built on Dierker after 2000

In 2001, the Astros had to get back into the postseason and finally win a round or two. The pressure was building. Dierker was feeling it, and in his book recalled the 2000 offseason was the first in which he realized the job wasn't as much fun anymore. Some of his non-traditional moves and decisions were criticized by his players. Craig Biggio was one of them, but not alone. Owner Drayton McLane noticed. "He just got out of focus and he alienated a lot of key players. He didn't communicate well. Craig and Jeff were great baseball people and they understood it from tradition. Larry was a forward thinker. He was one of the first that really concentrated on statistics. When bringing in a reliever, he had done great research. He might not bring in a lefthander to pitch to a certain left-handed hitter if the numbers showed a particular right-hander might do better. But by the end of 2001, he had worn out his welcome as a manager."

Enron Field Had Some Changes for 2001

To help the Astros bounce back after 2000, some adjustments were made to Enron Field. The nickname "Homerun Field" was not something the Astros were proud to hear. So the fence in left field to the right of the Crawford Boxes and in front of the visitor's bullpen was raised at least ten feet. Now hitters would have to hit the ball onto the concourse for a home-run to left and left-center and not just over a six-foot fence. Since it was also determined the prevailing wind generally blew toward left field at a pretty strong clip, it was not surprising that the roof was closed more often.

The Astros Break Records and Bounce Back, But...

The "but..." was for something that happened on September 11, 2001 a long way from any Major League Baseball park. It will always be remembered as "9-11," the day the two towers of the World Trade Center in New York City would be felled by airplane attacks, the Pentagon in Washington hit, and a fourth plane kept from hitting its intended target by some heroic passengers on board.

The whole world stopped that morning. Barry Bonds attack on the homerun record, the Astros comeback, the early NFL season were all totally irrelevant. The Seattle Mariners were on the way to a record 116 wins. No one cared after 9-11.

Commissioner Selig first cancelled all games for that night. Then he cancelled all games for a week. Even after the games resumed, most fans were pre-occupied with the aftermath of the attacks and the United States' retaliation plans.

Baseball resumed its normal schedule on September 21 and tacked the games postponed after the attack to the end of the schedule. For the Astros, that meant a home series with the Giants and a road series at St. Louis would be played starting October 2. Both would turn out to be very significant.

Before the 9/11 attacks, the Astros had just finished winning two of three against Milwaukee. The Giants would be coming into Houston next. They arrived in the city the night of September 10. They would be stuck in the city for a while after the attacks as the government closed all airports until the extent of the attacks on New York and Washington could be determined. As soon as the charter could be cleared—which was before general flights were allowed in the air—they went back to San Francisco. However, they would not lift the restrictions on non-club media on the plane. San Francisco newspaper beat writers had to stay in Houston until commercial flights were again available. By the time of the 9/11 tragedy, the Astros baseball team had proven that the debacle of 2000 in Enron Field's first season was an aberration.

The makeup of the 2001 Astros included the return of Biggio to the lineup in fine form. The lineup also saw Lance Berkman move in as a regular in the outfield, the veteran Vinny Castilla was acquired to play third base, and Julio Lugo with a stronger bat moving in as the regular shortstop. But the most important improvement was the re-acquisition of Brad Ausmus to catch and help direct the pitching staff.

The previous season, catcher Mitch Meluskey had shown a very good bat. He had hit .300 with 14 homeruns and 69 runs batted in. He also had a superb .401 on base percentage. It was the best overall offensive season ever for a Houston catcher. But Mitch had shoulder problems and did not handle the running game well. His rapport with both his pitchers and his teammates was horrible. From getting into a row with teammate Matt Meiske at the batting cage, to demonstrating a "big league attitude" at other times, Meluskey was a distraction. His appearance at the same time the pitchers were shell shocked by Enron Field was poor timing for him, but he did little to assuage the situation. Bringing Ausmus back in a trade that sent Meluskey to Detroit was one of GM Gerry Hunsicker's best moves. In reality the Astros had to bring Ausmus back for another practical reason, Meluskey's ailing shoulder would sideline him all of 2001. He would appear in only 20 more major league games, the last 12 with Houston in 2003. His major league career was over before he was thirty years old.

The team pitching earned run average in 2001 was reduced from 5.42 to 4.37. That was the 10th best mark in the league after being dead last in 2000. The makeup of the starting staff was different, too. Gone was the shell-shocked Lima early in the season. Young Wade Miller won 16 games with a 3.40 ERA. Shane Reynolds bounced back for a 14-11 record and Roy Oswalt joined the rotation and went 14-3 with a 2.73 ERA. Billy Wagner recorded 39 saves. Things were not totally smooth as Larry Dierker used 25 different pitchers during the season. But everything fell together and a team that was 72-90 in 2000 rose to 93-69 and another NL Central title.

Whether he was putting it on himself or it was coming from outside or not, Manager Larry Dierker knew this team had to do something in the postseason finally. His veteran players knew it too. The biggest problem had always been the Astros did not hit or score when the chips were on the line.

Here Come the Braves Again

Alas for the Astros it would be more of the same. The Atlanta Braves, who had been catching a lot of heat from their fans despite winning the NL East annually, had only won one World Series despite having the strongest starting pitching staff in baseball for years. But the Braves could almost always win the first round of the postseason. Houston couldn't.

In 2001, Atlanta came into Houston on October 9 for the opener. The Astros had a 3-2 lead after six innings. Wade Miller had battled Greg Maddux to a standoff. Ausmus's two-run homer in the fifth had given the Astros the two earned runs off Maddux. The third run was un-earned as a result of an error by Atlanta shortstop Rey Sanchez.

After 92 pitches through seven innings, Manager Dierker elected to lift Miller for a pinch hitter in the bottom of the seventh with a runner at first and one out. Orlando Merced and then Craig Biggio both flied out. Biggio's ball to deep left had fans on the edges of their seats before it was caught. In the eighth, the Astros went to the bullpen. The first man called in by Manager Dierker, Mike Jackson, was ineffective. The first man he faced, Keith Lockhart, doubled. Then Braves manager Bobby Cox called on former Houston favorite Ken Caminiti to pinch hit. Jackson struck him out. The fans started to breathe easier, but only for a while. Giles grounded a single up the middle, scoring Lockhart and tying the game. Then another grounder off the bat of ancient Julio Franco was booted by Astro shortstop Julio Lugo. Even though the lead-off double was the only hard hit ball surrendered by Jackson, Dierker figured he needed a strikeout pitcher and went with Billy Wagner an inning earlier than usual. Future Hall of Famer, Chipper Jones, hit the first pitch for a three run homer. That was the ball game and the Astros were able to score only one more run with Castillo's homerun in the ninth. The Braves had won 7-4. The Astros had only six hits. Biggio was 1-4 and Bagwell was 1-3 with a walk.

Game Two was classic Brave pitching dominance, but the Astros arms were just as good. An unearned run scored on a double play ground out by Rey Sanchez in the second was the only run of the game. It was unearned because Lugo had made a throwing error earlier to extend the inning.

Dave Mlicki started for Houston against Tom Glavine. Glavine went eight innings allowing six hits and no runs. Mlicki was followed by four relievers. Octavio Dotel went the longest with two innings and 23 pitches thrown.

Of the seven Astro hits, Bagwell was on base with every at-bat. He was 2-2 and walked twice. No one else could get him around. Biggio was 0-4.

Now the Astros had to go to Atlanta down two games to none. Shane Reynolds would face John Burkett. Shane didn't have it and neither did the offense. Only a two-run homerun by Daryle Ward off Burkett in the seventh put any Astro runs on the board. That cut the Atlanta lead to 4-2 but they upped it to the final 6-2 with a two-run in the bottom of the eighth. Chipper Jones two-run homer off Octavio Dotel clinched it. Former Astro back-up catcher Paul Bako had hit a two-run homer and driven in another run off Shane Reynolds earlier, and Julio Franco had also hit a solo homer off Shane.

It was the fourth first round postseason failure for the Astros in as many tries over the last five seasons. Back-biting behind the scenes and in the clubhouse by some of the teams most respected veterans including Craig Biggio, Jeff Bagwell, and Brad Ausmus along with a number of pitchers against Manager Dierker for some of his unconventional, but actually well-reasoned moves, plus Dierker's own frustrations brought an end to the club's best five-year stretch in its history.

Dierker Showed Pressure Building during Bonds' Visit

Near the end of the season when Barry Bonds was going after Mark McGwire's single season homerun mark at the same time the Astros were still trying to stop a slide and clinch the National League Central title, the pressure on Dierker was starting to show. The club had been in first place only since August 17, but never with a lead of more than five and a half games. By October 2, they were tied for the lead, having lost five of their last six. The Giants and Bonds were a tremendous draw at the gate throughout baseball no matter how the home team was doing.

When Astro fans started showing love for Bonds at the expense of the home team Astros, Dierker was seething. He kept it inside, but when his pitchers either walked Bonds on the manager's order or unintentionally walked him, a large number of the fans in the ballpark showered boo's on the home team.

While the Astros kept Bonds from doing any damage by pitching him carefully, the Giants won the first two games in the series. That made it seven losses in the last eight games for Houston, but they held onto first place because the St. Louis Cardinals chasing them could not win either.

The mid-week series, even with school back in session, drew standing room sellout crowds every night. Attendances of 43,548, 43,630 and 43,734 were made up of many fans only lured to Enron Field to see Bonds. The Giants, who were in a battle for the postseason in the NL West, wound up winning all three. Dierker was feeling the pressure of his team on the way to possibly blowing the Central, but playing before sell-out crowds, with most of them rooting for Bonds and not the Astros, was extremely unnerving.

Dierker could never accept what Bonds's presence was doing to the fan base. In three games, Bonds was held to only three hits in only six official at-bats, but he was on base a total of 12 times since he walked six times and was hit by a pitch in another at-bat. With every walk, Astro fans booed. When the walk didn't work out strategically as intended and the Giant's next hitter Jeff Kent made them pay, the crescendo of boo's grew worse.

Following Bonds in the batting order, Kent went 5-14 in the three games with a homerun and six runs batted in.

Bonds came into the series needing one homerun to tie the major league record of 70 held by Mark McGwire. Although the Giants won the first two games and had a 9-2 lead to the top of the ninth in the final game, the Astros had won the battles while losing the war. He hadn't homered or had any big hits.

Then Bonds hit number 70 off Astro rookie lefty Wilfredo Rodriguez, leading off the ninth on a 1-1 pitch. As the ball soared toward right-center field, the crowd jumped and a thunderous roar made it hard to even think. The game and series had been long lost by the struggling Astros, but the majority of those nearly 131,000 fans who had crammed the park to see Barry Bonds at least tie the record saw it.

With the loss and a win by St. Louis, the Astros dropped into second a game behind the Cards. After the game in the clubhouse some of the players, including Craig Biggio, saw it for what it was—a memorable baseball moment. Dierker could not see it that way even if Bonds's homerun number 70 had no bearing in the series outcome. He just could not stand the home fans rooting so hard for an opposing player and booing his own players when they walked Barry.

He also saw his team blowing the pennant. But they still had a chance. The final three games were in St. Louis. If the Astros could win two of three, that would give them the division title and that spot in the postseason based on winning the season series from the Cards.

The day after the Giants had swept the Astros, a hang-over existed for the first seven innings in St. Louis. St. Louis, behind former University of Houston star and area resident, Woody Williams, led the Astros 1-0. Lance Berkman slugged the Astros to a comeback win. First was a solo homerun off reliever Jeff Tabaka in the eighth. Then in the ninth, he put the Astros on top with an RBI double off Gene Stechschulte to score Craig Biggio, who had led off the inning with a walk.

Now the Astros needed just one win to clinch a tie and division champion designation.

They didn't get it in game two. The Astros led early, but not late as the Cards evened the series with a 10-6 victory. Craig Biggio had two hits, scored three and drove in two, but shaky defense allowed four unearned runs. A throwing error by Bagwell to second base trying to start a double play in the bottom of the third led to three unearned runs. It had been during the 2001 season that Bagwell first had problems with his right shoulder. From that season on, Bagwell was no longer Gold Glove caliber at first base because of the deterioration of his shoulder. It would get worse and eventually end his career. This time it was just a costly error.

It didn't turn out to be so costly for long. The Astros took Game Three 9-2 thanks to homeruns from Bagwell and Richard Hidalgo and the strong pitching of Shane Reynolds. While the Cards and Astros were declared co-champion in St Louis with identical 93-69 records, Houston got the most important nod. For playoff purposes, they were the champ and the Cards were the wild card.

Then came the postseason and the end of the Dierker era.

10 Jimy Keeps 'Em near the Top

"It was a manager's decision"

– Jimy Williams anytime a reporter asked about a strategic move

Courtesy of Joel Dinda/Flickr

Dierker Turned In Keys to Manager's Office

A few days after the Astros were ousted by the Braves, the Astros called a news conference. Larry Dierker, General Manager Gerry Hunsicker, and owner Drayton McLane were on hand to announce that in a mutual decision, Dierker would not return to manage the Astros in 2002. Some insiders didn't think the move would have been made if owner Drayton McLane didn't start the conversation. If McLane had one fault during his run owning the Astros, it was his fondness for getting close to his star players. He would take idle conversation about the team and their frustrations more seriously than he should have. He also would decide to visit the clubhouse close to game time to chat with his manager. Drayton was proud of his closeness with his players, "I went into the clubhouse before every game and made every player stand up and shake my hand. Then I'd go in and talk with the manager to encourage him."

Some of his visits would be simple pep talks that the players and staff had heard so many times they went in one ear and out the other. In other instances, he might keep his skipper from doing the last minute pre-game research needed to cover for every possible match up or strategical move that might be called for in the upcoming game.

Larry Dierker had one year left on his contract. Though depressed more than anyone else about the club's inability to win in the postseason, he knew those thoughts would pass in a few days or weeks and he would be eager to get started on plans for 2002. When McLane decided the time to make a managerial change was now, he conferred with his team president and general manager. McLane remembered, "He [Dierker] just got out of focus and he alienated a lot of key players. He didn't communicate well. Craig and Jeff were great baseball people and they understood it from tradition. Larry was a forward thinker. He was one of the first that really concentrated on statistics. When bringing in a reliever he had done great research. He might not bring in a lefthander to pitch to a certain left-handed hitter if the numbers showed a particular right-hander might do better. But by the end of 2001 he had worn out his welcome as a manager."

After McLane made the call, Gerry Hunsicker told Dierker the news. As Larry remembered, "Gerry called me in to say I had the choice of re-signing or being fired. I would be paid the final year on my contract either way. I was frustrated enough that the idea of not having to try and win a fifth time and get another chance in the playoffs or still get paid for not managing was appealing. To be perfectly honest, managing was the least favorite thing I did in baseball. I didn't like the pressure from within the clubhouse and pressure from outside from the media. I also didn't like all the petty desires from the modern players compared to the way it was when I was a player. All of those things coming from different angles and I was just thinking, this isn't any fun."

So in his post-playoff depressed stage, it wasn't hard to convince Larry a change should be made. "In a sense, the Bonds series was a turning point and then being swept by the Braves in the playoffs and I lost my cool in the press conference again and that was two times in two weeks I kind of lost it after a big game. Of course, in between we won two of three in St. Louis and won the division. They'd won almost every game in September at home and we took them. I was part of that and wasn't upset then, but yeah I was mad about Bonds and mad about the playoffs. I was frustrated because we'd won a playoff spot four times and lost in the first round on all of them. "

McLane no doubt thought a change was needed for both Dierker's health and the team. Larry's outburst following the Bonds games and his depression following the post season concerned McLane as much as any complaints from the clubhouse leadership.

As Dierker said in his book, *This Ain't Brain Surgery,* "The burden of playoff failure had become an unbearable load. In our four failed attempts in October, we really never hit. I am frankly nonplussed to figure out why. Sure, the pitchers are generally better in the playoffs than the standard rank and file of the regular season, but there were times during our championship seasons where we hit good pitchers, even when they were throwing well."

The Astros were only 2-12 in 14 postseason games during the Dierker reign. So what would be the story for 2002? Who would manage the team? Had their window of opportunity passed or could a different skipper and a few personnel changes get the Astros past the first round and into the World Series?

Short an M but Long on Experience, Jimy Took Over

With the nucleus of a 93-game-winning team to work with, there was no shortage of men interested in being the next Astro manager. The ultimate selection would go to a real solid baseball man named Jimy Williams. He wasn't a real McLane man though. While the hiring of the totally inexperienced Dierker had worked in many ways, minus the postseason failures, with the club winning four division titles in his five years, Williams had nine years of experience managing in Major League Baseball, plus eight years serving on Bobby Cox' coaching staff in Atlanta. Of his nine years as a big league skipper, he had only one sub .500 season. He managed originally in Toronto, winning as many as 96 games in 1987, then after coaching with the Braves, got a second job in Boston. He was replaced by Joe Kerrigan during the 2001 season and was available for the Astros in 2002.

Williams, who only used one "m" in his first name starting as a prank when he was in grade school and later to differentiate himself from another minor league Jimmy Williams, had been in or around baseball since signing a professional contract at twenty-one years old in 1964. He had spent most of his playing career in the minor leagues. Unlike Larry Di-erker, who had been one of the National League's top pitchers during his career, Jimy played in only 14 major league games in 1966 and 1967with the Cardinals. He was 3-13 .231. All his hits were singles.

As a manager Jimy had weaknesses, but few in the main part of the job. He knew baseball and was considered by many the best teaching manager in the game. He would much rather be hitting ground balls to infielders before the game than making small talk with writers, broadcasters or players behind the batting cage. That small talk aversion also included the owner. Drayton McLane's frequent visits to the manager's office before games rarely lasted long. Jimy had a different focus. Perhaps because he joined the Astros after having to deal with the sometimes notorious Boston media, he was close to the vest with his comments during the times he had to grant media or even owner's access. Any reporter asking why a particular strategic move was made was almost guaranteed to get Jimy's favorite answer, "It was a manager's decision." Trying to follow that up was useless. But Jimy was a good man and was not reluctant to ask a long time broadcaster or writer for his opinion of a player. He was almost fired following a game of his first season because of a major error in his owner's eyes. He failed to start all of his star players in a home game. McLane said he complained to GM Gerry Hunsicker and told him they had an obligation to fans to have the star players in the lineup. And if Gerry wouldn't say something to Jimy, he would do it himself. The wrong answer could cut his managerial term short.

Fortunately for Jimy, he understood and never made the mistake again. But Jimy Williams, for whatever success he had achieved in the past, he was just not a Drayton McLane kind of skipper. "He was a player's manager and a real baseball guy, but managers need to be leaders," said McLane. "You've got to inspire people and push people hard and that wasn't Jimy. You've got to shake 'em up and sometimes make unconventional decisions."

What sort of team would Williams have to work with in 2002? In some cases, the age of the Astros was starting to show, starting with long time stars Craig Biggio and Jeff Bagwell. Biggio was now thirty-six years old. In 2002, he would record the worst single season batting average of his career to that point, hitting only .253. He hit 16 homeruns and drove in 58 runs, but his on base percentage of .330 was also the lowest of his career until then. He stole 16 bases in 18 tries, but was starting to show less range and arm defensively. He was still a good player but his great player years were over.

As for Jeff Bagwell, his ailing right shoulder was becoming more of a problem on defense. It also hurt, so it had some effect swinging the bat. Plus, the hard workouts he had been known for after games were getting harder and harder to handle. Pain pills before games and occasional cortisone injections allowed him to play. That would be the pattern until 2005. Offensively, at thirty-four he was still a very good player. He hit .291 with 31 homeruns, but dropped under 100 runs batted in (with 98) for the first time since 1996. His on base percentage was still a solid .401. He wasn't trying to steal bases much anymore with seven successes in only ten tries.

The greatest pain Bagwell may have felt had nothing to do with his shoulder in 2002, but with the unexpected death of a very good friend.

Darryl Kile Died of a Heart Attack in Chicago

On June 22, pitcher Darryl Kile was missing from the St. Louis Cardinals clubhouse prior to a game in Chicago against the Cubs. He was found in his hotel room dead. An autopsy revealed two coronary arteries 90 percent blocked and a heart attack (myocardial infarction) was ruled the cause of death. The night before, he had complained of shoulder pain and weakness. Whether that was a sign that something was wrong or not is only speculation. As a major league pitcher, having shoulder pain is not uncommon and Darryl was a seemingly very healthy thirty-three-year-old professional athlete. After his body was discovered, the game that afternoon in Chicago was cancelled.

Kile had come up through the Houston farm system and began his major league career the same year as Bagwell with the Astros. They, along with Craig Biggio, even had the same agent, Barry Axelrod. Darryl was part of the team's division championship in 1997 before moving to the Colorado Rockies as a free agent. He had struggled playing home games in Denver's altitude, but had resurrected his career with the Cardinals. While with the Astros, Kile had been one of the team's most popular players with his teammates and media. Bagwell had kept in close contact with Darryl and his family. When he received word of his friend's death, he was heartbroken in losing a friend and for Darryl's wife Flynn and their three children.

While the Cardinals game in Chicago was postponed due to news of Kile's death, the Astros were scheduled to play an interleague game with the Seattle Mariners at Minute Maid Park that night. Manager Jimy Williams decided to let Bagwell, Biggio, and Brad Ausmus have the night off. None were in the starting lineup. In baseball, though, having the "night off" doesn't mean the same as it does for "normal" people. Players are expected to report to the ballpark, put on a uniform and stay on the bench or in the clubhouse in case they are needed. A similar "day off" for an office worker would call for them to come to the office and hang around in case something comes up and they are needed to work.

Biggio, Bagwell, and Ausmus were there, but their minds weren't on the game that much. As it turned out, however, two of the three would make appearances. Jose Vizcaino started at second base in Biggio's spot and had three hits. Orlando Merced got the start at first base and Gregg Zaun was behind the plate.

The Astros scored first on a two-run double by Daryle Ward in the bottom of the third. However, in the top of the sixth the Mariners tied the game. After a lead-off double off Astro starter Roy Oswalt, John Olerud ripped a two-run homer. The game stayed 2-2 through nine innings.

When the game reached the 11th, manager Williams had to ask Craig Biggio if he could pinch hit. Batting for pitcher Billy Wagner, he flied out to left field. The inning was over, but instead of double-switching, Williams allowed Biggio to only pinch hit. He did not stay in the game.

The game moved on and reached the bottom of the 12th inning still even at 2-2. After singles by Julio Lugo and Vizcaino and an intentional walk to Lance Berkman to load the bases with one out, Williams wanted to go with the percentages and send a right handed pinch hitter to bat for lefty hitter Orlando Merced. Former Astro pitcher, left-handed John Halama, had been very effective so far. He had allowed only two hits and no runs in 2 ⅓ innings. The man he would face would be the grieving Jeff Bagwell.

Bagwell, trying hard to handle the job he had been given, ran the count to two balls and two strikes. On pitch number five, he lined the ball into short right-center. Lugo romped in with the winning run as the Astro bench emptied, leaving and cheering to go for a good natured pummeling of Bagwell, who had provided the Astros a walk off extra inning win on perhaps the longest day of his life. There were tears in his eyes as he left the field.

Bagwell had a game later that 2002 season on August 27 vs the Pirates that went into the list of Houston baseball legends. Before the game that day, an eleven-year-old bone cancer patient asked Jeff to hit a homerun for him. Jeff told him, "I'm going to try, but I'm not Babe Ruth." In the fifth inning, he hit a pitch from Mike Bynum over the left field wall and pointed to the child in the stands as he rounded third base. Later Bagwell said, "I hit the homerun and he felt it was for him. I'm glad of that. It made it special."

Biggio and Bagwell were past their peaks, but still dangerous for opposing pitchers. Lance Berkman was now the top hitter. In 2002 he hit .292 with 42 homers and 128 runs batted in. The team's only .300 hitter was super utility man Jose Vizcaino, who had 406 at-bats and hit .303. Richard Hidalgo hit 15 homers but was a pale impression of what he had been two seasons earlier. The team was pretty much in the middle of most offensive statistics in the league, but dropped off to 14th in stolen bases.

On the pitching staff Roy Oswalt, with a 19-9 record and 3.01 ERA, was the best on the club, although Wade Miller's 15-4 3.28 was impressive. No other starters really were. Billy Wagner collected 35 saves. A couple of pitchers of whom much had been expected, Shane Reynolds and Tim Redding, faded.

It all added up to a 84-78 record and second place in the NL Central, thirteen games behind the champion Cardinals. In addition to the Bagwell heroics, the club had some games to remember even without being a contender. Just five days after Bagwell's walk off hit that beat the Mariners, backup catcher Geoff Zahn hit a two out 0-2 pitch as a pinch hitter for a grand slam winning walk off homerun as the Astros beat Arizona 7-4.

The Astros may have finished a baker's dozen games behind the Cards, but they did provide excitement in 2002. Fourteen games were decided with walk off winning hits or plays. The Astros won half of them. Ward and Vizcaino, like Zaun, won games with homeruns while Biggio, Lugo, Mark Loretta, and Bagwell won games with walk-off singles.

Attendance at the newly renamed Minute Maid Park was 2,517,357. The park actually had three names during 2002. It was Enron Field until February when the disgraced company that had gone out of business following massive fraud was removed as the ballpark sponsor. For three months, the Astros played at the generic Astros Field while management desperately sought a new naming rights sponsor to replace the millions committed from the now defunct Enron.

After about three months as Astros Field, the Minute Maid Company came through. Minute Maid, a subsidiary of Coca-Cola, had been based in Houston since 1967. The hometown company would take on the naming rights and on June 5, 2002, Minute Maid Park, often shortened by fans to MMP, was officially the new partner of the Houston Astros. The newly named park finished ninth of 16 in the league in attendance. Most of the season the Astros were not in contention. The closest they came was within two games in mid-August. Then they played sub .500 ball in September.

Biggio Moved to Make Room for Jeff Kent in 2003

Time was starting to run out if the Astros were going to have success in the postseason while Biggio and Bagwell were still close to their peaks. Even so, the 2003 team which won three more games than the 2002 unit, was in contention all season. When they beat Milwaukee at home on September 25 they tied for the top spot. However, losing two of the final three games of the season left them one game off the lead. Houston had been in first place 100 days during the season. They had never led by more than four nor trailed by more than 4 ½. The season looked more exciting that it really was because, with only an 87-75 final record, they had not played as well as fans would have liked.

The team had a new look. Receiving a one-year contract extension Craig Biggio agreed to leave second base to accommodate Jeff Kent who had signed a two-year $18-million free agent contract over the winter. Biggio said the contract was not necessarily about the money but to get him closer to being able to finish out his career in Houston. "It's the only organization I have ever known and it's the only organization I want to play with," he told the media at the time. It did, however, follow the same pattern as when he moved from second base to catcher in 1992—a contract extension and salary boost to help make the move easier to accept. The public face for the move was perhaps much smoother than the reality. Biggio was not as much behind the action as was made public.

Without saying as much directly, it is not hard to deduce, from what he told Astro broadcaster Bill Brown, that the move to make room for Kent did not come without conflict. "I was able to meet with Drayton for a long time. Then my agent [Barry Axelrod] and I were able to meet with the GM and Drayton for a long time. And then when we left the room it was over. I'm not going to say there were a lot of things that…I mean…you didn't know about it. Nobody knew about it. And that's the way it should be. There's no sense to sling mud out in the media. Nobody's going to win in that situation. But we were able to communicate and get some things off our chest, then we moved out there to try to become the best center fielder we could. I think it went really well. When I was moved to left field that took a little more time, because I really wasn't ready for that." The quote from Biggio was typical Craig. He hates to directly call attention to himself and the word "we" or "our" is often substituted for "I" or "my" with his words.

Biggio had played some games in the outfield years before and did welcome the addition of Kent's bat. "With our lineup the way it was last year, if we had Jeff in our lineup we would have done a lot better than we did last year," Biggio told the Associated Press.

There had been some speculation of having Kent play third base and leave Biggio at second, but it was decided to keep Kent at the position he was most familiar with and move Biggio into an outfield position that had not produced offensively well in 2002 instead.

Kent was a great addition offensively. Hitting 22 homers to go with 93 runs batted in and a .297 batting average, Kent brought some numbers that Biggio could not pull off in his prime. Jeff didn't have Biggio's range during his early years and was not known for his defense, but his offense was what the club needed. Moving to the outfield, Biggio hit just .264 but hit 15 homers and drove in 62. At thirty-seven years old, he wasn't trying to steal bases much now, but he was getting to first base any way he could. He was hit by a team record 27 pitches.

Biggio may have not been initially happy being pushed off second base for Kent, but he was a team player and lifelong Houston Astro and quickly realized the addition of Kent helped the team greatly. Once the season began, his only frequently heard complaint was how much extra running was involved going in and out between innings. Biggio had taken the time to put a real mileage count on it. He had even altered his offseason physical conditioning to include more distance running to get in shape for it.

Bagwell, now thirty-five years old, saw his batting average and on base percentage continue to decline a bit, but he still had the long ball. Jeff hit 39 homers and drove in 100. He also scored 109 times.

Other offensive stars included the star in the making, Lance Berkman (.288, 25HR, 93RBIs), Morgan Ensberg (.291, 25HR, 60 RBIs), and a bounce back year from Richard Hidalgo (.309, 28HR, 88RBIs). As a team, the Astros hit .263 and were fourth in the league in runs scored (805) and fifth in homeruns (191).

Early in the season, slick fielding Adam Everett replaced Julio Lugo at shortstop. Then Lugo was totally dropped from the club when he was accused of physically attacking his wife in the Minute Maid Park players' parking lot.

The Astros pitching staff was what likely kept the team in contention all year. The team ERA was fifth best in the National League at 3.86. They were third in fewest runs allowed and fourth in fewest hits allowed. The problem was that the sum totals were better than the staff itself. The plan was to hang close or in the lead to the seventh. Then the bullpen would take it to victory. Roy Oswalt was the best starter, but injuries limited him to only 21 starts. Rookie Jeriome Robertson won the most games and set a new Houston rookie record with 15. Nobody knew how he did it. His earned run average was a very weak 5.10. No starter pitched more than Wade Miller's 187 innings. Miller averaged 5⅔ innings per start. Robertson almost exactly only five. The 2003 Astro bullpen worked a lot. Fortunately, it was one of the best pens in the league, and far more often than not, if they club could get to the seventh with the lead, they won. Lidge, Dotel, and Wagner were nearly un-hittable.

History Was Made at Yankee Stadium

One of the most memorable games in franchise history took place on June 11 when the Astros visited the historic original Yankee Stadium for the first time. The series had opened the night before with New York taking a 5-3 win. In Game Two, Roy Oswalt started but suffered a groin injury in the first inning. Manager Williams would have to go to his bullpen far earlier than hoped. One advantage might have been the game being played under American League rules with the designated hitter. Pitchers would not have to be removed for strategic reasons offensively. Jimy had the option of going longer with his relievers if he wished to help make up for the innings lost from Oswalt departing in the first. Even so, Williams would still use a number of pitchers to finish the game.

After Oswalt, Jimy called on Peter Munro whose arm had been stretched out. He had been used in the rotation already. Munro, a New York area native, had some control problems in walking three, but he went two and two thirds innings. Had he not had shaky command and thrown fewer than 57 pitches during that time, he could have handled more work. He wasn't under great pressure since Houston scored in the first three innings and led 4-0 after three, but he was still struggling. He had been behind in the count way too much.

With two out in the fourth Kirk Saarloos relieved Munro. He got the final out and then worked an easy fifth. The Astros continued to hold the 4-0 lead heading into the sixth.

Instead of using one more bridge reliever to get to the Astros' big three at the end of the bullpen, Williams elected to bring in Brad Lidge in the sixth. Facing the minimum six hitters over two innings, he threw only 23 pitches, 15 of them for strikes, and fanned two of the six he faced.

Octavio Dotel was next for the eighth. In the meantime, the Astros had tacked on two more runs and now led 6-0. Dotel built a pitching line for his one inning rarely seen. In the inning he struck out the side, but it took him four hitters to do it! With one out after striking out Juan Rivera, he also struck out Alfonso Soriano, but the pitch was wild and got away from catcher Brad Ausmus. Soriano raced down to first base. That was no obstacle for Dotel. He struck out Derek Jeter and then Jason Giambi to end the inning.

The Astros added two more runs with a two-run double by Richard Hidalgo in the top of the ninth. The Astros were now leading 8-0 to the bottom of the ninth. It was certainly not a save situation or place to use a closer. But Jimy Williams knew what the scoreboard said and he frankly had used just about everyone else. The Yankees had no hits.

In came Billy Wagner to try to close things while Yankee owner George Steinbrenner was having fits with Williams's move. He complained later that the Astros were piling it on. It was unsportsmanlike. He thought Williams was doing it because he used to manage in Boston and the Yankees were the Red Sox's hated rivals. All fans of the Astros and most fans of baseball knew that opinion was his. You don't pass on trying to create an historic moment.

Often closers, when entering games not in normal closer's situations, have trouble, but not Wagner this time. He was trying to save a no-hitter. It was special. And he did it. Billy got Jorge Posada out on a swinging strike three. He did the same with pinch hitter Bubba Trammel. Then on the first pitch to Hideki Matsui, he induced a ground ball to Jeff Bagwell at first base. His easy toss to Wagner at the bag ended the game and preserved the no hitter. The Astros left the field whooping and hollering. Even Yankee fans (except for George) were applauding and giving the Astros their due. Only Jeff Kent didn't have the foggiest idea what was going on. He knew the Astros had won a game that wasn't all that competitive, but surely just winning a game at Yankee Stadium shouldn't bring that much joy?

Once he got into the clubhouse, he was filled in on what the six Astro pitchers had done and he understood.

Meanwhile out on the field the battle wasn't over. The game had been telecast by the Yankees, Astros, and ESPN. As the announcer who handled on-field interviews for the Astros, I had a hand held wireless microphone and a future game producer, Wave Robinson, in the television truck who knew the significance of this night. While a stage manager with ESPN was trying to get a headset microphone untangled so the announcers in the booth could talk with someone, the post-game had already started in Houston. I grabbed the last pitcher, Billy Wagner, and catcher Brad Ausmus and a conversation began. Then, out of the corner of my eye, all the other pitchers involved were on their way to the interview spot. Wave Robinson had gone into the clubhouse and rounded them up. It had not been easy. He had to battle with an ESPN producer and convince Oswalt he could avoid the mob of New York reporters gathering outside the clubhouse if he went on the field. On the field questions were doled out in a seven player interview. ESPN had to wait. When they finally set something up, all they could do was put the headset mic on one of the players with the others standing in the background.

The actual Astro interview total rose to eight when club owner Drayton McLane Jr. was spotted near the field and invited to jump over the barrier to put his two cents in.

That would turn out to be the only game the Astros would win on their first visit to Yankee Stadium, which was followed by the first trip to Fenway Park. Yet, they had come to New York and Boston and left the East Coast for home only one game off the lead.

Both Biggio and Bagwell Got Big Hits in Their Boyhood Shrines

The games were homecomings for both Biggio, a Yankee fan as a youth, and Bagwell, a die-hard Red Sox fan growing up. Both were able to hit homeruns in the ball parks of their dreams. Craig hit one off Mike Mussina in the first game in New York. Bagwell homered over the green monster in the second game in Boston. Craig was 5-13 with a homerun, two doubles, and two RBIs in New York. Jeff was 4-14 in Boston with a homerun, a double, and one RBI.

Richie Sexson Did Something That Will Never Happen Again

Another memorable game was on July 1 in Houston when the Astros beat the Brewers 6-5 on a walk off sacrifice fly by Gregg Zaun. It was a great game, with big hits and comebacks, but the biggest single play took place in the top of the fourth inning when Brewer slugger Richie Sexson hit a towering fly ball toward deep center field that was on the way to becoming a two-run homerun to give Milwaukee a 2-1 lead. But the ball hit the flagpole. At Minute Maid Park in 2003, the flagpole was adjacent to the outfield wall, but in play. Like many baseball parks in history, it was a conscious decision to put the pole inside the fence. The fact that it was located more than 400 feet from home plate meant it would rarely, if ever, have an effect on the actual game. This was the first time it would. When Sexson's ball hit the pole, it was like the goal posts in football. What the contact would mean would be determined by where the ball went. In football if the ball goes inside the pole, the points count; if it goes outside, the kick is no good. In baseball, something happens no matter which way the ball goes. If it hit the pole and went over the fence, it was a homerun. If it stayed in the field of play, it was a live ball.

Unluckily for Sexson, the ball stayed in the park. He had to hustle, but made it safely to third after driving in the tying run. He was on third with no outs, but the Brewers couldn't get him home. They lost to Houston by one run.

Drayton McLane remembers the game. "He hit it and it was a triple. About five minutes later, the commissioner [Bud Selig, former Brewer owner] called and said, 'Drayton, that's gotta be a homerun.' I said, too late the game has gone past that now. Now I know he hit the ball far enough for a homerun, but it hit the pole."

The point McLane was trying to make was that the play has been remembered far longer than the game—which was a good one—because fans saw something that rarely happens. It was a special event.

After the 2016 season, both the slope of "Tal's Hill" and the flagpole inside the playing field were removed from Minute Maid Park. Sexson will go in the books at the only player ever to hit the pole and be "robbed" of a homerun.

While the Astros were in contention most of 2003 and with a break here or there could have won the NL Central that season, the fact was the starting pitching was not healthy or strong enough. Had they won the division, they likely would have again been out-pitched and unsuccessful in the postseason. Time was running out with this nucleus of daily players. The starting centerfielder (Biggio) was thirty-seven. The second baseman and first baseman (Kent and Bagwell) were thirty-five. Bagwell was also having more and more problems with his right shoulder. Catcher Brad Ausmus was thirty-four. The farm system was lacking in can't-miss future stars. Lance Berkman, Morgan Ensberg, and Richard Hidalgo were still young and talented, but the Astros needed more, starting with pitching.

As the season ended in 2003 with a disappointing one game margin between the Astros and the winning Chicago Cubs, Astro GM Gerry Hunsicker and Owner Drayton McLane knew some changes were needed. So did the players. Billy Wagner was outspoken enough to punch his ticket out of town. He said the Astros would do something, but it would be nickel and dime patchwork repair. The inference, which many did not disagree with, was ownership in Houston was cheap; that the philosophy was to do the most you can for the least you can.

It was true the Astros normally were not considered as a likely home for big name free agents, yet in 1998 they had shocked baseball when they grabbed Randy Johnson. They couldn't retain him, but the reason was far more family lifestyle than lack of dollars. The club had made some good moves to acquire players like Moises Alou, Carl Everett, Bill Spiers, Jose Vizcaino, and the return of Ken Caminiti and Brad Ausmus. All had been good and key members of some winning clubs, so Wagner's comment was likely more out of frustration for how the season had ended than well thought out. No, the Astros weren't going to just throw money around, but if the right opportunity arose, the Astros would be a player.

On November 3, 2003, Wagner was traded to the Philadelphia Phillies for three pitchers the Astros hoped could compete for and improve the rotation. It is true Wagner was an $8-millonperyear pitcher, and his departure did give the Astros more room sign others, but his loss was also caused in part because it was time to elevate Dotel and Lidge in the late game pecking order.

The loss of Wagner was a matter of discussion in Houston, but soon fell off the sports pages when Houston signed two very well-known arms.

11   Andy and Roger Come Home

"People who aren't from Texas don't understand,
but this state has a powerful draw. I figured the good old state
of Texas would bring him home."

– Lance Berkman after Houston announced the signing of Andy Pettitte

Baseball fans are always optimistic. No matter how many holes your team has or how good other teams in the league may be, fans think that if things go right and this player or that player improves just a little bit, their team could win the World Series.

That is very rarely true, of course, but it has happened. Some of the thoughts about the Astros after the departure of Wagner were not that positive. That is, until December 16, 2003. The Astros had enticed New York Yankee free agent left-handed pitcher, Andy Pettitte, to come home and play for the Astros. A contact in November 2003, resulted in a contract offer from Houston. A contract was worked out in three weeks and in mid-December, Andy was introduced as an Astro. Pettitte lived in suburban

Deer Park just southeast of the city. Drayton McLane did the negotiating with Andy and his agents, Randy and Alan Hendricks.

Pettitte had played his entire career with the Yankees, starting in their farm system in 1991. He was not a top prospect having not been drafted until the 22nd round in 1990 out of San Jacinto Junior College. However, he worked his way through the farm system and made his major league debut with the Yankees in 1995.

He became a star right away and won 22 games the next season. Always a pitcher who gave up more hits than innings pitched with earned run averages rarely under 4.00, he was not the number one pitcher of the Yankee's staff, but a very solid veteran who rose to the occasion in big games. In 44 postseason starts, he was 19-11 with a 3.81 earned run average. The latter bested his career regular season mark of 4.27.

When the Astros signed the thirty-two-year-old Pettitte, they weren't signing their ace. Roy Oswalt already was that. They were signing an important piece for a full and improved rotation.

They also soon found they would be in line to sign someone else who could be their ace. Again, the owner himself did most of the leg work in bringing Roger Clemens to the Astros.

McLane remembered:

"Roger had retired and I really didn't know Roger. I'd met him before, but didn't really know him. I called him out of the blue. I left word that I had a Christmas present for him and his wife. I had my wife help me and we got them a real nice Christmas gift. I got in the car with the present and drove out to his big house on the west side, went up and just knocked on the door. He was there and they invited me in. That's how we got started. He was completely retired, but it still made George Steinbrenner really mad. Bringing Roger here really upset the Yankees."

On January 19, 2004, the Astros and six-time Cy Young Award winner Roger Clemens agreed on a new contract for him to pitch with Pettitte for the Astros. The contract was not for much money. He would make $5-million for one season as a pitcher with bonuses, plus a ten year personal services contract. Even the $5-million was not to be paid out in one season. He would get $1.5 million directly as a base for pitching in 2004 with the remaining balance paid in 2006. Even to get Roger Clemens, the Astros were not about to throw money around.

The Astros, because it was his home team, was the only team in baseball that could have lured Clemens out of retirement and signed him for such a low dollar amount. Plus, had good friend Andy Pettitte not already signed on, there was no chance Clemens would have come out of retirement. Roger's contract did allow him more control on his game prep and conditioning on days he was not scheduled to work, primarily to allow him to spend more time at home watching his boys play. He would often travel on his own and not have to be on hand till the day before he was scheduled to pitch. While not the norm, other veteran pitchers had had similar scheduling allowances. Nolan Ryan, for example, ran much of his own schedule during his days pitching for the Texas Rangers at the end of his career. Other starting pitchers had been given allowances in cutting road trips short or joining them late based on when they were scheduled to pitch. Clemens was sure to confer with team veterans to get their blessing since, as he told Alyson Footer what he had told his teammates, "I don't want you guys staring at me like I'm a prima donna. I want everyone to understand that I'm forty-one and have a seventeen-year-old son and I've made a commitment to him."

Jeff Bagwell had no problem with Clemens's special arrangements. "It's not a problem at all. This is a whole different scenario. This is a guy coming out of retirement…we're trying to win games. Nothing that Roger does is going to be out of whack. We are OK with it."

The Pettitte and Clemens acquisitions were mostly handled on the ownership level above that of General Manager Gerry Hunsicker. In baseball, GMs had traditionally been in full command of player moves, but in the free agent and high dollar era, there were more and more instances where agents had worked directly with owners. The finances involved made that necessary. Owners would have to approve large dollar acquisitions anyway, so the GM as middle man was often bypassed. That did not sit well with the general managers. Gerry Hunsicker and McLane clashed.

Their first public clash occurred after the 1998 season when Clemens had an option to leave the Toronto Blue Jays. A report had come out that Clemens would agree to be traded, but would require a major financial commitment from the team acquiring him to agree to the deal. Hunsicker, while at the baseball winter meetings, ripped Clemens for the request and Clemens ripped Hunsicker back claiming Houston was out of the running for his services. This was all going on while McLane had been talking directly with the Blue Jay owners about the possibility of a trade.

By the end of the 2004 season, Hunsicker and McLane parted company. Assistant GM Tim Purpura was promoted. However, before he left the team he had mostly built, sans Pettitte and Clemens, he had one more big move to make and the team would be back in the postseason.

Astros' Ticket Sales and Chances for Success Were Sky-High

Astros fans and most certainly manager Jimy Williams were ecstatic. The club had to hire additional staff to handle season ticket requests. Astros Vice-President of Ticket Sales, John Sorrentino, an eighteen-year team employee, said that the announcement of Clemens's signing resulted in the largest single day of season ticket sales in club history, and the second best day wasn't even close. "Days like this are what people in marketing dream about," added Sorrentino.

Even his new teammates were excited. Jeff Bagwell said, "How can you not be excited? You go to the grocery store and everybody's talking about Roger. This is something I thought really might happen. It's the culmination of what you've striven for. As a player, things change during your career, but for everything that's happened the last eight or nine years, this would be everything I've worked for."

Not only had the Astros come within one game of winning the NL Central the year before, but now with a rotation starting with Clemens, Oswalt, and Pettitte, they had to be the team to beat.

Things Started Slowly

As the 2004 season began, the Astros got off to a great start. They were a club record 21-11 on May 11 after 32 games. On the field they, were playing as well as the team looked on paper, but it quickly became evident a team can't win on paper or with off-season excitement and enthusiasm. It has to be done on the field and things didn't do as well as hoped. After the hot start, the club dipped under .500 and were just 44-44 at the All-Star break. The team had gone just 21-33 in their last 54 games. An early season elbow injury by Pettitte limited him to 15 starts. After Oswalt and Clemens, the rest of the rotation was unstable. Dotel got the closer role early, but had to surrender it to Brad Lidge, who was superb. He saved 29 to go with Dotel's 14. Dotel was traded mid-season. When Lidge came in it was "light's out." Which became his nickname. It fit. He struck out 157 in only 94⅔ innings pitched. Lidge threw more innings than all but four starting pitchers.

Oswalt won 20 and lost ten with a 3.49 earned run average. The forty-one-year-old Clemens was 18-4 with a 2.98 earned run average and 218 strikeouts in 214 and ⅓ innings pitched. It was good enough for his first National League and seventh Cy Young Award.

The Astros offense was keyed by Lance Berkman who hit .316 with 30 homeruns, 106 RBIs, and had a .450 on base percentage that rivaled the best of Bagwell during his prime. Bagwell, now thirty-six years old and requiring cortisone injections in his arthritic right shoulder two or three times per season to allow him to stay in the lineup, hit a career low .266 but contributed 27 homers and drove in 89 runs in 156 games. Biggio hit a then career high 24 homers while driving in 63 and hitting .281. During the spring, he had taken the left leg lift out of his stride. He originally had thought the leg kick was needed for him to generate more power, but decided at his now advancing age it was wearing him out and a less pronounced stride with a quicker bat was the key. The change paid off. He started the season in center field for the second year in a row, but would move over to left field while Lance Berkman moved to right just before mid-season. A major acquisition by the Astros would require Biggio make the fourth position change of his career. It would also send Jason Lane to the bench.

Carlos Beltran Came to Houston

The trade that brought center fielder Carlos Beltran to Houston from Kansas City in late June was made by Gerry Hunsicker, but again Drayton McLane had a strong hand in it.

"[Kansas City owner] David Glass is my best friend," said McLane. "I called him and said we'd like to make a trade for Beltran. So we got our two general managers together and we made the deal."

The Royals wanted to trade him to get some value before he moved on. Many teams were reportedly in the running. It was the Astros that pulled it off. Houston sent Octavio Dotel, who had lost the closers role to Brad Lidge, to Oakland as the main part of the three-way trade.

The Astros' stolen base totals had dropped off over the last two years, with both Bagwell and Biggio unable to run as well as they once did, and other players in the lineup not blessed with much speed. Plus, the defense with Kent at second and both Biggio and Berkman in the outfield was not top level. Bagwell with his ailing shoulder could no longer make the special plays he had been famed for making during his Gold Glove years.

Beltran would bring superb defense to the outfield, plus speed on the bases, and power to the plate. He was an all-tools player. But even a player as good as Beltran had to be instructed on the "Astros' Way" by Jeff Bagwell.

Gene Coleman remembers the lesson Baggie imparted, "We were fighting for the playoff position and Beltran got hit on the elbow by a pitch. In the post-game interview, he told the media he probably wouldn't be able to play the next day. Baggy's locker was nearby and he had heard what Beltran said. When the media left the room, he went over to Carlos, sat down next to him, and explained that if he and Craig could play, the team needed him and he needed to play. The next day Carlos Beltran was in the lineup."

When the deal was made on June 24, the Astros needed him. Craig Biggio had heard the rumors and knew acquiring a center fielder would affect him, but as he told the media, "If you're the guy that can move around, then you're going to be the guy. I heard other options about the infield maybe, this and that, but it never came about. This is what's going to be better for the club, and when you add a guy like Beltran, it's going to make us better." There had been some talk of Biggio moving to third base. Morgan Ensberg, who had hit 25 homeruns in 2003, had not hit a homerun yet. Although Ensberg never really found his homerun stroke in 2004, he held onto his job and would have a very good season in 2005.

The club was floundering in fourth place and five games behind the leader in the six-team NL Central. Beltran's appearance in the Astros lineup wouldn't turn things around immediately. The club was just starting a six game road trip in which they would win only two. When he played his first home game on July 2, the team would be in fifth place and six games out of first.

It was no surprise that Manager Jimy Williams was feeling some heat. Expectations were high before the season, but not being fulfilled. It didn't help that Williams was devoid of personality in the eyes of the public.

The addition of Beltran was not changing much. He had some good moments and made some great catches, but the Astros were still struggling.

Houston Hosted 2004 All Star Game

For one weekend, the focus in Houston shifted to the All-Star Game. The Astros would be the host for the third time. In two games staged at the Astrodome in 1968 and 1986, pitching had dominated. Perhaps that was no surprise since it was always the Astrodome's forte. In 1968, the NL won 1-0, and in 1986 the American League took a 3-2 victory. Roger Clemens was the winning pitcher in 1986.

However, in Minute Maid Park's first game, the offense prevailed. In fact, Clemens was the losing pitcher this time as the American League took down the National 9-4. Clemens gave up homeruns to Alfonso Soriano, Ivan Rodriguez, and Manny Ramirez in the first inning. David Ortiz homered later against Carl Pavano, while Albert Pujols hit the only NL long ball off C.C. Sabathia.

The Astros were represented by Clemens, Jeff Kent, Lance Berkman, and Carlos Beltran. Beltran had actually been selected because he would have been an American Leaguer, but moved to the Astros less than three weeks before the game. So he was added to the National League roster. Kent and Beltran both had hits.

Berkman had used up his heroics the day before. He had worked his way through the Homerun Derby using his right handed stroke to the final round. Some of his homers were among the longest ever hit in the competition. One of the five homers he hit totaled more than 459 feet, and was estimated to have gone 493 feet! He would face Oakland's Miguel Tejada in the finals. Tejada had hit 22 homers in the earlier rounds. Berkman's total was 17. However, in the finals, things went right to the wire. Berkman blasted four more long balls putting the pressure on Tejada. Miggy was up to it. He still had five outs left when he ripped his fifth homer in the final to beat Berkman 5-4. A couple of ironies from that match up: Tejada and Berkman would be teammates in Houston in 2008 and 2009, and Berkman was the only player who finished in the top five that was never linked to or suspected of using anabolic steroids or any other performance enhancing drug. Tejada was and so was number three finisher Rafael Palmiero, number four Barry Bonds, and number five Sammy Sosa.

End Of Jimy

By the All-Star Game break, the Astros had decided to make a managerial change. Since Jimy Williams was going to be a coach for the National

League team, his firing would be held off until the day after the game. If the Astros needed any extra reason to let Jimy go, the reaction of the fans when Williams was introduced before the game confirmed their decision. Jimy heard boo's showering from the stands. It was unfortunate and in many ways undeserved. However, so much had been expected from the 2004 team and the budget to make it happen had been stretched. A change had to be made. Williams wasn't the only victim. Pitching coach Burt Hooton and hitting coach Harry Spilman were replaced by Gary Gaetti and Jim Hickey.

Former Astro Favorite Phil Garner Signed on as Williams Left

Veteran player and former major league manager Phil Garner, who lived in Houston, was named to replace Williams. He was hired as an interim replacement since the hiring was done without following the Commissioner's mandate that minority candidates be considered. He took over with the club 44-44, 10 ½ games off the lead in fifth place. It took quite a bit of convincing to get Garner to leave his business interests and take over the Astros job. Garner had played for the team, had been on Art Howe's coaching staff, and later managed in both Milwaukee and Detroit. His last job had ended six games into the 2002 season in Detroit when he was fired. As a player, he had hit .500 for the Pirates in the 1979 World Series when they won over the Baltimore Orioles and had been a .260 career hitter over 16 seasons, including seven with the Astros. Garner was McLane's type of manager. He was outgoing, aggressive, and had a better report with his players. McLane remembered, "He worked well with Andy and Roger, which Jimy didn't."

The team didn't start winning more games right away when Garner took over just like when Beltran joined the club. (They had gone 6-9.) From 44-44 they dropped to 44-46. From that point, they would win a game, lose a game, win a couple, lose two, win two. They hovered on or near .500 until August 23. That night behind Clemens, they beat the Phillies 8-4. Their record was 62-62 and they were 20 games behind the leading Cardinals.

The game that got the Astros rolling featured a 3-4 night for Craig Biggio. Two of his hits were doubles. Carlos Beltran had a three-run homerun.

After that game, the Astros got red hot. They won 30 of their last 38 games. They still finished 13 ½ games behind St. Louis in the division, but their 92-70 record was good enough to clinch a wild card spot by one game over the San Francisco Giants

Astros Made the Postseason but Could They Win a Round?

The Astros were now back in the postseason for the fifth time in the last eight years. It would be the long-time nemesis Atlanta Braves in the first round.

The Braves were a division champion with 96 wins and would have the home field advantage. These were not the same Braves though. Their starters would be Jaret Wright, former Astro Mike Hampton, John Thomson, and Russ Ortiz. John Smoltz was a reliever, and Maddux and Glavine were gone. It was almost guaranteed the Astros would be better offensively against Atlanta than a few years earlier.

In Game One, Atlanta scored first, but the Astros got four in the third and three in the fifth and never looked back. Clemens got the win with Ausmus, Beltran, Berkman, and Lane all hitting homers. Jeff Bagwell was 2-5 with an RBI and two runs scored. Biggio was 1-5. Beltran was 3-3 and his incredible postseason was underway.

In the second game, the Braves took an 11 inning 4-2 win. The Astros were held to just four hits. Bagwell and Raul Chavez both hit homers. Rafael Furcal's two-run two-out homer off Dan Miceli in the last of the 11th inning won it for Atlanta.

With the series shifting, the Houston Astros were confident. Brandon Backe started and gave up only two earned runs in six innings. Biggio was 1-3 with a walk and run scored and Bagwell was 1-4 with a walk and a run scored. Beltran had a double and a homerun with two runs batted in to lead to an 8-5 Houston win.

With a chance to finally win a postseason series in Game Four, it wasn't to be. The Braves took a 2-0 lead in the top of the second, but the Astros scored five in the bottom of the inning. Then they didn't score again while the Braves plated three in the sixth and one more in the ninth to even the series 2-2 with a 6-5 victory.

A three-run homer by Adam LaRoche off Chad Qualls was the Braves only homer. Craig Biggio was 3-4 with three runs batted in on his homerun in the second. Jeff Bagwell was 2-4 with one RBI.

With Roy Oswalt on the mound and Braves pitching no longer as dominant, even though the series had to return to Atlanta for Game Five, the Astros were confident. It was well founded. Houston had a 4-2 lead until the seventh. Then the offense blew it open. Five runs in the seventh and three more in the eighth. When Dan Wheeler got Chipper Jones out on a fly ball into Jason Lane's glove in left field, the Astros had finally won a playoff series after eight tries.

Beating the Cards in the Next Round Didn't Work Out

Next up for Biggio, Bagwell, and the rest of the Astros would be the National League Central rival St. Louis Cardinals.

The Cardinals had won 105 games during the regular season. They had scored just under 200 more runs than they had surrendered. They were loaded with power. Albert Pujols had hit 46 homeruns. Jim Edmonds had slugged 42, and Scott Rolen hit 34. All three had driven in more than 100 runs.

The pitching staff featured five double figure winning starters led by Jeff Suppan with 16 wins. Chris Carpenter, Matt Morris, and Jason Marquis won 15 each. Jason Isringhausen was closing the door for a deep bullpen with 47 saves.

Still, the Cardinals would have to win the series on the field. Carlos Beltran made sure of that.

Despite four homeruns by the Astros (Beltran, Berkman, Kent, and Lamb) it wasn't enough as St. Louis won the opener 10-7. Chad Qualls took the loss in relief of Brandon Backe.

The second game was also taken by St.Louis 6-4. The game was tied at 4-4 until the eighth when the Cards pushed home the winning runs off reliever Dan Miceli. Back-to-back homers by Pujols and Rolen won it. Beltran and Ensberg both homered for Houston. Biggio was 1-5 with a run scored. Bagwell was 0-3 with two walks.

With the best of seven shifting to Houston on October 16 and a full house waiting to see Roger Clemens make his debut in the series, the Astros did not disappoint. Clemens went seven innings and allowed just two runs with Lidge closing out the last two innings and the Astros won 5-2. Biggio and Bagwell were both 1-4, but Beltran and Berkman, both with two hits and a homerun, each represented the "killer B's" well. Jeff Kent also homered.

In Game Four, the series was tied when the Astros took a 6-5 lead in the bottom of the seventh and held on. Roy Oswalt was not sharp, surrendering five runs in six innings, but Dan Wheeler and Brad Lidge shut the door. Jeff Bagwell was 2-3 with a run scored and an RBI double. He also walked once. Biggio was 1-4. Beltran homered again. It provided the game winning run in the seventh.

In Game Five, the Astros had a chance to take a three to two game lead into St. Louis. And they did it. Brandon Backe was superb. In eight innings, he allowed no runs and only one hit. Brad Lidge pitched the ninth and that was it in a 3-0 Houston victory. Jeff Kent's only hit in three at-bats, a three-run homer off Jason Isringhausen in the last of the ninth, was the winner. The walls of Minute Maid Park almost came down from the roar of the crowd and the sight of Kent approaching the plate to the crowd of teammates circling. The Astros needed only one win in two games to make their first World Series appearance.

The series shifted back to St. Louis on October 20. Pete Munro started for the Astros, but Phil Garner was going to do all he could to win game six. Other than those who might be needed for Game Seven, it would be all hands on deck. After 2 ⅓ innings and eight hits and four runs allowed, Munro was pulled. The next four pitchers, Chad Harville, Qualls, Wheeler, and Lidge all did the job. In fact, the game was tied 4-4 all the way until the bottom of the 12th when Jim Edmonds hit a two-run homer to win it.

So it would to a deciding seventh game between the NL Central champs and the team that finished second 13 ½ games behind.

An ailing Roger Clemens took the mound for Houston. Jeff Suppan would work for the Cards. Houston took a 2-0 lead into the last of the third. St. Louis got on the board by squeezing in Tony Womack in the bottom of that frame to make it 2-1. It stayed that way until the last of the sixth when an RBI double by Pujols tied the game and then a two-run homer by Scott Rolen put the Cards on top for good.

The Astros had only three hits. Biggio had one of them, a lead-off homerun in the first inning, but Bagwell, Beltran, Berkman, and Kent were all hitless. Kent and Beltran drew the only walks issued by four St. Louis pitchers.

One of the turning points in the game was in the Astros second. Already leading 1-0 Ausmus was hitting with two on and one out. His line drive appeared to be headed to the left center field gap, most likely to the outfield wall. Two runs likely would have scored, but center fielder Jim Edmonds made a dive for the ball extending his body almost perpendicular to the ground. He made the catch. A photo of that catch has hung in the St. Louis press box for years.

In their first ever NLCS series since the wild card six division era, the Astros took the Cardinals as far as they could. It was maybe not the best and most consistent regular season, but it was the most successful postseason in Astro history. Beltran had hit eight postseason homeruns. Could they go one step further in 2005 or was this the limit?

A lot would have to do with whether the club could retain Beltran and Kent and the return of a healthy Pettitte, and whether Jeff Bagwell's shoulder was totally shot. After winning the NL Cy Young Award, Clemens knew he'd work out something to return. But even if Pettitte returned healthy, could the Astros be as good as their injury plagued unit in 2004?

Like Johnson in 1998, Astros Couldn't Convince Beltran to Stay

Having finally gotten past the first round of the postseason in 2004, the Astros had a higher goal in 2005, but they handicapped their chances as a result of some offseason actions. Carlos Beltran and his agent Scott Boras passed on the Astros interest to re-sign him to a long term contract and instead signed with the New York Mets. Beltran had been reportedly offered a competitive contract, especially when cost-of-living was factored in, but the Mets still beat it. McLane said, "They had an un-announced deal with the Mets and I kept talking with Scott Boras and making offers and making offers. He let me keep talking, but be had already made a deal with the Mets. Boras absolutely wanted to get him into the New York market for more endorsement dollars. The Yankees weren't interested, but Beltran wasn't really a New York kind of player. He was quite reserved and I think his career would have been much more successful if he had stayed in Houston."

As McLane remembered, the stumbling block was Boras, "I tried very hard to convince Boras Houston would be a better fit. I met with him twice personally, but he was not willing to let me talk directly with the player. I got Beltran's number from either Biggio or Bagwell and I left word I'd be willing to fly anywhere to talk with him, but he was totally dominated by Boras."

In addition to not being able to bring Beltran back, the club declined to pick up Jeff Kent's option for 2005. Kent had made approximately $10-million in 2004, and presumably would have made more had his option been picked up. Kent wasn't washed up. Though he would be thirty-seven-years-old in 2005, he hit .289 with 29 homeruns and 105 RBIs for the Dodgers that year.

If losing Beltran and Kent wasn't enough, young star Lance Berkman injured his knee in the offseason playing touch-football. He would need surgery and miss the start of the 2005 season.

The Astros even changed General Managers. Gerry Hunsicker, who had been at the held during all the championship years of the Larry Dierker reign and who was running the club to its first postseason win in 2004, resigned. Officially the resignation was called a mutual decision to give his heir apparent Tim Purpura an early chance to take over since Gerry had planned on moving out after the 2005 season anyway. Not everyone believed that was really the case. Some thought it was time for Gerry and owner Drayton McLane to part company. McLane's feelings were that, "I think with Gerry the pressure of the job won out. Remember his wife was ill part of the time and I think he was worn out. Negotiating with the players, especially when we got involved with Roger Clemens and Andy Pettitte, took some of the traditional GM roles away and into ownership which was an adjustment."

There were many instances where Hunsicker and McLane collided. Often it was over the budget. Hunsicker was very much aware the Astros couldn't and the owner wouldn't over-spend on free agents or even re-sign the team's own players. Gerry was a master of finding the right player to fill holes. He had found a number of outstanding players from the beginning of his run as GM. Moises Alou, Carl Everett, Brad Ausmus, and Mike Hampton were only four of many acquired from other organizations during his watch. His first huge move that caught the attention of all baseball fans everywhere was in 1998 when the club made the trade for Randy

Johnson at mid-season. All he had to do was convince his owner to take on the last half of Johnson's contract. The rest of the deal, including what players to send to Seattle, was all Gerry. Owners always have final approval on contracts and McLane was OK with the signing of Moises Alou in the 90's, the Johnson deal, and the Carlos Beltran acquisition in 2004.

But also like all owners. McLane sometimes he worked on things on his own and didn't always keep his GM in the loop. The greatest failure in this regard was the original talk with Roger Clemens agents. Clemens became an Astro in 2004, but McLane had some contact with Roger's agents after the 1998 season. Hunsicker was not originally part of it.

How Clemens Might Have Become an Astro in 1999

In 1997, Clemens had signed a free agent contract with the Blue Jays after the Red Sox elected to pass on their former ace who had only won 29 games over the last three seasons and was now thirty-three-years-old. After two years, he had the option of staying for two more or requesting a trade.

In Toronto, he bounced back to win two straight Cy Young Awards, but after the second year and upset with Toronto budget cuts, he demanded a trade after the 1998 season. The Hendricks brothers, Clemens agents, originally talked with Astro owner Drayton McLane. McLane let his team president Tal Smith and general manager Gerry Hunsicker know shortly after. Both Smith and Hunsicker were in agreement that Clemens would be a great addition, but that the figures and possible bonuses included were not right for the franchise. When they called a news conference at the 1998 winter meetings in Nashville to criticize a reported Clemens's proposal for $27.4 million in bonuses as part of a new deal, Smith and Hunsicker felt the move was un-called for since he was already under a contract for two more years, for one thing, and to Smith and Hunsicker, that sounded like a player and his agents just being greedy.

Admittedly, the Astros brass from owner McLane on down was a bit touchy at that time. Randy Johnson had snubbed a good offer from the club to sign a long term contract with the Diamondbacks. The story circulated was that his wife didn't like Houston's weather in the summer. The reality was weather had little to do with it. Randy eventually signed with the Arizona Diamondbacks, where the average daily temperature in the summer is north of 100 degrees, because Randy, his wife, and family simply wanted to play at home. They had made their home in the Phoenix area for years not far from the spring training home of the Seattle Mariners for whom he had played most of his career.

The Astros, especially its owner, wanted a pitcher who could replace Johnson. And in Clemens's case, it would give him a chance to return home. McLane's contacts with the Hendricks brothers turned out to be in vain after the Smith-Hunsicker news conference in Nashville.

In an Associated Press story of December 23, 1998 Clemens said, "I am very upset about what Mr. Smith and Mr. Hunsicker said and how they directed things toward me as a person."

"I don't know them personally and they don't know me as a person. This disappointment I feel is that I have no interest in playing for two individuals like that who would make a statement like that and don't know me." In this case, Smith and Hunsicker may have not even known their owner.

McLane, while standing behind his executives, still hoped something could be worked out. He had remained in contact with the brothers floating some dollars around to see if the Astros could make a trade with Toronto. Both the Hendricks brothers said, while they were upset with all the goings-on, that didn't sever their relationship with the Astros in the future. Just this time.

According to the Associated Press, the Astros reportedly (through McLane himself) had made a $43.5 million three-year offer. However, with the attainable bonuses, it would more likely average nearly $20-million per year. There is some question about whether McLane realized it would be that much.

Clemens walked away from the Houston offer after the Smith-Hunsicker comments, but he did not stay with the Blue Jays either. They had options on two more seasons, but Clemens had a right to leave if a trade could be worked out.

As history shows, he did leave after being traded to the Yankees. They signed him for less than the Astros had offered, but on a longer contract. Houston would have another chance prior to 2004.

2005 Looked Like It Might Be Tougher to Win

In 2004 Clemens was superb for the Astros. In 2005 he would be solid again. Winning a seventh Cy Young Award in 2004 he followed by leading the NL in earned run average in 2005. However, he won five fewer games. The loss of both Kent and Beltran from the batting order, the creeping age affecting Biggio, and the continuing pain and weakness of Jeff Bagwell's shoulder made the club far less potent offensively.

Andy Pettitte had recovered from his elbow injury and may have had the best over all season of his career with a 17-9 record and sparkling 2.39 earned run average. Roy Oswalt won 20 and lost 12 with a 2.94. Clemens was 13-8 with a 1.87 earned run average, and Brad Lidge truly was "lights out" with 42 saves and 103 strike outs in only 70⅔ innings pitched. The pitching had the second lowest team earned run average in the league and gave up the second lowest run total as well.

Things were not so well offensively. The team was shut out 17 times in 2005. A major reason was that the great career of Jeff Bagwell was ending. Continuing shoulder pain and weakness plus a lot time on the disabled list limited Jeff to only 37 games and 100 at-bats. He hit just .250 and collected the last three homeruns of his career.

Craig Biggio, now thirty-nine years old, moved back to second base with the non-retention of Kent. He was looking like his age defensively, often replaced late in games for defensive purposes. His range was reduced and his arm had weakened. As a hitter, he had learned how to "cheat" at the plate. Essentially that meant he would look for a particular pitch in a spot and start the swing a bit early to be able to get around on it. He did it well, hitting a career high 26 homers to go with 69 runs batted in while hitting .264.

Lance Berkman was able to begin playing in May after his offseason knee surgery. In 132 games he hit .293 with a fine .411 on base percentage. He also clubbed 24 homers and drove in 82.

The biggest offensive star was third baseman Morgan Ensberg. The twenty-nine-year-old product of the Houston farm system bounced back from a ten-homer 2004 to hit 36 homeruns, and drive in 101 runs while hitting .283. Fellow farm system alum, Jason Lane, finally got a chance to play every day. He hit 28 homers, drove in 78, and batted .267. Left field was shared mostly between Chris Burke and Orlando Palmiero.

The Astros unfortunately were 11th in the league in scoring runs (693) and were only 13th in team batting average (.256). With 161 homeruns, the club was only ninth playing in a home ballpark not unfriendly to power hitters.

For the 2004 season, the team had hit eleven points higher and scored 114 more runs. They also hit 26 more homers. The 2005 team certainly was not as strong as what was on the field in 2004.

Still, they only won three fewer games. An 89-73 record was not good enough to win the NL Central. It wasn't even good enough to contend for the top spot. Houston finished eleven games behind the champion Cardinals. However, it was good enough to squeeze past the Philadelphia Phillies by one game for the wild card.

To make the postseason field, several things had to happen. And they did. On May 24 after a loss in Chicago dropped the Astros to 15-30, the *Houston Chronicle* printed a gravestone for the Astros on the front page. They were in last place in the division and 14 games off the lead. The team was not showing an ability to score. In most cases, Astro pitchers had to hold their foes to three runs or less or chances to win were slim.

Even before the Astros had fallen all the way, rumors were spread all over the media around the country that the Astros would throw in the towel and trade Clemens and maybe others before the trading deadline. In the internet media age, most of the reports were written based on past history in baseball and were pure speculation with no solid facts behind them. The Astros stood pat.

After 15-30 the Astros won the next game in Chicago, but dropped back to fifteen under .500 the next day. On May 27, the Astros hit bottom. At 16-31, they were now 15 games behind the Cardinals and not even considered a wild card option.

Not Zombies Rising from the Dead: Astros Just Came Alive

Then they started to heat up. In September alone the Astros won 20 games. They were not catching up to St. Louis at all, but remember they would eventually catch the Phillies for the wild card. They beat Philadelphia all six times they met. That was the difference. Pettitte, Oswalt, and Clemens beat them in a sweep in Houston in late July by scores of 7-1, 2-1, and 3-2. The second game on July 26 was a walk off victory. Mike Lamb's homerun leading off the last of the ninth off Ryan Madson gave Oswalt the win in a game that only took 2:11 to play.

Biggio Led to Key Wins Against Phillies and Billy Wagner

When the Astros met the Phillies in Philadelphia starting on September 5 it was the same result—a three game sweep by the Astros. Brad Lidge, who would later work for the Phillies on a World Champion team, saved all three games. Billy Wagner, who had proceeded Lidge in the role in both Houston and Philadelphia, was the losing pitcher in two games that he had a chance to save.

Andy Pettitte, with Lidge, won the opener. In the second game, Jason Lane singled home Eric Bruntlett off Wagner to put the Astros into a 2-1 lead. Lidge saved the game. Craig Biggio homered for the Astros other run, but he wasn't finished with heroics in Philly.

In Game Three, the Astros won another in the ninth. Trailing 6-5, the Astros were facing Wagner again. He got Adam Everett and Brad Ausmus for the first two outs. But then pinch hitter Jose Vizcaino hit a ball toward third baseman David Bell who booted it. With a runner on first and one out, speedy Willy Taveras chopped a ball on the ground. He beat it out for an infield single. Now with two on and two out Craig Biggio strode to the plate to face long time teammate Wagner. With the count at 1-1, Biggio started his swing a bit early to compensate for Wagner's fastball and found one right in the sweet zone. The ball rocketed to deep left field before slamming into the fans sitting in the bleachers. Houston led 8-6. Lidge made short work of Philadelphia in the last of the ninth. The Astros had beaten Billy Wagner twice, had swept the six games with the Phillies and were on their way. After the game, Houston was 75-64. They would go 14-9 the rest of the way to edge out the Phillies. The Phillies put on a run to catch the Astros the last four games of the season. They won all four. The Astros needed to win two of their last four. Facing the Cubs at Minute Maid Park, they did exactly that.

Here Come the Braves And Maybe the Cardinals, Too

Now came the 2005 postseason. First the Astros would have to beat the Braves. Then, if they won, a matchup with the Cardinals was likely. Both of Houston's most difficult opponents over recent years would have to be overcome to get the team into its first World Series.

How hard would that be? The Astros had good pitching but a much less skilled offense than in 2004. They had to expend a lot of energy just to get into the postseason. Catcher Brad Ausmus spoke for the whole team after the club clinched the postseason berth. "Thank God it's over! We've been in a playoff atmosphere for month, it seems like. Or at least the last month. It's nice that it's over and nice that we won." This was not the 2004 team. The offense without Kent and Beltran was weaker. It was shut out 17 times during the season and had the bad habit of leaving a lot of runners in scoring position. Plus, Jeff Bagwell could do nothing but swing a bat occasionally, forty-one-year-old Roger Clemens was battling several aches and pains and the club needed to hope adrenaline kicked in because they were tired.

Few were worrying about what the Astros could not do at the time, but rather that now an experienced team would be in the postseason again. For Craig Biggio, it was not just the immediate future that loomed. The pressure of whether, as a high-priced veteran, he would be still an Astro in 2006 was taken care of when, on the night of the clinching, General Manager Tim Purpura announced Biggio and the Astros had agreed on a one-year contract for 2006 at $4 million. Both Biggio and the Astros were well aware that the veteran second baseman had a strong run going for 3,000 hits in his career. Achieving that magic number would almost certainly be worth induction into the Baseball Hall of Fame someday.

Bagwell Kept Trying but His Shoulder Pain Was Too Great

As for Jeff Bagwell, he had been sidelined for more than half the season and only played in 39 games. He had homered off Greg Maddux on April 29 for his career 449th. It would turn out to be the last homerun of his career. He was only hitting in the .230s and was in almost constant pain. In early May, he had actually felt his career could be over due to the continuing and more severe pain in his right shoulder. At that point, he was put on the disabled list for 15 days with no treatment planned, only to rest it. As Bagwell pointed out when talking with the media on May 10, he had tried just about everything including cortisone injections and even acupuncture to be able to play. Treatment had started with surgery on the original torn labrum in 2001 and the ensuing rehab and treatment just didn't work. With cartilage removed, his shoulder was basically bone on bone with arthritis flaring up to cause the continuing and rising pain. By 2005, Bagwell had been playing in pain for about 3 ½ years. It was getting worse. He was hurting and his throwing arm was gone. He was once the best fielding first baseman in baseball with his range, skill at scooping up low throws, and his ability to start double plays and make the tough throws. Now he couldn't throw the ball much better than a six year-old. Even fielding a sacrifice bunt and making the throw to the pitcher covering was sad to see. Jeff had to almost shot-put the ball since he couldn't use his shoulder.

After the rest period did nothing, Bagwell elected to try a new surgery in an effort to salvage his career. The surgery was to provide range of motion, something Bagwell no longer had at all. Called Arthroscopic Capsular Release surgery. It was a last ditch option. Even if successful, it would not cure Bagwell's shoulder, but if it gave him more range of motion he might be able to play again. As Bagwell put it at the time, "I think it's the best possibility for me to play again. I have to do it. I think that's the only way I can continue to play this game. I owe it to the Astros and I owe it to myself to give it a try. I think the best chance for me to play again is to have the surgery." The surgery was performed in early June.

Jeff flew to Spartansburg, S.C. and the Steadman Hawkins Clinic. Dr. Richard Hawkins, assisted by Astros medical director Dr. David Lintner, conducted the surgery. The process was declared a success. The procedure loosened the tendons surrounding Bagwell's degenerative shoulder. Tendons surrounding the shoulder were cut, giving it more room to move. Several bone chips were removed and significant arthritis was observed. While still under anesthesia, the physicians tested and found much greater range of motion than before the procedure.

The surgery was not intended to solve all of Jeff's problems, but only to see if the shoulder could be usable for baseball activities again with less pain.

Hero One Last Time

As the Astros and Bagwell would find when he rejoined the team in September, his shoulder was still a major problem. He just couldn't throw. He would be a pinch-hitter. He would have one pinch-hit shortly after he returned that won a game. On September 16, he was called on to pinch-hit with two on and two out in the last of the ninth against Milwaukee. On a 1-1 count Bagwell ripped a pitch from Dana Eveland into right field driving in Willy Taveras with the winning walk-off run. It was Bagwell's first hit since May 2 in his third plate appearance since returning from surgery. He had been called out on strikes and walked in his earlier at-bats.

"It's been a long road back, a lot of questions whether I was going to be able to make it," Bagwell told the media after the game. "I'm still not all the way back, but when you sit on the DL for four months rehabbing, you don't feel like that much a part of the club…Tonight at least I came and did something to help this club get closer to the postseason."

Since the Astros made the postseason by only one game, what would turn out to be his last heroic moment helped his team a great deal.

Astros and Braves Met in the Postseason for the Fifth Time

These weren't the same Braves and Astros. The biggest different was that, although Atlanta won 96 games, their pitching staff was not as dominant. John Smoltz was back in the rotation as a starter, but there was no Maddux or Glavine. The Astros had a Clemens, Oswalt, and Pettitte main rotation.

Pitching did not dominate in game one. The Astros won 10-5. Biggio was 2-3 with a walk, three runs scored and one driven in. Morgan Ensberg drove in five. Ailing, Jeff Bagwell did not start, but appeared as a pinch hitter and drove in a run with a single. Pettitte was the winner after pitching seven innings and allowing four hits and three earned runs.

Atlanta bounced back to win game two 7-1. Smoltz bested Clemens who gave up five earned runs in five innings. Biggio was 1-4 and Bagwell did not play.

With the series shifting, the Houston Astros were ready. Houston won 7-3 with Roy Oswalt allowing three runs in 7 ⅓ innings. Led by Craig Biggio's three hits and two runs scored, and two hits from Willy Taveras, Ensberg, and Jason Lane, along with a homerun from Mike Lamb, Astro bats put Houston over the top. Bagwell again did not see action.

Leading two games to one, the Astros wanted to clinch Game Four to not only end the series, but to keep it from moving back to Atlanta. What resulted may have been the greatest game in Houston baseball history.

With the Astros "big three" Pettitte, Clemens, and Oswalt having already started games, it would be up to Brandon Backe to toe the rubber in game four. Backe had been impressive.

Minute Maid Park was jammed. In the top of the third inning, the Braves jumped on Backe for four runs. Two walks and a hit batter loaded the bases off with two out. Then Adam LaRoche hit a 1-1 pitch over the fence in right-center field for a grand slam homerun. As the four baserunners trotted to the plate, Minute Maid Park got quiet.

Backe was relieved in the fifth when the Braves added another run. A single by Marcus Giles and a double by Chipper Jones put runners on second and third with no outs. Andruw Jones hit a fly ball to left field that was foul, but Lance Berkman elected to get an out instead of letting the ball drop and Giles scored. That, hopefully, would help keep the Braves from another big inning. Backe was relieved by lefty Mike Gallo. Jones had moved to third on the sacrifice fly but Gallo was up to the task. Despite having to battle around an intentional walk and hit batter, he got the final out and surrendered no more runs when Brian McCann grounded out to end the inning. Gallo had a tremendous season in keeping inherited runners from scoring, coming into a number of games with runners already on second or third. He had come through again.

In the bottom of the fifth, the Astros finally scored. However, the inning also was similar to so many during the regular season. It should have provided more than the lone run they got. Mike Lamb, Adam Everett, and Brad Ausmus had all singled. However, the only run they scored came on a sacrifice fly by Orlando Palmiero who was pinch hitting for Gallo.

Things were not looking good in the top of the eighth when the Braves upped their lead to 6-1 on a solo homerun by McCann off Wandy Rodriguez, the Astros fourth pitcher.

No doubt some fans were leaving the park, or intended to after the Astros hit in the last of the eighth. Then they changed their plans. Ausmus led off the Astro's eighth when Atlanta starter Tim Hudson walked him. Eric Bruntlett then grounded a 1-2 pitch for a single with Ausmus moving to second. The Braves elected to bring in hard-throwing reliever Kyle Farnsworth. He got Craig Biggio to hit the ball to Chipper Jones at third to force out Ausmus. With one out and Luke Scott at the plate, Bruntlett and Biggio orchestrated a double steal. Bruntlett to third and Biggio to second.

Whether that unnerved Farnsworth or it was just the frequent wildness featured by the big right-hander, the result was that Scott walked on a 3-2 pitch loading the bases for the Astros best hitter in 2005, Lance Berkman.

On a 2-1 pitch, Lance hitting left handed against the hard throwing right-hander, lined a ball toward the Crawford boxes in left field. His opposite field drive made it several rows deep and the grand slam homer put the Astros back in the game. It was now 6-5 Braves.

"It was probably the quickest trip around the bases I've made in a long time," Berkman told the media after the game. "It was a very exciting and emotional moment."

The Astros kept their momentum when Chad Qualls entered to pitch the top of the ninth and faced only three hitters. After a walk to Chipper Jones leading off, Biggio was the middle man on a 5-4-3 double play off the bat of Andruw Jones. Then, forty-one-year-old Julio Franco grounded out to end the inning.

In the last of the ninth, with the Astros only one rally from closing out the series and heading to St. Louis for round two, things were not looking good when Jason Lane grounded out and Jose Vizcaino struck out against Farnsworth. Two out, no one on base, and Ausmus against Farnsworth. The usually light-hitting low-power veteran was up to the task. The count was 2-0 and Ausmus knew Farnsworth would be coming with a fastball to get a strike. Ausmus was ready. As the ball he hit sped into left center field toward the 404-foot mark, the main question for all was would the ball reach home territory or bang off the wall on the wrong side of the yellow line that defined the promised land? Although Andruw Jones was baseball's top defensive center fielder at the time, he was not going to be able to reach the ball. So would it be a homerun or double?

The thousands at Minute Maid Park roared when the ball hit the façade of the wall and the second base umpire Sam Holbrook raised his hand and arm in the air and made a circling motion signifying homerun. The Astros had come back from a 6-1 deficit to tie the game in the last of the ninth. Later Ausmus told the media, "I don't think he [Farnsworth] was particularly concerned about me hitting a homerun to center or right field. That was probably the biggest I've had."

But the game wasn't over yet, not by a long shot.

Qualls stayed in the game for the Braves 10th, and after a one-out double by Ryan Langerhans, had no problems retiring the side. In the Houston 10th, Chris Reitsma got the first two outs then Lance Berkman doubled. Astro manager Garner brought in Chris Burke to pinch run. That would turn out to be a decision second-guessed for a few innings, but not permanently. Burke was faster and the Astros were going for the win now.

Morgan Ensberg was intentionally walked and Jeff Bagwell was brought off the bench to pinch hit and hopefully win the ball game and series. That dream faded when Baggie hit a soft fly ball to the left to end the inning.

Brad Lidge came into the 6-6 game in the 11th and was wild. He walked two, but survived. He had to throw 34 pitches.

Lidge was still on the mound in the 12th and threw 12 more pitches. He gave up a single, but again no runs. Meanwhile the Astros were retired in order in both the 11th and 12th.

Neither team mounted a threat in the 13th. In the 14th, with Dan Wheeler working his second inning for the Astros, the Braves had the bases loaded with one out. Then Wheeler struck out McCann and got pinch hitter Pete Orr on a ground out to Ensberg at third to end the inning.

Both teams were starting to run short of pitchers. Andy Pettitte, who had left the clubhouse before the game feeling a bit under the weather and was set to start the Astros next game, got in his car in suburban Deer Park and started to head to Minute Maid Park in case he was needed. Roger Clemens sidled up to manager Phil Garner and pitching coach Jim Hickey and said since it was his day to throw between starts, he could work an inning or so if needed.

In the meantime, when the Astros went out 1-2-3 in the last of the 14th and Wheeler had to pitch the top of the 15th, the Astro bullpen cupboard was bare. Clemens put on his spikes while Wheeler was retiring three of the four he would face and started to warm up. Roger noted the bullpen was a lonely place. Only bullpen coach Mark Bailey and bullpen catchers Stretch Suba and Javier Bracamonte were there.

Clemens would actually enter the game in the bottom of the 15th. Out of position players, Garner decided to let Clemens swing the bat for Wheeler as a pinch hitter. The strategy was sound. Biggio had led off the inning with a walk. Wheeler was due up, but as a reliever had not batted in two years and had only one sacrifice bunt in his whole career. Clemens, as a starting pitcher, had eight sacrifice bunts in two years with Houston. He got the job done moving Biggio into scoring position. Then Chris Burke walked and, with Ensberg at the plate, Clemens thought he might not have to pitch after all. A base hit by Ensberg could win the game.

Alas, Ensberg slapped a ball to shortstop that was turned into an inning-ending double play. The game would move to the 16th and Clemens would pitch—being the seventh pitcher used in a game that was still not over.

Clemens was strong with two strikeouts in a 1-2-3 16th. Brower followed with the same in the bottom on the 16th. In the Braves 17th, pinch hitter Brian Jordan hit a one-out double, but he was stranded on the bases when Giles struck to end the inning.

The Braves' Joey Devine pitched the bottom of the 17th and had a 1-2-3 inning. Houston had 10 1-2-3 innings in what would be an 18 inning game. Atlanta went down in order four times.

Clemens, working his third inning in relief, had to work around a throwing error by shortstop Jose Vizcaino to pitch a scoreless 18th. He would lead off the bottom of the 18th. Knowing that he was running out of gas on the mound, he elected to take big swings at the plate. It would be game-winning homerun or nothing. With his growing fatigue and tender hamstring, he did not want to run bases. He wanted to trot.

The big swing strategy was fun for the fans, but it didn't work. Devine struck him out. Next was Chris Burke, who had entered the game back in the ninth inning as a pinch runner for Lance Berkman. Phil Garner's decision to make that switch was a significant subject of conversation and complaint.

However, Devine made the same mistake on Burke that Kyle Farnsworth had made with Brad Ausmus back in the ninth. He fell behind on the count. On a 2-0 pitch, Burke hit the ball toward the Crawford boxes in left field. The crowd was both excited and nervous. Would the ball be high enough to make it into the first row or bang off the big scoreboard?

For the second straight year after so many seasons of first round frustrations, the baseball gods were working for the Astros. Homerun! The Astros had beaten the Braves in a record long 18 inning postseason game and were heading to St. Louis to see if they could get past the Cardinals and into their first World Series. Inside Minute Maid Park the fans couldn't stop roaring. Outside the park in downtown Houston, horns were being honked. Fans and just those walking the streets were whooping it up and exchanging high fives. Once the sell-out crowd started emptying the ball park, the number celebrating in the streets grew. For the second straight year and first time at home, the Astros had won a first round playoff series.

For the record, the 18 inning game was played in five hours and fifty minutes. Brad Ausmus had caught sixteen innings. He had spent two innings at first base with Raul Chavez catching. Then they switched spots when Clemens entered the game. Five different players spent time at first base. Three different players did time at shortstop with both Jose Vizcaino and Eric Bruntlett playing it twice. Bruntlett also played center field twice and was involved in four position shifts. Twenty-three of the Astros twenty-five players saw action, with only starting pitchers Roy Oswalt and Andy Pettitte not in the lineup.

Jeff Bagwell pinch hit and flied out. Craig Biggio played the whole game and was 1-7 with a walk and a stolen base. Even so, just being on the field and involved in such a game was exhausting. "I'm doing everything I can just to stand upright! This team never does anything easy, but we never gave up on each other. To come from as far back as we have, there's no doubt about it. This year has been the most special," recounted Biggio after it was all over.

Next up were the St. Louis Cardinals, who had won the Astros National League Central Division by eleven games over the wild card Astros. The Cardinals had been 100-62 for the best record in the league and had beaten the Astros in eleven of sixteen meetings.

Astros Were Again Underdogs in Series with St. Louis

The effect of the Astros' 18 inning win over the Braves figured to add yet another reason why the Cardinals would win the series. Add to that the emotional impact of the fact that Busch Stadium II was going to host its final games either during this series or in the World Series. The new Busch Stadium III was being constructed adjacent to Busch II. The Cards had been playing in Busch II since 1966 when it was one of the early round "cookie-cutter" stadiums built to accommodate both baseball and football. The new stadium would be for baseball only. Much of it had been built when the NLCS began. What was missing was the left field area, which would be built once the right field portion of Busch II could be demolished.

The focus for both teams would be inside Busch II and not on its eventual fate.

The best of seven NLCS began in St. Louis on October 12. The Cards showed the Astros who they were by scoring in both the first and second innings off Andy Pettitte and rolling to a 5-3 win. Chris Burke homered for his second game in a row for the Astros as a pinch hitter in the seventh inning, but the Astros managed over seven hits. Reggie Sanders hit a two-run homerun off Pettitte for two of the five earned runs that he surrendered in six innings.

The Astros had Roy Oswalt rested and ready for the second game. He and Brad Lidge limited St. Louis to only six hits, one of them a homerun by Albert Pujols. The Astros were racking up eleven hits and four runs off Cardinal pitchers Mark Mulder and Julian Tavarez. Craig Biggio had two hits and an RBI. Willy Taveras, Lance Berkman, and Chris Burke all had two hits each as well. The series was now even and heading back to Houston.

In Game Three, Roger Clemens told himself his ailing hamstring didn't hurt as much as it did and got through six innings allowing just two runs. The Astros scored two runs in the last of the sixth to break a 2-2 tie. Clemens was the pitcher of record when Chad Qualls and Brad Lidge came in to wrap up a 4-3 victory. It was not easy.

Mike Lamb had a big game with a double and a two-run homer. Biggio, who was 2-4, was the only other Astro with two hits.

In the ninth inning, with Astros leading by two runs, Lidge ran into trouble. After retiring the first two hitters, he walked pinch hitter John Rodriguez, who was allowed to go to second base on fielder's indifference. Then John Mabry doubled to score Rodriguez and put the tying run on second with two out. David Eckstein, who had given the Astros fits all season with a successful slap hitting style, did not do it this time. After working the count to 2-2, Lidge got him and the Cardinals out on a fly out to center field. The Astros now led the best of seven series two games to one. Next up would be Brandon Backe for the Astros against Jeff Suppan. Not much offense was expected from either team. Not much resulted.

St. Louis scored a run in the fourth on a sacrifice fly by Albert Pujols. The Astros tied the game on a homerun by Jason Lane in the bottom of the inning. The game remained 1-1 until the last of the seventh when Morgan

Ensberg's sacrifice fly with one out and the bases loaded brought home Willy Tavares.

There would be no more runs. However, it took a good decision and play by Ensberg in the top of the ninth to keep the tie. After singles by Pujols and Larry Walker found runners on the corners with no outs, Ensberg took a ground ball off the bat of Reggie Sanders and nailed Pujols at the plate trying to score. Then Mabry hit a ball to Biggio which was turned into a game-ending 4-6-3 double play. The Astros now led the series three games to one and were just one victory away from the franchise's first World Series.

Pujols and the Homerun That Never Came Down

Knowing they only needed to win one game with three available if needed, the Astros and their fans fervently wanted to win their World Series berth at home. What a celebration downtown Houston would see— even grander than after Chris Burke's homerun to beat the Braves—IF the Astros could now oust their archrival Cardinals. St. Louis, on the other hand, even with its great division championship series and 100 wins, was still smarting about what happened to them in the 2004 World Series with Boston. After knocking out the Astros in the NLCS in 2004, they were swept in the Series by Red Sox.

Now to stay alive for a chance to redeem themselves, they had to battle back to take this series with the Astros. As Game Five began, they were in good shape. Although the Astros scored a single run in the second inning when Craig Biggio singled home Brad Ausmus, the Cards knew they were not in any real trouble. Houston had opened the inning with a single by Lane and double by Ausmus, but lost Lane when he tried to score on a throw to the plate by Pujols on a grounder hit by starting pitcher Andy Pettitte. The Astros got only one run out of the inning.

Then St. Louis took the lead in the top of the third on a two-run single by Mark Grudzielanek. Pettitte and Cardinal starter Chris Carpenter traded zeroes on the scoreboard until the bottom on the seventh when the Astros fans started smelling a World Series after Lance Berkman cracked a three-run homer. It was a "Killer B" special. Berkman hit it with Biggio and Burke also scoring.

From that point on, the bullpens took over. Heading to the top of the ninth, Houston was three outs from the World Series with ace closer Brad

Lidge on the mound. Lidge was pumped. He blew away both Rodriguez and Mabry with swinging strikeouts. The pesty David Eckstein was able to dribble a grounder into left field for a hit. That, however, may have unnerved Lidge for, facing left-handed hitter Jim Edmonds who could tie the game with one swing, he lost the strike zone. On a 3-1 count, Edmonds walked.

Under the stands, those who were involved in post-game shows on television for both St. Louis and Houston were watching a monitor near the press elevator when Albert Pujols came to the plate. So far, Pujols was hitless in four at-bats and might be St. Louis' last chance. After a first pitch strike, it was a vast understatement to say he was ready for the second offering. Under the stands, the TV people heard the crowd seconds before the picture appeared on the screen. Houston folks knew the sound was not the crowd cheering from victory, but more in the massive groan category. Then seconds later, all saw on the TV screen just how hard Pujols hit the ball. The ball was well more than 100 feet off the ground when it soared over the Crawford boxes in left field. Some would later swear it was still rising when it flew past the short railway behind and above the left field wall. The ball just disappeared.

Under the stands with the TV folks gathered, one St. Louis post-game host clenched his fist and softly exclaimed, "All right…way to go!" Realizing who was around him and that those reactions are considered inappropriate for media members, he tried to apologize, but a member of the Houston contingent quickly jumped in to let him off the hook. After all, it WAS quite a timely and well-hit homer. "Don't worry about it," said the Houston announcer, who had seen what Chris Burke did in the previous round, "I can imagine how you feel."

Of course, the homerun didn't officially keep the series alive yet. The Astros still got to hit in the last of the ninth. And even if the Cards held on, the Astros still needed to win only one game—even if now it would have to be in St. Louis.

As it turned out, that was necessary since the Cards' ace closer Jason Isringhausen retired the Astros in order in the bottom of the ninth. Taveras, Vizcaino, and Burke were retired on just nine pitches. That hardly gave equipment manager Dennis Liborio and his staff time to tear down the plastic sheeting and champagne bottles that were all iced down for a clinching celebration from the clubhouse. Both teams would have to go back to St. Louis.

At this point it must be pointed out that professional athletes think differently about action on the field than most fans. Fans live or die with what players do or don't do. They have no control. Players have success or failure in their own hands. When they win, they are happy; but when they lose, they tip their hats to the players that beat them. The agony of defeat exists but doesn't last long. In baseball, there is usually another game to play the next day.

Such was the case with the Astros. Disappointed and taking the loss harder than most in the long 162 game regular season, they still knew they just needed one more win to take the National League pennant. The club was quiet and subdued when they got on the bus to head to the airport for the flight to St. Louis. The mood was too gloomy for a couple veterans. At one point during the team flight, Jeff Bagwell and Brad Ausmus asked team traveling secretary Barry Waters to ask GM Tim Purpura if it was OK to pull a prank on Lidge. They actually wanted the pilot to pull it off. Purpura gave the OK and a few minutes after the chartered plane was in the air, the pilot turned on his microphone and made an announcement that if they looked out of the left side of the plane, they could see the ball Albert Pujols hit flying past them.

At first, many on the plane were not happy. Pitching coach Jim Hickey was reportedly the most upset. However, it didn't take long for laughter to break out once they found that Bagwell and Ausmus were behind the joke. The rest of the flight was NOT the funeral flight it could have been. The Astros were disappointed, of course, but loose and ready to take on the Cards, beat them in their own place, and close down Busch Stadium II for good.

Bagwell contributed to the Astros in the series in a way that could not be measured by statistics or any analytic. He helped keep them loose.

Astros Waste Little Time in St. Louis

There was going to be no stopping the Astros this time. In Game Six played in St. Louis, Roy Oswalt pitched seven innings, allowing only three hits and one run. Rodriguez's sacrifice fly in the fifth would be the only Cardinal run. Meanwhile, the Astros pounded out eleven hits: two more by Craig Biggio who upped his 2005 postseason batting average to .326. Brad

Ausmus had three hits and Willy Taveras, two. Jason Lane hit his second homerun of the series.

Dan Wheeler closed it out on the mound. The last out was a soft fly ball that nestled into Lane's glove in right field two hours and fifty-three minutes after the first pitch. The Astros, for the first time in the franchise's forty-three-year history, were the champions of the National League and heading to the World Series. Busch Stadium II had seen its last game.

The atmosphere in the clubhouse was exciting. Champagne flowed, but was drunk in moderation by most. No time for over indulging. The World Series was starting in Chicago in less than three days.

The club would take a chartered plane from St. Louis to Houston for one day, then to Chicago to check into the Westin Hotel across the street from the Hancock Tower. They had a workout schedule and even media sessions already scheduled by the folks with Major League Baseball. Once the postseason gets past the division series stage, MLB takes full control. They tell the teams where to be, what to do, and even how the stadiums are operated.

While the Astros were taken care of, the local media had a different problem. Most were not pre-booked in Chicago. Sports desks and program directors scrambled to get last minute credentials plus hotel bookings for many who had not covered the team all year, but now, with the World Series looming, were going to jump on the bus.

Lost in all the excitement was that fans might have already seen the last of one of the franchise's great players, Jeff Bagwell. He had only one at-bat in the St. Louis series and only three at-bats in the whole postseason. He was incapable of playing first base due to his shoulder and lack of an ability to throw the ball. Even as a hitter he could no longer swing the bat with as much strength. After all the years with the Astros, would Bagwell be on the World Series roster?

Manager Phil Garner answered that question before the series began. The games in Chicago would feature the use of the designated hitter. Jeff Bagwell would handle that role. Garner assured Bagwell the assignment was not just for sentimental reasons. As Bagwell told the media, "Phil's been nothing but great with me. He's really been straight up with me. He's helped me along at times here, and I appreciate the confidence. That's why I'm in there and get the opportunity to play. He thinks I can do something, and I hope I reward him for it. I was excited. This is what I tried to come back for. The thing in the back of my mind was if I get to the World Series, I could DH and I'm going to get the opportunity."

Astros Had Chances in Four Games, but Were Swept

The World Series in Chicago was played in two nights of horrid weather. Not only was it cold, in the 40s, but also wet. Not wet enough to threaten the games, but wet enough with on and off light drizzle, to be very uncomfortable for fans and players.

If that wasn't enough, Astro pitcher Roger Clemens was still trying to pitch through a hamstring injury that had been hurting for several weeks. The injury was a major factor in Game One and thus perhaps the whole series.

It was Clemens against the White Sox's Jose Contreras making the pitching matchup in Game One. In the first inning, Jermaine Dye hit a solo homer, but the Astros got the run back in the top of the second on Mike Lamb's solo homerun.

In the second inning, former Astro Carl Everett singled and scored on a ground out. With two out, Jose Uribe doubled home a second run and Chicago led 3-1.

The Astros tied things in the third after singles by Ausmus and Biggio when Lance Berkman doubled them both home.

Clemens, bothered by the cold and wet weather, felt his hamstring tighten and had gone as far as he could go. Wandy Rodriguez replaced him on the mound in the fourth. In the fifth inning, however, he surrendered a solo homer to Joe Crede putting the White Sox back on top. Trailing 4-3 in the eighth, the Astros had runner in scoring position with two out after a Berkman lead off single. Then came strike outs of Morgan Ensberg and Mike Lamb by Neal Cotts. Bobby Jenks relieved Cotts. Pinch runner Chris Burke then stole second, but Bagwell struck out to end the inning. Chicago added a fifth run in the last of the eighth on a two out RBI triple by Scott Podsednik off reliever Russ Springer. The Astros were retired in order on only eight pitches by fireballing Jenks in the ninth.

A healthy Clemens could have made the difference in Game One, and eliminating one bad inning in Game Two could have made a different outcome in the Chicago-based games. Andy Pettitte started Game Two, but struggled and had ineffective relief.

Pettitte Gave the Astros a Chance, but Bullpen Crashed

Pettitte started against the White Sox's Mark Buehrle. Andy gave up some hits allowing eight in just six inning of work. But he allowed only two runs. Four relievers were used with three (Wheeler, Qualls, and Lidge) giving up runs. Houston took a 4-2 lead in the fifth that lasted until the bottom of the seventh.

The Astros got their first run on a Morgan Ensberg solo homer. But the White Sox got two in the bottom of that second inning. Three straight singles, and some heads-up base running by Chicago catcher A.J. Pierzynski, gave the Sox the lead.

Berkman's sacrifice fly untied the game in the third and his two-run double in the fifth put the Astros on top 4-2.

Then the wheels fell off Astro pitching in the seventh. With two out and two on, Chad Qualls came in to replace the faltering Dan Wheeler. Then Qualls made his first pitch to Paul Konerko who ripped it for a grand slam homerun. The White Sox now led 6-4.

Leading off the ninth, Bagwell got his only World Series hit with a single to center. It would be the last hit of his career. Lane struck out, but Burke walked. Ausmus grounded out but both runners advanced and Jose Vizcaino came in to pinch hit for Adam Everett. On the first pitch from Bobby Jenks, he lined a single to left field that scored both Bagwell and Burke. The game was tied 6-6.

Alas in the last of the ninth with Brad Lidge on the mound and one out, slap hitting Scott Podsednick ripped a ball to right field that made it over the wall. The game-winning walk-off homerun, the second Lidge had allowed in his last three appearances, ended things with a 7-6 White Sox victory. It was the only the second homerun Podsednik would hit in 141 games in 2005. He had not hit any during the regular season. His only other homerun had been in the American League Division Series earlier in the postseason. Now down two games to none, the series shifted to Houston.

Game Three: Oswalt Had a Meltdown Inning

As in Game Two, the Astros had a good chance to win, but one bad inning and an inability to get key hits later did them in. What was worse was this was a Roy Oswalt start.

Now back in Minute Maid Park, the Astros had their home field, sort of. Major League Baseball had dictated that since the weather in Houston was quite suitable, the roof would be open for the game. If the Astros had their way, it would have been closed. They preferred the lack of wind and the increased noisy atmosphere with the roof closed. Open roof games tended to result in higher scoring games as well. As it turned out, MMP did not become "Homerun Field" in Game Three. Only one homer, a solo shot off White Sox starter Jon Garland by Jason Lane, was hit. But twelve runs would be scored, even if did take extra innings.

The Astros scored in the first after Biggio led off with the double and, one hitter later, Berkman singled him home. The Astros got their second run in the third when Biggio and Ensberg both singled with two outs to drive in two un-earned runs. However, in the top of the fifth, the wheels fell off for Oswalt.

It started when Joe Crede picked on an 0-1 pitch leading off the inning for a homerun. Uribe singled before Garland struck out. Then the Sox strung three singles in a row that drove in two more runs. After a second out off a fly ball hit by Konerko, Pierzynski drove in two more with a double. That was the last of the scoring, but Oswalt struggled to end the inning and when it was over, the White Sox had scored five and Oswalt had thrown 46 pitches in the inning. Chicago now led 5-4.

Oswalt was able throw another 1 ⅓ innings of scoreless ball before relieved by Russ Springer in the seventh. Roy was able to pitch only six innings, but was charged with five earned runs. He was the first of eight Astro pitchers. With Springer and Wheeler keeping the Sox in check, the Astros tied the game in the eighth after two-out walks to both Ensberg and Lamb were followed by an RBI double by Lane.

The Astros might have won the game in the last of the ninth. The White Sox again opened the door thanks to two walks and an error. Burke reached first on a one-out walk. On a pick off attempt at first by Orlando Hernandez, the throw got away. Hernandez was charged with an error as Burke went to second. Then, with Biggio at the plate, he stole third. Winning run now at third with one out. Biggio walked.

Willy Taveras did not make contact. He struck out on a 2-2 pitch. Berkman was walked intentionally, but Ensberg struck out on a 2-2 pitch and the game went to extra innings.

The rest of the Astro offense would consist of five walks and a hit batter. The White Sox would win the game in the 14th when rookie pitcher Ezequiel Astacio threw a ball in former Astro Geoff Blum's sweet spot, down and in, and Blum hit a high fly just inside the right field foul pole to give the White Sox a one-run lead. The homerun would be immortalized as part of the statuary art work outside the White Sox home ballpark. Chicago added one more run with a bases loaded walk to Chris Widger by the shaken-up Astacio.

While the Astros got two runners on base thanks to a walk and error by their shortstop in the last of the 14th, they could not score and Chicago had a three game lead.

In Game Four, Brandon Backe gave the Astros a chance to win. He allowed five hits and no runs in seven innings. Brad Lidge, unfortunately, was not as effective. He gave up one run in two innings and took his third loss in the Series. Jermaine Dye had three hits, including a two-out single off Lidge in the eighth that drove in the game's only run.

The Astros were held to five hits by starting pitcher Freddy Garcia and four relievers. In somewhat of an irony, Garcia was one of the Astro farmhands traded for Randy Johnson in 1998, when most thought the Astros had their best team ever and the best chance to win a World Series. Then, seven years later against an Astro team few thought would be in this position, Garcia, now with the White Sox, was the winning pitcher in a Series game that sealed Houston's fate.

Mike Lamb's double was the only hit for extra bases. Biggio had one of the singles. He finished the four game series hitting .295. Willy Taveras also had a single and the best Astro average in the series at .349. Lance Berkman was 0-1, but walked three times and hit .333. The rest of the club was not effective and the team average for the four games was just .172. The White Sox hit just .235.

Jeff Bagwell had the last official at-bat in his career in the seventh inning against Garcia. He grounded out to second base pinch-hitting for Backe.

Being Swept Was Not Fun, but It Was a Close Sweep!

Losing a World Series in four straight is embarrassing, but the 106 game winning Cardinals had lost in four straight to Boston the year before. This four game sweep at least was close, much closer than most. Chicago outscored the Astros by just six runs. The Astros had leads at some point in three of the four games and one game went 14 innings. Roger Clemens's ailing hamstring and two big innings were the difference. The White Sox, for this series, played better baseball and rightfully won the World Championship, but the Astros went much further than anyone would have expected before the season.

Craig Biggio, at thirty-nine, had learned to adjust to advancing age and had a good season. Craig actually led all MLB players in postseason hitting in 2005 with a .295 average while also scoring the most runs: eleven. The story for Jeff Bagwell was not as good. Still under contract for one more year, there was great doubt he could actually play again. As it turned out, the numbers he had at the end of the World Series were the statistics that would go on his permanent record. No one knew for sure quite yet, though.

12 Baggie and Bidge Reach Big Numbers as the End Nears

"I just hope this all gets worked out some way.
That's my boy [Jeff Bagwell]. I hope he's given an opportunity
to go to spring training. I love this guy, and he's made
a lot of sacrifices for this city and organization."

– Craig Biggio on Jeff Bagwell's desire to try to play in 2006

As the excitement from the Astros finally winning a National League championship and going to the World Series ended in the disappointment of being swept, it wasn't long before fans and Astros management had to start thinking about 2006. And what the management determined was that not many changes were needed. Clemens, Pettitte, and Oswalt would again lead the starting rotation. Although none of them had been impressive in the four game sweep at the hands of the White Sox, Brandon Backe, who had been the fourth starter, had been and he was also back. Younger pitchers like Wandy Rodriguez, Taylor Buchholz, and Matt Albers offered some promise for rotation depth. An outfield of Willy Taveras, Jason Lane, and Luke Scott would not be ranked as one of the best in the game, so the club added veteran Preston Wilson and, during the season, Aubrey Huff.

On the infield, Lance Berkman would move to first base permanently with Biggio, hoping to pile up more hits in his quest for 3,000, at second. Everett and Ensberg still manned the other spots. Brad Ausmus would catch. A notable absence was Jeff Bagwell. His career officially ended during spring training.

Since Bagwell had only been involved in 39 games in 2005, this team was not much different. The problem was that the 2005 team was quite weak offensively. The pitching, while it may have failed the Astros in the World Series, had won the postseason bid for the team in the first place. Now both Pettitte and Clemens were a year older. And so were Biggio and Ausmus. Was there really much hope for 2006?

In spring training the usual optimism existed, of course. After all, the Astros were the National League champions. Never mind that in the regular season they had finished well behind the Cardinals. Furthermore, behind the scenes there was activity that made some fans wonder if the team would do what was needed to get to the next level.

Farewell to Jeff Bagwell

Jeff Bagwell wanted to come to training came just to see if he could play. The Astros wanted him to retire due to his chronically damaged shoulder. That would have allowed the club to collect on the insurance policy, which would have reimbursed the team for the most of the nearly $17-million he was owed. Astros owner Drayton McLane wanted Jeff to stay home. In that case, a declaration that he was physically incapable of playing would have been an easy call for insurance adjusters. However, if Bagwell came to camp and performed well enough to be considered a possible player, but was cut by the team as a matter of opinion that he was not capable of making the team, the Astros might have a battle with the insurance company. Bagwell would have gotten his full money in either event, but the Astros might have been responsible to paying all of it without insurance help. This matter was not a minor one.

As agent Barry Axelrod remembered, "Our negotiations with the Astros were never difficult up to then. During his career, we never got to free agency with Jeff. The Astros were always interested in extending his contract and he was always interested in talking with them. The most significant time was during the strike of 1994-95 when we tried to get a multi-year deal in spring training and they decided they wanted to go one year at a time. Then Drayton called and asked if we still wanted to talk about a multi-year thing. I said sure and we went back there and got a multi-year deal done in about ten minutes."

A significant problem in 2006 was that the insurance policy expired on January 31, nearly a month before camp was to open. The Astros filed a claim prior to that date, but Bagwell still planned on showing up to training camp on February 23.

As Barry Axelrod, Bagwell's agent, told the *New York Times*'s Murray Chass on February 2, 2006, "Dr. Andrews saw him last month [January 2006]. He said Jeff has a bad shoulder with degenerative arthritis and bone spurs and has limited mobility. But he's had that for several years, and he's averaged 160 games, 600 at-bats, 100 runs batted in, and 30 homers a year, so he has shown he's capable of playing through the thing."

"I don't blame someone for wanting to save $15.6 million," Axelrod said, "But it's the cost of doing business. I haven't seen any team take such drastic steps to be out from under a deal as we've seen here."

Continuing the Chass article was a comment from Axelrod that the Astros would have a public relations nightmare if Bagwell, "shows up and says, 'Here I am.' And they say, 'You're not welcome here.'"

Bagwell himself was quoted by Axelrod through Chass as saying, "It's amazing how badly they don't want me to play."

"That was probably the most difficult thing I ever encountered with Jeff and maybe with anyone," said Axelrod years later. "They (Astros) really didn't want him to come to spring training in 2006 because they felt if he got out on the field, got in uniform, tried to play, and failed then the fact that he had got out there would delay the finding that he was totally disabled.

"I actually went down to spring training and went in with Jeff the first day. It got pretty contentious. I consider Drayton McLane a friend, a good friend, and we talk about that day once in a while. I didn't know whether they were going to have a security guard there and not let Jeff in the gate or what was going to happen," recalled Axelrod.

Barry used the story of one of his other noted clients, Olympic champion figure skater Michelle Kwan, to explain how Jeff would decide whether he could play or not. "I told Drayton that Michelle Kwan was a good person and Jeff is a good person. Michelle Kwan, when she realized she was injured and couldn't go, was the first one to say it. She wasn't going to take up a space on the Olympic team and take it away from someone else when she knew she couldn't perform up to her personal standards. I said that Jeff was exactly the same. He'll be the first one to let you know. And that's exactly what happened."

As Jeff said at the time, he was taken off the active roster, "I came down to spring training to see if I could still make it as a first baseman with the Astros. There were times in the offseason where I felt like I could do this. But with the condition of my shoulder, I'm not going to be able to start the season with the Astros."

During the early spring, his teammates protected him. They made it so he would not have to make any throws at first base. He could not toss the ball overhand at all. Biggio would race over near first base after any out recorded at first so Jeff could underhand him the ball to start the standard around the horn throws. Jeff would not be used as the cut-off man on throws from the outfield. The third baseman Morgan Ensberg, or even Biggio in some circumstances, would take over the role.

The author witnessed the last game with Bagwell in a uniform as a player that spring. He could not make the most basic and simple throw after fielding a bunt. Every throw had to be underhand. At the plate, his bat was slow, but defensively it was almost sad. He left the game well before the point when most starters are pulled in the spring. He never played again. For the spring, he hit only .219 with two runs batted in. He never had to make a tough throw. The decision was made for Bagwell to start the season on the disabled list.

In a news article published by the *Florida Times Union* on March 26, 2006, he said, "I may never play again. It's been fifteen years with the Astros. I came down to spring training to see if I could still make it as a first baseman with the Astros, but with the condition of my shoulder, I'm not going to be able to start the season with the Astros."

The insurance question would be solved in the team's favor if Bagwell stayed on the DL all season. Then it would be admitted his career was cut short by the shoulder and $15.6 million of the $17 million contract would be reimbursed to the Astros. That is exactly what happened and after the season Bagwell retired.

For his career, Jeff had played fifteen seasons with the Houston Astros. He had a career .297 batting average with 449 homeruns, 1529 runs batted in, 202 stolen bases, and a career .408 on base percentage. He won an NL Gold Glove Award for defensive excellence at first base. He was NL Rookie of the year in 1991, NL MVP in 1994, and finished in the top five in MVP voting two more times. He remains the only first baseman in baseball history with more than 400 homeruns and 200 stolen bases.

As his last manager, Phil Garner told ESPN.com in 2006, "I can't imagine what the Houston Astros would have been the past fifteen years without Jeff Bagwell on this ball club. He made the Houston Astros what they are today."

2006 Astros Were'nt Really Good, but They Competed

The Astros in 2006 were able to adjust without Bagwell. They had Lance Berkman now operating at first base full time. The thirty-year-old self-dubbed "Big Puma" had a Bagwell-in-his-prime type season. Lance hit .315 with 45 homeruns, 136 RBIs, and a .420 on base percentage. The problem was that the holes were elsewhere. At forty, Craig Biggio dropped to a career low .246 batting average although he did hit 21 homers and drive in 62. He only attempted five stolen bases in 145 games and swiped three. Brad Ausmus, now thirty-seven years old, hit only .230 and eighth place hitter, shortstop Adam Everett, hit only .239. The bottom three in the Houston batting order, Everett, Ausmus, and the pitcher, did not threaten many opposing pitchers.

Third baseman Morgan Ensberg dropped down to .235 with 23 homeruns. Jason Lane in left field hit only .201 with 15 homeruns. Newly acquired Preston Wilson hit .269 with only nine homeruns. Mike Lamb and Chris Burke added solid offense off the bench, but too many regulars came up short. A bright spot was Luke Scott who hit .336 with ten homeruns in 65 games. But it was not an offense that many feared.

As for the pitching, the team ERA was 4.08. Not good for most seasons, but good enough for second best in the NL in 2006. Oswalt was the best of the starters, winning 15, losing eight, and registering a 2.98 ERA. Andy Pettitte was very hittable, giving up 238 hits in just over 214 innings pitched. He was 14-13 with a 4.20 ERA. Roger Clemens had a good 2.30 ERA, but at forty-three-years-old, he was frequently not healthy and limited to just 19 starts while going 7-6.

After his failures in the 2005 postseason, many considered Brad Lidge shell-shocked. He saved 32 games but had a whopping 5.29 earned run average. His record was 1-5. Most observers felt Lidge's problems were with location and predictability. He had games in which he had command of only one of his two pitches: either the fastball or slider, but rarely both. Hitters recognized that and looked for the other. He was also often pitching behind in the count too much.

Even with the mediocre record, the Astros could have won the National League Central. At 82-80, they were beaten out by the Cardinals, who came back down to earth from 2005 by only one and half games. And it would be the 83-78 Cardinals that would ultimately win the World Series.

The Astros were never in first place during the season, but put on a rush down the stretch—a Phil Garner Astros trademark. The club had not been over .500 since June 22 and were under .500 from July 4 until September 25. They won nine straight games from Sept 20 through Sept 28. That moved them from 7 ½ games behind to just one-half game off the lead with three games to play. The Astros were 81-78 with three games left—all in Atlanta.

The way things turned out, an Astros sweep could have put the Astros into the postseason. They won only one of three while the Cardinals swept the Brewers in St. Louis.

The Astros got back in the race when they swept the Cardinals in a four game series in Houston. When the Cards left town, their 7 ½ game lead was down to 3 ½.

That series was keyed by Lance Berkman. He homered twice and drove in four runs. His second homer—a two-run shot in the bottom of the eighth—won the game 6-5.

In the second game, the Astros won by the same score when Craig Biggio singled home Orlando Palmiero in the last of the ninth for a walk off victory. Biggio had three hits and three RBIs in the game.

Late heroics were evident again in game three. Luke Scott sent Astro fans home happy with a three run homer in the last of the ninth to break a 4-4 tie and give the Astros a 7-4 walk off win.

In the final that secured the four game sweep, Roger Clemens went five innings and allowed only one run, but Chad Qualls got the win in relief as Houston exploded for a four-run seventh, breaking a 3-3 tie. Berkman drove in the first run with a ground out and Aubrey Huff, whom the Astros had obtained from Tampa Bay mid-season, smacked a three-run homer.

The sweep got the Astros back in the hunt. They just weren't able to make it over the top.

On the excitement of the Astros having made the World Series in 2005 and the fact that the club was continuing the best period in Houston baseball history, the Astros played before more than 3-million fans for the third time in franchise history. That was great, but as is always the case with fans: "That was last year. What are you going to do for me next year?"

Biggio Ended His Career with Passing 3,000 Hits

Manager Phil Garner was in a bit of a quandary. His team had rallied in each of this three years as manager to either make the postseason or come very close. But none of Astros teams had been really good. One of the biggest weaknesses was the lack of a clutch offense. Lance Berkman was the only solid hitter who was still in his prime. Morgan Ensberg had been on a decline. Jason Lane had fallen further than that. One-time prospects like Chris Burke and Eric Bruntlett had shown to be utility-role players and not future stars. And now on the pitching staff, both Andy Pettitte and Roger Clemens were gone. What ultimately happened with the club could easily have been expected. But that was somewhat in the background; 2007 was the season in which Craig Biggio would reach 3,000 hits and then was expected to retire.

This would be the season of Biggio.

Astros Brought in a Big Hitter but He Wasn't Enough for 2007

The Astros ownership did get involved in off-season bidding for a big hitter for the outfield. Alfonso Soriano and Carlos Lee were the top sluggers on the market. The Cubs would sign Soriano for $136-million for eight years. Soriano had more skills. He could steal bases as well as hit for power and average. He could play infield or outfield, but not particularly well in either. Lee was an outstanding hitter, but was not in Soriano's class, at the time, as an overall player. The Astros signed Lee to a six-year, $100 million contract. The average salary per season was virtually identical. Both players were thirty years old. Lee had driven in 100 or more and hit more than 30 homeruns four times during eight previous seasons, most with the White Sox. He was not a fast runner, nor did he have any range in the outfield. The latter would be of little negative effect at Minute Maid Park. Playing left field, Lee would have less ground to cover.

Lee Had a Great Offensive Season in 2007

Lee did his job in 2007 for Houston. It may have been his best year in the majors. He hit .303 to go with 32 homeruns and a personal career high of 119 runs batted in while playing in all 162 games. Rookie Hunter Pence was called up after the season had begun and made an impression. He had been outstanding in spring training, but the Astros decided to save some free agent eligibility time by having him wait about a month before being put on the major league roster. That is a ploy used by many teams, but for Astro fans it was a sign of not wanting to do the utmost to win.

The Astros largesse with Lee's contract was made possible by Bagwell being off the books and both Clemens and Pettitte gone. Plus, Biggio was signed to another one year contract for $5.2 million. They had money to spend.

Pitching Was Abysmal

Making the team good enough was another thing. The 2007 Astros weren't very good. Roy Oswalt was the only starting pitcher with an earned run average under 4.58. He was also the only starting pitcher to win more than he lost. Oswalt was 14-7, 3.18. The rest of the regular starters didn't compare: Woody Williams (8-15, 5.27); Wandy Rodriguez (9-13, 4.58); Chris Sampson (7-8, 4.59); Matt Albers (4-11, 5.86); Jason Jennings (2-9, 6.45.)

Williams and Jennings were acquired in the offseason. Both had local or regional connections through their birthplace, high school, or college.

The Astros team ERA was 12th in the National League at 4.68 and were last in homeruns by giving up 206.

The Astros wound up well out of the pennant race with a 73-89 record. Yet the team drew more than 3-million fans for the fourth time. Strangely, of the four times the club had drawn over 3 million in a season, two of the clubs were sub .500 and not in pennant races.

Biggio Became Baseball's 27th 3,000-Hit Man

There were 42,537 fans in the stands on June 28 when the Astros hosted the Colorado Rockies. The club had just come off a poor road trip in which Houston had lost six of nine, but during the trip, Craig Biggio closed in on 3,000 hits for his career. He needed three hits, but whether he could get it done in this game was in question. Before the game, long time teammate Jeff Bagwell, who had flown in from out of town to see the series, told Craig, "Kid, I'm here for only three days. Dude, you got to get that hit by then otherwise I'm leaving." Biggio reportedly replied, "You can't tell me that. Seriously, it's not easy."

No problem. Not only did Biggio make it that night, but he accumulated five hits in one game for only second time in his career.

With the fans cheering his name with the famed "BEE-GEE-OH… BEE-GEE-OH" and with signs all over the jammed ballpark offering praise and encouragement, Craig went to work. In the first inning, he grounded out. However, in the third he singled off Rockie starter Aaron Cook. In the fifth inning, he singled into left field. Now at 2999 hits and at least four innings to play, the fans knew Craig would have at least two more at-bats. The atmosphere in the park with thick with anticipation.

In the last of the seventh, Biggio came to the plate with the tying run at second base. On a 2-0 pitch from Cook, he looped a liner to center field. The hit drove in the tying run and the crowd was wildly excited. So was Biggio, who thought it might be possible to stretch the hit into one of his almost patented doubles. He didn't make it. Out at second, but with a run scoring, the game was tied and there was time for celebration.

Jeff Bagwell, in civilian clothes and standing in the runway just behind the dugout, wiped a tear after seeing what his long time teammate had accomplished. He had run down from the suite area to see if he could congratulate Craig when he came in to the dugout before the game continued. Bagwell admitted to Jesus Ortiz of the *Houston Chronicle* that emotion had taken over. "I'm sitting up there and he got the 3,000th hit, and I was like, 'Oh my God.' I sat there and I sat there, and then I said I had to go see him. I just wanted to see the man and give him a hug. I cried when I sent down from the box because I was so freaking happy for him. That's a big deal."

The game had been stopped to allow the fans to honor their hero—Mr. Astro. Wife Patty and the children, Conor, Cavan, and Quinn, all made their way to the field.

Whether one of his teammates pointed out to Biggio that Bagwell was in the far corner of the dugout or Craig surveyed the scene himself and saw Baggie may be in question, but what happened next was a great moment in Astro history.

Biggio moved toward the bench and motioned. He wanted Bagwell on the field with him. According to the Ortiz article, Bagwell tried to rebuff Biggio, "Dude, stop it. Stop it." It was Biggio's moment, but he wanted to share.

"No, you're coming out here one last time." Bagwell relented, and the full house roared with approval. The two greatest Houston players of all time were on the field together for one of the greatest baseball moments in Houston history.

The original "Killer Bs" The first two Hall of Fame bound Houston Astros.

The Game-Winning Grand Slam that No One Remebered

When the game resumed, now tied at 1-1, the focus was still on Biggio. He had two more at-bats and added two more hits, but the Rockies led 4-1 to the Astros eighth. Then Berkman and Mike Lamb both homered off LaTroy Hawkins to tie the game again. A Troy Tulowitzki solo homer off Brian Moehler in the top of the 11th gave the Rockies a 5-4 lead.

This was Craig Biggio's night. He wasn't done being a star. With two out in the last of the 11th he singled for his fifth hit of the night. Rookie Hunter Pence doubled and Lance Berkman was hit by a pitch to load the bases for Carlos Lee.

Carlos unloaded them with a long and high fly ball homerun down the left field line for a grand slam game-winning walk-off homer. The Astros won a thriller 8-5. It was the most ignored game-winning grand slam in history.

Everyone wanted to talk to Biggio. That included me as I handled postgame hero interviews for Fox Sports. Lee may have been the man who won the game, but he won Craig Biggio's game.

The Astros won the next night on a two-run walk-off homer by Mark Loretta that both erased a Colorado lead and gave the Astros the win. Biggio was 0-3 and saw his overall average drop to .247.

Garner Run Ended

In 2007 there were not enough games like those two. After 131 games, the Astros were 58-73 in fifth place and nine games off the lead. Phil Garner was replaced as manager by his bench coach Cecil Cooper. Cooper would bring the team home at 15-16 for an overall disappointing 73-89 record.

In Craig Biggio's final game on September 30, Minute Maid Park was jammed with 43,828 fans. The Astros scored three in the bottom of the first inning off Braves starter Buddy Carlyle. Biggio hit the last of his 668 career doubles—the most ever by a right-handed hitter and fifth most all-time—his 3060th hit, and later scored his 1844th run in the inning. That would be Craig's last hit and run scored.

In a twenty-year major league career, Biggio had hit .281 with 3060 hits, 668 doubles, 291 homeruns, 1844 runs scored, 1175 runs driven in, 414 stolen bases, a career .363 on base percentage, and a modern major league record of 285 times being hit by a pitch.

Biggio had been an all-star at two positions and a four-time Gold Glove winner at second base. He also played all three outfield spots. He won five Silver Slugger awards. He was on the All-Star Team seven times and finished in the top ten in MVP voting three times. In his final game, he even donned his catcher's gear for an inning recalling how it all started.

Craig was ready to move on with his life. When he was offered the job as head coach at private St. Thomas High School in Houston, he grabbed it. Both his sons, Conor and Cavan, would be playing there, and it was a great way to give back some of the time lost while Biggio was in the major leagues. It would also be a great way to teach the game he loved. As it turned out, it was memorable for everyone involved. In both the 2010 and 2011 seasons, Craig, with Conor and Cavan contributing, led St. Thomas to back-to-back state championships in the private school category. After both sons had graduated and moved on to college at Notre Dame, Craig retired and re-joined the Astros in a support capacity. Meanwhile, daughter Quinn was showing great skills in both volleyball and softball, keeping up with the guys. She, too, would be Notre Dame bound.

With Bagwell and Biggio now both gone after the 2007 season, the Astros would have to almost start over. Part of that was because the team was now for sale.

13 The Golden Era Ended as McLane Sold the Astros

Courtesy of Linda Presson

"We had a tentative deal"

– Drayton McLane admitting in late 2009 that he
and Jim Crane were close in 2008

End of an Era Concludes as McLane Sells Astros

Much like the line in singer Kenny Rogers's song, "You've got to know when to hold 'em know when to fold 'em," applies to gamblers, it applies to many businessmen as well. Drayton McLane Jr., the owner of the Astros from 1993 to 2012, is certainly a businessman. He knew very little about either the sport or the business that runs it when he bought the team and the Astrodome lease from John McMullen in November 1992 for a reported $117 million. At the end of the Astros most successful run in franchise history, McLane was ready to move on by the end of 2007.

Perhaps disillusioned by the performance of the team after he had opened the checkbook to sign slugger Carlos Lee and by the rising costs for top-level players, McLane figured the time was right. Neither of his two sons were interested in taking over, and if Drayton died while still owning the club, the inheritance tax bite would have been hard to manage. The problem was finding a buyer. He wasn't going to advertise his desire to sell. If the right deal was presented, he would consider it. He wasn't going to give the team away. If he was going to come out ahead on the deal and money invested in the club over the years, McLane needed to sell the team for no less than double what he paid and preferably for considerably more. Major League Baseball preferred local, or at least regional, buyers. Unless playing facilities were below par in the city where the team was located, they didn't want to see teams jumping around as much as the NFL had dealt with in the recent past. Baseball had had some jumping in its history, but preferred stability. In Houston's case, the Major Leagues losing a top ten television market and the country's fourth largest city would be a major blow. McLane would just have to take his time to find a buyer.

That meant McLane's biggest job was finding folks from Houston, or at least Texas, that would not be buying the club just to move it to their favorite locale. When McLane bought the club, there were few in Houston interested. Prices for professional sports franchises were rising faster than the water in some of Houston's downtown streets during a tropical storm. Most teams now were so expensive that a single buyer was very scarce. That applied to Houston; the nation's fourth largest city was loaded with Fortune 500 businesses. Some potential owners were not comfortable with the power the player's association had over running the business. Then there was the continued rising costs for players.

Although McLane never admitted the team might be for sale, he almost had a deal in place during 2008, but the potential buyer backed out. The potential buyer was named Jim Crane.

The financial crash the country experienced in 2008 made Crane unsure whether the time was right even after a tentative deal had been worked out. Regardless of the reason McLane was not happy with Mr. Crane.

Crane had pitched in his younger days and was pretty good. He once struck out 18 in a college game for Central Missouri. He was also a long-time fan of the St. Louis Cardinals and dreamed of owning a Major League Baseball team. His negotiations with Drayton McLane marked his first effort to get into the owner's club, but in later years he would make bids for both the Chicago Cubs and Texas Rangers. He was a self-made multi-millionaire through an energy services company and a world-wide freight shipping company. He lived in Houston and all his businesses were located in the city. His biggest weakness was the amount of cash he could put up and how much of his purchase would be from loans. Major League Baseball had some rules on that. Consequently, there were some who wondered if a Crane offer would be approved at that time.

McLane may have been angry in 2008, but he and Crane would be doing business again in a few years.

Limbo: Not a Good Place for a Sports Franchise

No one who worked in the Astros' front office at the time remembers when Drayton McLane may have told them the club was for sale. Sometime before it happened, however, he had started investigating a way to make the club more money and increase the club's worth. At this time, both the Houston Astros and the NBA Houston Rockets had separate contracts with Fox Sports to telecast their games on Fox Sports Southwest. Negotiations when contracts came due involved few people from Fox actually in Houston. The regional network had moved its headquarters from Houston to Irving, Texas, near Dallas, in the early 2000's. And large decisions such as rights fees were negotiated with higher management from Los Angeles. Neither Houston team was comfortable with that. So, at some point, a meeting was held in 1999 between the higher management and/or ownership groups of the two teams to consider breaking free from Fox and forming their own network. At that point, the Astros passed on the offer. However, four years later, the Astros were ready to listen.

It was decided that when contracts expired with Fox, the two teams would put their games on a new network that both teams would own and run. George Postolos was the chief executive officer with the Rockets who first tried to sell the Astros on the idea. He had seen how lucrative the networks owned and run by the Boston Red Sox and New York Yankees had been. He wanted the same thing in Houston, but for it to work both teams had to work together. He had an idea how to increase revenues by both teams.

With a contract renewal date looming, the new partnership starting making plans. At the time, Postolos was gone, but the same team ownerships were in place from when the idea was first proposed. A few hires were made, and Fox was notified of the plan. Then Fox took them to court, claiming their contract had a right of refusal match clause. Further, they could not terminate the deal in place prematurely. Fox and the teams opened re-negotiations and signed a deal for a reported $600-million over more than ten years. There was little chance that the contract would run out, though, since the two teams were given an option to terminate the deal and negotiate with other networks starting in 2009.

One of the complaints of the Houston teams was that Fox Sports Southwest had studios in Irving, Texas, near Dallas. All pre-game, post-game, and other programming was produced and aired from Irving and not Houston. Furthermore, as part of the Fox Sports family, major negotiations had to go through Los Angeles headquarters. The Astros and Rockets wanted a Houston base. Fox agreed and created Fox Sports Houston with an office and small studio presence in downtown Houston.

At this point, it looked as though the status quo was to continue. It is also possible that the actual cost of starting a new network and having to sign up affiliates and negotiate rates might have been more than both teams wished to spend. As part of Fox's concession, all pre-game, post-game, and special team shows would be produced in Houston. A fully-ranked General Manager would be put in charge of the Houston operation. Both teams agreed to continuing working under the Fox banner and negotiate a new deal. However, when Fox submitted bids for a new deal with the Astros that would have tripled their current rates, the Astros/Rockets were not interested.

Cable company Comcast had moved to Houston in a swap with Time-Warner cable and was already running regional sports networks in other cities. At that time, Fox would not partner with teams. That may have been the last ditch deal-killer for the Astros and Rockets. Fox would pay rights fees, but keep control of the telecasts. Comcast had no such restriction. While Fox Sports's DFW and Houston operations covered a five state area and more than 3-million homes, Comcast would be starting from scratch except for those who were on Comcast's Infinity Cable. That meant only about 40% of Houston, and virtually nowhere else in Texas, could see Astros baseball. The 40% also applied to the Rockets, but their out-of-region coverage was already limited by NBA territorial restrictions. Even so, Comcast reportedly sold the teams on the idea that they would make the network Houston specific with more local programming and a larger staff to provide a first class Houston operation. They gave the impression they would be able get better coverage eventually, and the teams would be able to make up to $100-million a year.

However, in other Comcast markets, they had considered their rights "exclusive" and did not even try to sell games to satellite or other carriers that would be competing in the same market. Under those terms, there was no chance the Astros primarily, but also the Rockets to a lesser degree, would ever reach as many homes as they did while they were affiliated with Fox. The teams would have two wishes fulfilled. They would be running the show from Houston and not the Dallas area or Los Angeles. They would have an ownership stake, too.

It sounded really good to the Rockets and Astros. And, as far as McLane was concerned, owning a percentage of this new network would increase the value of the Astros when he finally did sell them. The value was only on paper, though, and never reached fruition. Well, it never reached fruition to anyone but McLane. This story will continue later.

The bottom line was that the new television network was being planned, as was the eventual Comcast hook-up, while McLane still owned the team but was hoping to soon find a buyer.

Meanwhile, his team was mediocre, but again a contender in 2008.

Cecil Cooper's First Team Hung in There

During the off-season of the first year, there would be no Jeff Bagwell or Craig Biggio on the team, and for the first time since 1989, the Astros made some moves to rebuild the team. The starting lineup included new faces at second base, shortstop, third base, and center field. The pitching had a new closer and two new starters. One of them was Shawn Chacon for a while. After 15 starts, his record was only 2-3, and his earned run average was 5.04. He had been signed as a free agent in the offseason to join the starting rotation, but was re-assigned to the bullpen in late June. Feeling he had been promised to be a starter when he signed with the Astros, a confrontation with General Manager Ed Wade resulted in Chacon body-slamming his much smaller boss. That resulted in Chacon being granted his release on June 26.

This would also be the first full season with Cecil Cooper managing with Wade as general manager. Cooper had finished 2007 as interim manager after Phil Garner was fired. He had compiled an outstanding playing career with the Boston Red Sox and Milwaukee Brewers. In eleven years, he hit .298, averaging 21 homers and 98 RBIs per season. He had seasons in which he hit as high as .352, and hit as many as 32 homeruns and 126 RBIs. He had managed in the minor leagues. Ed Wade, former GM of the Philadelphia Phillies, was hired on September 20, 2007 after Tim Purpura was let go about a month before. Under Purpura, the team had not put much money in the farm system, so there were few real prospects waiting in the wings. Hunter Pence had broken in during the 2007 season from the farm and looked solid, but after him not much was there. Pence, however, was very impressive. In fact, during the waning days of 2007 when asked who would be the next Astro leader, Craig Biggio bypassed Lance Berkman and pointed at the rookie seated a few seats away. He was pointing at Hunter Pence. Pence played the game, even then, as though his hair was on fire and he was looking for a wall to run through to put it out!

Watching Pence play for the first time, the impression was that he didn't know how to throw, didn't know how to wear his uniform, had a funny stance at the plate, and should be playing in a park recreational baseball league.

Then when one followed him longer, they found that despite a throwing motion that brought pain into the elbows of those watching it, he had a very strong arm. Despite wearing his baseball socks sometimes over the top of his knees, he could really run. And despite a slash and run style at the plate, he hit a lot of balls very hard. And he never let up. Hunter Pence was a player!

There is no surprise why Biggio named Pence. Like Craig, he took the game very seriously. Lance was a superb talent and the best player on the team, but also a jokester and not one of those players who would spend more time in the clubhouse or weight room than necessary.

Oh, but Lance could hit. In 2008 he would register a .312 batting average and a .420 on base percentage while hitting 46 doubles, 29 homeruns, and driving in 106 runs. Lance was the best, but far from the only offensive hero. The team was old, with only two regulars, Pence and newly acquired center fielder Michael Bourn, as young as twenty-five, but it had some hitters.

Kazuo Matsui, a long time Japanese star who had been with the Colorado Rockies, came in to play second base. He put up good numbers with a .293 batting average and 20 stolen bases. Unfortunately, his season was limited to only 96 games. He had opened the season late after undergoing surgery to repair an anal fissure then, later in the season, missed more time with an irritated disk in his back and was also out with a strained hamstring.

Matsui's injury plagued season was the rule rather than the exception. Other players who put up good numbers missed a good deal of time. Matsui's new double play partner, Miguel Tejada, was not one of them. Signed as a free agent, Tejada's name came up as a possible steroid user at about the same time. The publicity was not good, but the Astros had acquired Tejada to put more punch in the lineup. Fans in Houston had seen Miguel beat Lance Berkman in the Homerun Derby at the All-Star Game in Houston in 2004. He was now thirty-four years old and on the down side of his career, but still hit 13 homeruns with a .283 batting average for the Astros in 2008. Tejada had hit as high as .330 in his career and hit 34 homeruns while driving in 150 runs to lead the league in 2004 in his first year with Baltimore. He had had some big years, but they were in the past.

Behind the plate, Brad Ausmus had come back to help tutor the future. The future included catchers J.R. Towles and Humberto Quintero. Neither could claim the job, and Brad wound up behind the plate for more games than either of them. Now thirty-nine, he hit just .218.

Ty Wigginton played third base and hit 23 homeruns, drove in 58, and batted .285. Pence hit .269 with 25 homers and 83 RBIs. Michael Bourn came home to the city where he grew up, stole 41 bases, and covered the large acreage in Minute Maid Park better than anyone ever had.

The bench was solid with Geoff Blum, at thirty-five, back in a Houston uniform. He provided some power with 14 homeruns, while veterans

Mark Loretta and Darin Erstad brought solid bats and great veteran leadership. Pence soaked up as much as he could from Erstad, who has once led the American League with 240 hits while hitting .355 for the Angels in 2000. Now he was primarily a pinch hitter.

Erstad got a bit more playing time for a while as starting left fielder Carlos Lee was put on the disabled list and never played again after being hit by a pitch that broke his left little finger on August 9 at Cincinnati. Lee's loss was huge, although few thought so at the time. His season would show a .314 batting average, 28 homeruns, and 100 RBIs in just 115 games. He was projecting to have an even better season than in 2007. Had he not been hurt, the Astros could have won the division.

The reason his injury was a small footnote was that when it happened no one was thinking of the Astros being in contention, let alone winning. Their pitching had been below par and they were in fourth place, 12 ½ games off the lead. The author remembers Lee commenting at his locker after the game of August 10 that he hoped he'd be able to play again in the playoffs. The media scoffed. The Astros won their fourth straight victory that night , but were still one game under .500 and all those games off the lead.

But like so many Astro teams of the last decade, they saved their best for last. From the Lee injury, the Astros went 28-16 to finish the season. From being as many as 16 games back on August 29, they got to within 8 ½ games, and thirteen games over .500. Whether they could catch the leading Cubs or not may not have been possible, but a wild card spot was still a solid possibility.

During their hot streak, Mark Saccomanno was called up to fill the void caused by an injury to Ty Wigginton and hit a homerun. It was not just any homerun. He hit it on the first pitch he had ever seen in the major leagues. The Astros beat the Pirates September 8, 2008, 3-2. After the game Saccomanno told reporters, "I went up there very nervous. I don't even remember it, my legs were so weak. It was a great feeling to hit it out. It was like a dream."

The former Baylor star will never forget that dream. It would turn out to be the only homerun he would ever hit in the majors, and one of only two hits in ten at-bats. The homer came off Ian Snell in the fifth inning. Mark was hitting for Astro starting pitcher Alberto Arias, who sustained an arm injury. The number of players to hit a homerun on the first pitch seen in the major leagues was only 24 after Saccomanno joined the club. Teammate on the Astros, Kaz Matsui, had done it in the MLB debut with the Mets in 2004.

Few remembered what Saccamanno had done for long for a good reason. There was a big storm in the Gulf of Mexico headed toward Houston.

The Astros had a three game series set with the Cubs for Minute Maid Park starting Friday, September 12. And the Astros were hot. They had won 14 of their last 15 games including a sweep of the Cubs in Chicago two weeks earlier.

Then Hurricane Ike hit the Gulf Coast.

Hurricane Ike Landed on September 13

Because of the imminent arrival of Hurricane Ike, which was scheduled to come aground in the United States on Galveston Island less than 40 miles from downtown Houston, the Astros' upcoming series with the Cubs was cancelled at Minute Maid Park and Major League Baseball tried to make arrangements for the games to be moved. Several possible locations were discussed, but finally Miller Park, with its retractable roof, in Milwaukee was selected. While it was a park both the Astros and Cubs were used to playing in when they faced the Brewers in the National League Central Division, the Astros were not pleased to be going there. Milwaukee is only 90 miles from Chicago, and the series would almost result in extra home games for the team the Astros were trying to run down.

The storm came aground on Friday night. Those who were located far enough north in the Houston area and had power were able to follow the storm on television. The rest had to batten down the hatches and keep their fingers crossed.

No members of the Astros or their travelling party knew what was next. But in baseball, like show business, the show must go on. Early Saturday morning, phone calls were sent out to players, broadcasters, media relations staffers, and anyone else who normally travelled with the team. The Astro busses would be leaving from Minute Maid Park for Bush Intercontinental Airport later that day. Then all would fly to Milwaukee.

Everyone made the plane, but for some they had to work hard. Some players who were living in downtown high-rise apartments or condos had to walk down many flights of stairs since power was out and no elevators were working. Pitcher Randy Wolf said his journey took him down fourteen flights of stairs in the dark with bags in hand followed by a walk of several blocks to the ballpark. Two broadcasters, Jim Deshaies and Dave Raymond, who lived in The Woodlands forty miles north of downtown, elected to find their way to northside-based Bush Airport and meet the team at the airport.

Those who drove in to the ballpark or looked outside the bus windows on the trip to the airport saw a dead-looking city. Debris was everywhere. Broken and fallen trees lay next to roofs torn from buildings. Billboards were in shambles, and everything was dark. There were no lights anywhere, no power for miles and miles, and very little automotive movement. Harris County's 4 million residents were nowhere to be seen.

Upon arrival at the airport, the busses pulled up to the gate. The Astro's Continental Airlines charter was in its usual place on the tarmac. There were no other planes. There was nothing going in or out. Presumably the lack of planes was a result of the airport being vacated before being shut down in advance of Ike. It was eerie.

After the bus pulled up to the gate, everyone grabbed their carry-on items and went up the stairs into the terminal. The required security check would be conducted inside. Normally, teams going on road trips are checked at their ballpark prior to boarding busses for the airport. Then, when they arrive, the bus can pull up straight to the plane and all can board. This time, it was impractical to bring the TSA screeners to Minute Maid Park with all the destruction. Everyone passed through rapidly enough and re-boarded the busses for the 200-yard drive to the plane. While the party had been screened, the equipment truck had unloaded the Astro's gear and personal luggage onto the plane.

Upon liftoff, those on board kept their eyes to the windows to see just what sort of destruction Ike had left. From the Northside it was not that bad. Power may have been out in large areas, but other than some tree damage and an occasional roof, most of the destruction was further south near Galveston and the Gulf. For one Astro, that was his greatest concern. Pitcher Brandon Backe grew up and lived in Galveston County. After the storm hit, he spent hours driving around the area to check on friends. The storm had unleashed its greatest fury and damage to the Galveston area. Backe was in no mood to leave and play a baseball game, but as he said, "I felt obligated. I have heard from some of my friends, but others I don't know if they are O.K. or not."

Those in the Astro party were leaving others behind to cope with the power problems and clean up. More than 80 people in the region were not so lucky. They died in the wake of the storm. There was nearly $40 billion in damages.

After the series in Milwaukee with the Cubs, which had been shortened to two games, everyone was going right to Miami to start a scheduled road trip. Some wives and family were left behind without any electrical power for days. Even getting back into a pennant race was over-shadowed by concern for those left in Ike's wake.

Astros Were Not Ready for Zambrano in Milwaukee

What no one knew at the time was that the two games played in Milwaukee would mark the last time the Houston Astros would have a chance to think about winning a spot in the postseason for seven more years. What they did know was that they were very mad at Baseball Commissioner Bud Selig for putting the games in a division rival city against another rival only 90 miles away. The Astros would have rather played in Arlington, which was closer, and would certainly not have been as much of a home site for them as Milwaukee was for the Cubs. And it was supposed to be a Houston home game anyway. The problem was that while the stadium in Arlington was open on Sunday, the Rangers were scheduled to play there on Monday.

So the two games would be played in Milwaukee. And as the Astros and their fans had feared, Miller Park was loaded with Cubs fans. More than 23,000 fans (23,441) lined up outside to buy tickets to the game. Inside, they got their money's worth and then some. The Cubs won, took only 2 hours and 17 minutes to do it, and their starting pitcher, Carlos Zambrano, threw a no hit game. It was a perfect day for a Cub fan.

Zambrano was only one hit batter (Pence) and one walk (Bourn) from a perfect game. In the nine inning complete game, he struck out ten Astros and threw only 110 pitches. He was never under pressure after the Cubs scored five runs off Astro starter Randy Wolf in the first 2⅔ innings. Alfonso Soriano's two-run homerun in the first off of Wolf was all Zambrano needed, although the final score was Chicago 5, Houston 0. The Cubs' lead over the Astros was now 9½.

The next day was barely better. The Astros only got one hit—a single by Loretta in the bottom of the seventh—as Ted Lilly, with some bullpen help after the seventh, led Chicago to a 6-1 win. Jim Edmonds, Derek Lee, and Geovany Soto all hit homers for the Cubs before 15,158 mostly Cub fans on Monday.

Now 10 ½ games behind and only thirteen games left to play, the Astros' last chance for a championship under Drayton McLane's ownership was over. The Astros would split their last twelve games and not play a 13th, since a makeup of the Cubs game skipped in the move to Milwaukee would not be needed. Fans didn't know it, but an effort to sell the team had almost come to fruition and then died during 2008. It would not be the last time, but the club had to prepare for a new owner. Drayton McLane was ready to get out of baseball.

Patchwork Teams Were The Rule at the End of the McLane Era

The 2009 Astros—two years past the end of the Biggio-Bagwell era—was when the McLane ownership record would start to fade. From his gaining ownership in 1993 through the 2008 season, the Astros had the fifth best record in all of baseball. The Houston win-loss record of 1350-1176 for a .534 percentage was bested only by the New York Yankees, Atlanta Braves, Boston Red Sox, and Cleveland Indians. The record was better than such traditional winners like the St. Louis Cardinals, Los Angeles Dodgers, and San Francisco Giants.

In 2009, the wheels started to fall off. Manager Cecil Cooper was relieved with 13 games to play. He had been very critical of some of his players and the way they were performing to the media. Fans loved that he was emotive. His players did not. Cooper had been an outstanding player for the Milwaukee Brewers for year. However, like many great players who try to manage he was not always happy with what he saw on the field and lost patience. He wouldn't criticize naming names, but some of the things he complained about allowed those who were paying attention to know exactly to which player or players he was referring.

The highlight of 2009 may have come in the second game when Jeff Keppinger, an offseason acquisition, hit a walk-off game-winning single to beat the Cubs', and even the Astros', record at 1-1. The lost the next five games and didn't reach .500 again until July 12. They got as far as four games over .500 at 50-46 on July 24 and were within 1 ½ games of first place before the wheels fell off for the last time.

They would go 24-42 after July 24 to end the season at 74-88, in fifth place, and 17 games off the lead. Cooper was replaced by coach Dave Clark when the team was 70-79.

Want A Positive? Carlos Lee Hit Well

Positives for 2009? Carlos Lee had a full season and hit .300 with 26 homers and 102 RBIs. Up through this season, Lee's $100 million contract was paying dividends. He had put together three solid seasons. However, he was now thirty-three years old and the contract still had three years left.

Lance Berkman had a down year for him. Missing time with a left calf strain, he was limited to 136 games. His average was only .274 with 25 homers and 80 RBIs. Hunter Pence hit .282 with 25 homers and 72 RBIs, while Michael Bourn jumped up to .285 and stole 61 bases. Miguel Tejada showed he could still hit for average by hitting .313 to go with 14 homers and 86 runs batted in. Kaz Matsui hit only .250 but reached a milestone combining his hits during his Japan and MLB careers and was honored by the Japanese equivalent of the Hall of Fame as a Golden Player.

Career Milestones for Three Astros

Three Astros reached milestones during the season. Berkman, Lee, and Ivan Rodriguez all hit their 300th career homers while they were wearing a Houston uniform. Rodriguez had been acquired during the off-season and was dealt to his first team at Texas before the season was over. He still caught more games than any other Astro catcher in 2009 (93).

Only Wandy Rodriguez stood out on the mound. He was 14-12 with a 3.02 earned run average. Roy Oswalt dropped off to 8-6 with a 4.12 in 30 starts. No other starter had an earned run average less than 5.30. As a team, the 5.54 team earned run average was 13th in the National League.

14

Hitting Bottom and the Plan to the Top

"We've thoroughly enjoyed owning the team and it has been one of the highlights of my life."

– Drayton McLane on announcing sale of Astros to Jim Crane

With a Sale Being Worked on, Astros Watched Costs

Sometime during the 2010 season, Houston businessman Jim Crane started thinking of the Houston Astros again. He wanted into baseball. He had put in bids for the Chicago Cubs and was in one of the bidding groups for the Texas Rangers when they were up for sale. In Chicago, the Cubs went to the Chicago-based Ricketts family at the end of 2009. In Texas, the Rangers were sold to a local group headed by Ray Davis, Chuck Greenberg, and Nolan Ryan in 2010. Crane knew Drayton McLane would be open to an offer since Crane had made one in 2008 before backing out when the financial market crashed. The only question was whether he had burned any bridges with McLane.

Courtesy of Delaywaves

He found out that was not the case. Money really does talk. And McLane would now start doing all he could to get the best price. Instead of spending money on long term free agent contracts or long extensions for players already on the team like Lance Berkman, Roy Oswalt, and Michael Bourn, the club would trim the budget and start putting more money into scouting and the farm system. This would give a new owner few multi-year commitments and hopefully some players in the system with promise. It would also start implementing a plan McLane knew Crane wanted to follow if he was able to take over.

Building the farm system sounded good to General Manager Ed Wade and team President Tal Smith. Of course, both of them also knew the club would be even worse on the major league level than it was in 2009. They were in baseball operations. Whatever McLane was doing in the background as far as selling the team was concerned was on the business side. They would keep doing their job under the guidelines sent down from the top as effectively as they could.

Starting in 2007 with Biggio's quest for 3,000 hits and continuing into 2008 and 2009, the importance of Craig and Jeff Bagwell on Astro history were not forgotten. Two statues were erected outside the ballpark showing Biggio at second base making a throw to Bagwell at first. In addition, several bobble head and other memorabilia giveaways were part of some nights at Minute Maid Park. Both Biggio and Bagwell were listed in the media guides as special assistants to the General Manager. The club couldn't cut away from the past because they had no present.

Brad Mills Came in to Manage Under Major Handicaps

For 2010, GM Ed Wade hired rookie major league manager Brad Mills to take over. Ed also tried to improve the starting pitching by bringing in Brett Myers and, during the season, J.A. Happ, whom he had known well during his days running the Phillies. He picked up Matt Lindstrom and Brandon Lyon to man the back end of the bullpen. Youngsters from the Astro system, Bud Norris and Felipe Paulino, were given shots in the starting rotation. Farm product Chris Johnson was given a chance at third base for more games than anyone else who manned the spot. The same was the case for Tommy Manzella at shortstop.

However, not was all well. Lance Berkman, now thirty-four years old, was limited to only 85 games and not performing to his standard, then was traded to the New York Yankees for pitcher Mark Melancon and Jimmy Paredes on July 31. Pitcher Roy Oswalt had been dealt two days earlier to the Phillies for Anthony Gose, Jonathan Villar, and J.A. Happ. Gose was then turned over to Toronto in a deal for first baseman Brett Wallace.

The salary dumps and acquisition of young low-paid prospects was underway. It didn't hurt that both Oswalt and Berkman, who was battling leg problems, were older and appeared past their prime. Big money contract extensions might not have been a good move even if they had been playing well, but they weren't. They were both also ready to move on. Michael Bourn would be next to go after the following season.

What did all this maneuvering do? Even with good seasons from Hunter Pence, Michael Bourn, and 14 wins from Myers, it didn't do enough. It gave Mills a rookie manager record of 76-86. The team actually played better after both Berkman and Oswalt were traded, winning 32 and losing 27 after July 31. Nothing got the team into the pennant race. From May 22 through the end of the year, the club was always double figure games behind the division leaders. After three very good seasons from Carlos Lee, things fell off greatly in 2010. Now thirty-four years old, he saw his average drop all the way to .246. He hit 24 homeruns and drove in 89 runs, but he was becoming less mobile and was a liability in the field. Lee still had two more years on his contract.

From the salary dumps of popular Astros into the offseason prior to 2011 fans knew something was up.

Astros Had Worst Season in History

Only the most die-hard Astro fan would have expected the 2011 team to be very good. But only the most pessimistic would have expected the team would be the worst in Houston major league history. That, however, is what fans saw. Dead last in the six team National League Central, the Astros lost over 100 games for the first time. And like Ted Williams said when he was hitting .39955 on the last day of 1941, which would have rounded up to .400, and elected to play because he didn't want to hit .400, "with my toe nails on the line," the Astros did not leave their toe nails on the line. They lost 106 games.

During the offseason, the talk had been about whether the team would be sold. Word was that Jim Crane was back and negotiating with Drayton McLane again.

Meanwhile, the efforts to clean the deck of long term obligations continued. The TV rights would leave Fox Sports Houston after the 2012 season, and plans were moving forward with Comcast to start up on October 1, 2012. Berkman and Oswalt were gone, both big dollar earners. Michael Bourn was traded to keep from having to deal with him as a free agent. He was traded on July 31 to the Braves for Juan Abreu, Paul Clemens, Brett Oberholtzer, and Jordan Schafer. Schafer would handle center field the rest of the year. The others were prospects to continue the rebuild of the system.

The Astros were building their system and giving some younger players a chance in the majors. They got experience. They just didn't get to learn how to win much.

Saying the pitching was mediocre might be over-rating it. The team earned run average was last in the National League at 4.61. They gave up the most runs and homeruns. Wandy Rodriguez was the best starter, and he was just 11-11 with a 3.49 earned run average. Twenty- year old Jordan Lyles made an early debut probably sooner than he should have and was 2-8 with a 5.36 earned run average in 20 games.

Offensively, the club hit .258, fourth best in the league and led the league in doubles. They were 13th in runs scored and 15th in homeruns. The 2011, Astros only hit 95 homeruns. They were not a scary team for opposing pitchers to face. Carlos Lee led the club with only 18 homers. He drove in 94 and hit .275. Only shortstop Clint Barmes with 12, Hunter Pence with 11, and utility man Matt Downs with 10 hit double figures in homeruns.

There was one player who debuted in 2011 that showed long term promise. He was a twenty-one-year-old second baseman from Venezuela who had proved he could hit. Jose Altuve was only about 5'5' tall and had been over-looked the first time scouts saw him. But after signing with the Astros as a free agent in 2007, he kept showing more than expected in the Houston farm system. In five minor league seasons, he hit .327. Prior to getting the call to Houston, he had hit .408 in 52 games for Lancaster in the Class A California League. Then, after being promoted to Class AA Corpus Christi in the Texas League, he hit .361 in 35 games.

Altuve played the last part of the 2011 season with the Astros. The major leagues were not too much for him. In 57 games, he hit .276. The

Houston farm system may have produced a future super star to join such stars of the past like Biggio, Bagwell, Berkman, and Oswalt.

The excitement that Altuve brought was not the only positive from the field in 2011. There was one memorable game that proved the old adage, "You can't beat fun at the old ballpark, because you are likely to see something you never have before."

Bogusevic Had the Ultimate Hit

That occurred on the night of August 16. The Cubs led the Astros 5-2 to the last of the ninth. Brett Myers had started for Houston and surrendered four runs in seven innings. Meanwhile, Ryan Dempster had kept the Astros in check. He allowed only four hits and two runs through his seven innings on the mound. Kerry Wood threw an inning of relief. Closer Carlos Marmol was called on to go for the save in the ninth.

After a lineout to left field off the bat of Jimmy Paredes, J.B. Shuck grounded a ball to right field for a single. With Clint Barmes at the plate, Marmol threw a wild pitch that moved Shuck to second base. After another ball, Barmes singled to left field, but trailing by three in the ninth, third base coach Dave Clark held Shuck at third. Matt Downs was called on to pinch hit for catcher Humberto Quintero and worked a walk on a 3-2 pitch. Brian Bogusevic was next, tabbed by manager Brad Mills to hit for pitcher Aneury Rodriguez.

Then, with the count reaching 2-2 and the bases full, Bogusevic did something he will remember forever. He drove the ball to deep left-center field. It was high. It was far, and it was over and out! A super grand slam walk-off homerun! The Astros won the game by a 6-5 score. Every one of the four runs Bogusevic drove in were needed to wipe out the 5-2 deficit. The Astros won the game 6-5. It was only the Astros' 39th win. They had already lost 84. But it was the most thrilling comeback of the season.

Behind the scenes, something was announced early during the season that had been expected for some time. The Astros were going to have a new owner.

McLane Ended Ownership. Jim Crane Took Over

On Monday, May 16, 2011, with the Astros about to begin a seven game road trip starting in Atlanta, the team called a news conference for Minute Maid Park. The sale of the Astros was going to be announced.

Drayton McLane Jr., who had owned the club since November 1992, was selling the club to Jim Crane and partners.

Crane had tried to put a deal together in 2008, but reneged. Then he was rebuffed on bids for both the Chicago Cubs and Texas Rangers. But now he had fulfilled a long time goal. He was buying a major league baseball team.

McLane had owned the team during the most successful period in the team's nearly fifty- year history. The Astros had been in the postseason in 1997, 1998, 1999, 2001, 2004, and 2005. They had made it to the World Series in 2005. During McLane's reign, such stars as Craig Biggio and Jeff Bagwell had been with him all way until their retirements. Attendance had set records, and the new ballpark he championed for downtown Houston came into being. As he said, "One of the responsibilities of good leadership is to hand off better than you found it." Some questioned that statement when they looked at the team the Astros were putting on the field at the end of the McLane reign. However, he was right when one considered all features of the Houston Astros compared to what he bought all those years ago.

Despite the Astros on-field struggles since 2008, that was what Crane was getting. The rebuilding of the farm system had started. Other than Lee's contract, which still had some time to run the decks, had been cleared for the new ownership. The club was profitable with expectations that it would be even more so when the new Comcast TV partnership kicked in following the 2012 season.

As for Crane's thoughts during the announcement, "As the new owner of the Astros, I want to let you know I love baseball. Baseball has had a big impact on me—from the time I was little—and for the better."

McLane indicated the actual hand-over of the team would take place once the sale was approved by Major League Baseball in 60 to 90 days. He would turn out to be a bit optimistic about that. The sale price was for a reported $680 million and would include the club's stake in the future regional sports network to be run by Comcast with both the Astros and Houston Rockets as partners. The network share was as much as $300 million of the selling price.

George Postolos, who had helped get the idea of the teams owning all or at least a share of their network in the early 2000s and who had worked with Crane in his unsuccessful attempts to buy the Cubs and Rangers, was designated by Crane as the president of the club once the Crane Group took over. He had no baseball experience and did not have a good reputation as a people person with the staff during his days running the Houston Rockets. However, he was a loyal number two man for a powerful owner and would serve Crane as he had Rockets' owner Leslie Alexander for a few years.

As it turned out the Astros would remain under McLane's control through the whole season because the other owners didn't approve the sale until November 17, 2011. A major reason was that it took time to vet Crane and his minority owners. That included background and financial research and telling Crane something he was not happy hearing. Jim Crane had negotiated a deal with Drayton McLane to buy a National League baseball team, the Houston Astros. Crane had grown up a National League fan both as a youth in the St. Louis area and in Houston with the Astros. But Baseball Commissioner Bud Selig was determined to balance the leagues. Ever since the team he once owned, the Milwaukee Brewers, had moved to the National League from the American, the National League had two more franchises. Since there was no talk of expansion, and contraction had even been considered a few years before, he wanted both leagues to have the same number of teams. He also wanted all divisions within the leagues to have the same number of teams. He wanted to expand inter-league play, which would become season-long with 15 teams in each league.

He had power over Jim Crane to make it happen. If the Astros didn't agree to switch leagues, the sale would not be approved. He couldn't force the Arizona Diamondbacks or Colorado Rockies to move to the AL. But a new owner seeking approval had less power. Furthermore, the Texas Rangers were in favor of having Houston join their division to give them one less opponent based two time zones away. The Astros would not only have to leave the NL Central division, but also the Central Time Zone for far more road games. They would also have to use the designated hitter.

Houston was stuck. Even if they could have stayed in the NL and either Arizona or Colorado moved to the AL West, the Astros would have had to leave the NL Central for the NL West anyway. The time zone problem was a certainty. When the National League had only two divisions, the Astros were in the West. The difference was that in those days the West had six teams and only three on the west coast. Atlanta, Cincinnati, and Houston were in the division. Only the teams in Los Angeles, San Diego, and San Francisco were really in the West, and the number of trips and games two time zones away were fewer.

Crane surrendered to the move to the American League West, but he wouldn't do it for free. As he pointed out, he agreed to pay Drayton McLane $680 million for the National League Houston Astros. He wanted a rebate. McLane wouldn't pay it. Major League Baseball would. News reports indicated $20 million would be headed to Crane to help with his debt to McLane.

Starting in 2013, the Astros would leave the National League. Most fans were irate at the change. Houston had been a National League city for decades before they actually had the Colt 45s. The Houston Buffs minor league team had been an affiliate of the Cardinals since the 1920s and, in the team's latter days, was signed on with the Cubs. Houston was a National League city, and now they would have to use the designated hitter, which the majority of National League fans abhorred.

For the 2012 season, the Astros would be owned by Crane and his partners during the last season in the National League. The process started by McLane and his baseball operations folks was continued and expanded. In the meantime, unlike when McLane had bought the team from John McMullen and made few changes in the front office and staff, Jim Crane and George Postolos had many changes in mind. New employees replaced the holdovers in nearly every department. Most of the changes came after the 2012 season, but new team President Postolos and new General Manager Jeff Luhnow brought in their people as quickly as they could. Whether McLane knew this might be coming or not, he showed class when, before leaving, he granted bonuses to the employees who had been with the club for years under his ownership.

Then things started to move quickly.

15 The New Era of Astros Baseball: Rocky Start

"Our style will be smart, and it starts with the draft. We want to make sure we're building a team for the future."

– Jim Crane on taking over ownership of the Astros from Drayton McLane

New Management Wanted a New Look

If the Jim Crane ownership did one thing, it was clean the deck of most management from the Drayton McLane era. For some this was a shock since it was not what McLane had done when he bought the team. The vast majority of employees inherited from John McMullen retained their jobs as McLane tried to learn how major league baseball worked. In Crane's case, he had been a fan all of his life, and as a successful businessman, he already had strong ideas about what he wanted to accomplish. He and his new team president, George Postolos, started surveying season ticket holders, fellow stock holders, and others who contributed heavily to team charities. They asked questions ranging from the fan experience in the ball park to whether they liked the radio and television announcers. In most cases, they got responses that mirrored opinions they already held.

The pair changed the baseball operations by hiring former St. Louis Cardinal assistant general manager Jeff Luhnow. He won the job by overwhelming his interviewers with a detailed report analyzing the Astros system and explaining in detail what it would take to re-build the baseball operation from scratch. The Luhnow plan would actually continue what McLane and his staff had started when he made the decision to sell. Veterans would not fit unless they could be signed to short contracts as spacefillers. Young players would be elevated to the major leagues, but would be expendable if they appeared unable to handle the major leagues. The system would be built so deeply that the club would not only have prospects for their team in multiples, but also many players with great value usable as part of future trades with other major league clubs.

Following this plan would require most of the scouts currently with the Astros be replaced and new ones, who were more geared to scouting by statistical models, be brought in. Part of baseball had always been playing the percentages. Now it would extend into more areas than just on the field.

After working on the transition for the new owners, General Manager Ed Wade and both the Presidents for baseball and business operations, Pam Gardner and Tal Smith, were let go. Jay Lucas, head of media and communications, was axed, as was Barry Waters, who had been travelling secretary for the club for over twenty-five years. Scouts were dropped and replaced. Even the radio announcers, Brett Dolan and Dave Raymond, were fired and Hall of Fame honoree Milo Hamilton was retired. On the television side, popular analyst Jim Deshaies jumped to the Chicago Cubs after the Astros were slow in opening negotiations. Bill Brown would remain in the lead role, but the field level commentator game announcer, Greg Lucas, home game reporters Patti Smith and Bart Enis, and pre and post-game hosts, Kevin Eschenfelder, Lucas, and Enis were changed. That had nothing to do with the Astros. Those changes came due to the demise of Fox Sports Houston for whom they had been employed. Enis and Eschenfelder joined Comcast in different roles, Smith stayed as the Fox Sports Southwest bureau chief in Houston. Lucas started writing books. The new network planned to change things and would be re-formatted with their own faces. Change is what Comcast SportsNet Houston did.

The Astros Were Hard to See on TV, but Weren't Worth Watching Anyway

From the outset of the new television deal, a few things were evident. Comcast was going to make its network first class. There would be very few limits on spending while they built the programming. In addition to Houston Rocket and Houston Astros games, they would also carry Houston Dynamo games from Major League Soccer. They would produce and air high school and college sports and have a number of studio programs including daily sportscasts and talk shows. The staff would be much larger than anything Fox had. There was one major problem, though.

The network didn't have any major affiliates other than Comcast's own Xfinity Cable. In the Houston market, only 40% of the homes had any cable access. Comcast had the exclusive rights to the city of Houston, but suburban areas had deals with other cable companies. Those systems were much smaller than national power Comcast and were very reluctant to sign on to carry Comcast Sports Net-Houston due to the price demanded. Comcast was quite willing to sell the network to anyone who was not a direct competitor, but was not so quick to work out deals with competitors like DirecTV, Dish, and AT&T U-verse. Satellite and video streaming services were also competitors. Viewers in the Houston market could subscribe to either of them and not Xfinity.

Herein lay the main difference between a network production and a provider production. Fox Sports Net was a network that provided its products to carriers. Cable systems, satellite, and streaming systems were where they sold their product. They didn't own one or the other, and thus were not a competitor. Fox was not seeking exclusive coverage, just coverage.

At its peak, Fox Sports SW, which included its Fox Sports Houston affiliate, was available to more than 10 million homes. The majority of those homes, encompassed in a five state area, had access to Houston Astros baseball. When Comcast Sports Net-Houston took over, the coverage was available to only 40% of the Houston population—perhaps less than 400 thousand homes and to no one much outside the Houston market.

This cut out major regional markets such as San Antonio, Austin, New Orleans—which did not have Major League Baseball and had many long time Astros fans—as well as the populous Dallas-Fort Worth market which had its own team in Arlington, but also had a number of National League and Astro followers. Of course, the National League option disappeared when the Crane ownership group was forced to change leagues.

Astro management was not concerned at first. They knew under their rebuilding plan the club would be losing a large number of games and might not be drawing good ratings on television. By the time the team started to improve, surely the folks with Comcast who were in charge of gaining affiliates would be making progress. And the Astros were supposed to be making about $80 million a year off the contract anyway. That would be more than double what the last Fox contract had paid.

One problem was that the fee the partners (Astros, Rockets, and Comcast) were requiring from affiliates was more than cable/satellite systems felt the product was worth. DISH network was so aghast at what new networks around the country were demanding, they pulled out of the sports business for the most part. The strategy was sound in one way. There are more people that don't follow sport than do by a large margin. If DISH could provide their service for considerably less than cable or satellite competitor DirecTV, they would have a market. The one possible weakness in their plan was that a high percentage of subscribers to satellite or cable services are doing it because of sports.

That corporate decision by DISH took their service off the table even if Comcast had been willing to put the games on a competitor. DirecTV and Comcast could not agree. Some of the other cable systems around the city and region balked. If availability of games for viewers in the Houston area was limited, the games were effectively totally unavailable outside the immediate area.

Meanwhile Comcast Sports Net-Houston was soon bleeding money. The partners had to contribute to keep the operation going. Rights fees due to the teams were not paid. The $80 million per year was only a dream.

Fortunately, the Astros could cover the loss of local TV revenue and even the huge drop in attendance due to putting poor teams on the field. They had very few financial obligations to players.

Crane Figured He Over-Paid for the Team and Sued McLane

There is little question Jim Crane and his fellow minority owners were well vetted by Major League Baseball before he was allowed to purchase the Astros from Drayton McLane. However, many were not sure how well Crane vetted the deal he made to buy the club.

As an example, many in the television sports business, both nationally and locally, questioned the value placed on Crane's purchase of the team's share in Comcast Sports Net-Houston, which had never gone on the air or signed a single affiliate yet. The original total purchase price for the team and network was reported at $680 million. It was first cut when Crane objected to the club being forced to move to the American League. Of the $615 million left, it was reported that $326 million of that was for the share of Comcast Sports Net-Houston.

Crane filed a lawsuit against McLane, Comcast, and NBCUniversal, the division that built the sports network, charging that McLane sold an asset that all knew at the time was overpriced and "broken" and that Crane was "duped" when he bought the interest in the network based on "falsely inflated subscription rates."

McLane's early response only was that Crane and his partners had access to all materials and Crane's complaint that he had not received a business plan for CSN-Houston prior to the purchase was not true. The lawsuit was only the beginning of continuing problems for the network.

Less Than One Year from CSN-Houston's Birth —Bankruptcy Filed

Comcast Sports Net-Houston had been on the air for only eleven months when, on September 27, 2013, bankruptcy was filed according to NBCUniversal to, "resolve structural issues affecting CSN Houston's partnership."

The Astros protested the move as a ploy to keep the team from ending its role in the partnership. Jim Crane realized the Astros would never reap the income estimated in the original plan and wanted out. The legal situation, lack of affiliates, money lost, and all the disagreements between the three partners ultimately doomed the network.

In August, DirecTV and AT&T proposed a reorganization plan. The two companies, which were in the process of merging, would acquire CSN Houston in a 60/40 joint venture. If approved, that would keep games on Comcast's Xfinity cable but also add DirecTV and AT&T. The network operations would be down-sized with over 75 employees let go and all non-game studio shows shut down.

By 2015 the Astros, on the newly branded Root Sports SW, would reach 63% of the Houston market and now also be available in all the other large regional markets in which they were not seen in 2013 or 2014. The timing was perfect. After the lowest point in Houston's baseball history—three straight season with 100 or more losses—things were going to turn in 2015. Some new potential super stars were or would soon be wearing Astro colors.

16 Things Aren't Pretty on the Field Until 2015

Courtesy of Keith Allison

"This was a great ride. What a great group of guys we have.
I didn't want it to end."

– Astros outfielder Colby Rasmus after NLDS
elimination loss to Kansas City, 2015

The four seasons prior to Colby Rasmus being able to make that statement were horrible for Astro fans. Starting in 2011 and continuing through 2012 and 2013, the team had records of 56-106, 57-107, and 51-111. Things were much better in 2014 when they were still 22 games under .500, but even a 70-92 record gave some hope.

2012 Crane and Company in Charge

When the Astros opened the 2012 season, Jim Crane was the owner and Jeff Luhnow was running baseball operations. Brad Mills had been fired as manager late in 2011. The Astros new manager would be Houston resident and long-time major league coach Bo Porter. Fred Nelson and Bobby Heck would remain in charge of the farm system and scouting operations for one last year. Their edict was to continue to get and develop the best young talent. In addition to Jose Altuve, who was already in the major leagues, they had some other potential major leaguers in the system. Even so, both Nelson and Heck would be gone by 2013 as Luhnow continued to bring in his people more attuned to the "new" analytic scouting and development methods being developed by highly educated fans of the game who may not have ever played it in college or professionally.

The Astros would have a very young lineup. Only Carlos Lee at thirty-six would be older than the twenty-eight years of shortstop Jed Lowrie and outfielders Justin Maxwell and Brian Bogusevic. Lee was in the last year of his six-year contract and didn't have much left. He would be traded to Florida before the season was over after playing his last 66 games in Houston and hitting a credible .287, but with only five homeruns and 29 runs batted in.

The team recorded a franchise low .236 batting average and was last in runs scored. Astro hitters struck out more than any team in the National League. Altuve kept showing promise, though. He hit a team high .290 and stole 33 bases. Justin Maxwell hit the most homeruns, 18, but batted only .229. J.D. Martinez, who would later star in Detroit after being let go by the Astros, didn't show much in 2012. In 439 at-bats he hit just .241 with 11 homeruns and struck out 96 times.

The pitchers were not much better. The pitching staff's 4.56 earn run average was 15th in the 16 team league. Lucas Harrell, with 11-11 with a 3.76 earned run average, and Brett Myers, converted to a closer with 19 saves, were the best of a generally ineffective crew.

Manager Brad Mills was fired before the season was over with Triple A manager Tony DeFrancesco taking over for the final 41 games. Under DeFrancesco, the team was 16-25.

Astros Hit a New All Time Low in 2013—111 Losses!

Houston had already lost 100 or more games for two seasons in a row when they made it a trifecta in 2013. This would be a record for ineptitude. The club would not only lose 111 games with only 51 wins, but they would finish the season on a fifteen game losing streak.

This would be the first season with the Crane/Postolos/Luhnow trio in charge from the end of one season to the start of the next. It would also be the first in which few could watch the team on television. It would mark the end of George Postolos as team President and the return of Nolan Ryan and more importantly his son, Reid Ryan, to Houston.

While the season was still in its early stages, Postolos, under pressure from many complaints for his heavy-handed style of management, resigned as President of the Astros. In May of 2013, Reid Ryan was named to replace Postolos.

Reid Ryan Changed the Atmosphere with Front Office and Fans

The appointment of Ryan, eldest child of Hall of Fame pitcher, Nolan Ryan, was an immediate success and hailed by fans as the best move Crane had made since taking over the team. Ryan had experience running teams in both the Texas Ranger and Houston Astro farm systems at Round Rock and Corpus Christi. His father, after his playing career, had been both an executive and part owner of the Rangers. Reid was also a fans' owner. While his job primarily would deal with business matters, he knew the game and was not hesitant to talk about it. Like the team's previous owner, Drayton McLane, Ryan was fond of walking the ballpark and conversing with the fans. Jim Crane, a much more introverted man, was not as comfortable in that role. Under Reid, the Astros made a strong effort to bring players from the past back to the park and be invited to take part in promotions, off-season caravans, fan fests and special promotions.

While the franchise now was making better moves off the field what fans were seeing on the field was still pretty miserable.

Manager Bo Porter, a former college football player at Iowa, had a lot of football coach in him despite all his years in baseball. He tried to fire his team up. He tried to be positive. He spouted the company line about building for the future. But his team lost a lot of games.

There was little secret to why they lost. They just weren't any good. Chris Carter, acquired from the Oakland A's during the offseason, led the team with 29 homeruns. But he only drove in 82 runs and hit just .223. And he struck out a whopping 212 times.

No one of the entire roster, including players with limited at-bats hit .300. Jose Altuve was best at .283 among everyday players, and he stole 35 bases, but since his hitting philosophy was to swing at anything he could reach, his .316 on base percentage was only sixth-best among everyday players. The team batting average of .240 was fourteenth in the American League. They scored 610 runs and surrendered 848. That was the second most given up in the league, as were the number of homeruns surrendered. Individually, the most effective starter had been Bud Norris. In 21 starts, he was 6-9 but with the only sub 4.00 earned run average at 3.93. He must have been too good for this team. He was traded to Baltimore on July 31. Actually, though, it was a salary dump primarily, with Houston getting a minor league player named Josh Hader and a player to be named later, which turned into outfielder L. J. Hoes.

They lost 111 games by dropping their last fifteen. Their last win had been on September 23 vs the Los Angeles Angels. Lefty Dallas Keuchel was the winning pitcher. Few may have been following the Astros in person (1,651,883—15th of 16 AL teams) or on TV, but Keuchel would turn out to be someone to follow in the future for sure.

Improvement Started to Show in 2014

In 2014, front office changes including Quinton McCracken in as farm director and Mike Elias as scouting director. Both were numbers guys who wanted to help the club find the best prospects for the best price based on statistical evaluation. The Astros were not generating the revenue necessary to compete with the big guys in the game for high dollar free agents. But they also weren't looking for them yet. They had to build enough pieces in other spots first.

In 2014, the plan seemed to be to play the youth to find out who could play well enough to be part of a contending team in a year or two. Jose Altuve continued to shine. He won the American League batting championship with a .341 batting average at age twenty-four. His batting title was the first ever won by a Houston player. His 225 hits set a new franchise record. Unfortunately, the rest of the team hit little. Seven of the nine regular players struck out over 100 times, with four of that number whiffing in more than 125 at-bats. Names like Jason Castro, now in his third season as the number one catcher; Jon Singleton; Altuve; Jonathan Villar; Matt Dominguez, who had been acquired in the late season trade of Carlos Lee to Florida in 2013; Robbie Grossman; and George Springer joined more veteran players like Dexter Fowler, Chris Carter, and Alex Presley in seeing the most action. Except for Fowler and Altuve, none of them hit much. Carter tried to counter 181 strikeouts by hitting 37 homeruns, but his batting average was only .227. The team batting average was not impressive at .242. Without Altuve's numbers, the team hit just .228! They hit 163 homeruns, third best in the AL, but with 1,442 strikeouts heavily contributing, they were third-worst in the league in runs scored. There was something more positive from the pitching staff.

The pitcher's ERA of 4.11 was 12th best, which equaled their ranking for number of runs allowed. It was not good, but did show improvement. Twenty-six year old lefty Dallas Keuchel started to blossom. He was 12-9 with a solid 2.93 earned run average. Colin McHugh, selected off waivers from the Colorado Rockies in the offseason, won 11, lost 9 and registered a 2.73 ERA.

In 2014, Nolan Ryan rejoined the team of his son, Reid, as an advisor after having resigned as CEO of the Rangers a few months before.

Manager Bo Porter, reportedly running afoul of the "plan" with baseball operations, was removed as manager of the club 138 games into the season. The Astros were 59-79 at that point and had won three of their last four games. Minor league manager Tom Lawless took over for the final 24 games. Houston would have a new skipper in 2015.

17 Biggio Makes Hall of Fame as Astros Return to Postseason

Courtesy of Arturo Pardavila III

"We played fifteen years together and changed the culture in Houston by making it a baseball town. We both got to live our dreams together by playing in the big leagues side by side. Thanks for being here today. It really means a lot."

– Craig Biggio in his Hall of Fame induction speech to Jeff Bagwell 2015

It had taken Craig Biggio a few years of eligibility before he was finally elected to join that august group in 2015. His career batting average of .281 was not among the highest. He never won a batting championship or played on a World Series champion team and was in only one Series. Yet Biggio was exactly what a Major League Baseball professional was supposed to be. He played the game hard every night. He played for his team, accepting changes in position on three occasions. And he was a leader on the field, in the clubhouse, and in real life. Yes, he had more than 3,000 hits. That had to count for something. So did all the other numbers he accumulated from doubles, to stolen bases, to being hit by pitches. No right-handed hitter in baseball history had more than his 668 doubles. He was the only MLB player ever to hit at least 600 doubles (668), 250 homeruns (291), 3,000 hits (3060), and have 400 stolen bases (414). Even being hit by pitches for the modern record of 285 times was worth noting. Craig Biggio was a cumulative Hall of Famer.

When all-time starting lineups are named, Biggio won't supplant players like Rogers Hornsby or Joe Morgan or Frankie Frisch, but like those three, he is a Hall of Famer and very deserving of the honor.

From his boyhood when he befriended neighbor Chris Alben in his losing fight with leukemia and took over as the mentor for his younger brother Charlie, Craig devoted a lot of time to service.

After he joined the Astros, he quickly became involved with the Sunshine Kids' local chapter. Several Astro players including pitchers Joe Sambito and Larry Andersen helped get him involved. By the time Biggio had established himself in Houston, he was the man in charge of the players' participation. Always active in the local chapter even after his playing days, he continues to be a national spokesperson for the group that tried to put a little sunshine in the lives of children having to battle cancer.

In 1997, he was named the Branch Rickey Award winner for the major leaguer most dedicated to service off the field. That elevated him into the Baseball Humanitarians Hall of Fame established by the Denver Rotary Club in 1992. Through 2016, seven members of the Baseball Humanitarians Hall of Fame are also in the Baseball Hall of Fame in Cooperstown. These two-way Hall of Famers include Biggio; John Smoltz, who was inducted in Cooperstown with Biggio in 2015; Paul Molitor; Tony Gwynn; Ozzie Smith; Kirby Puckett; and Dave Winfield.

In 2015, the Astros honored Biggio's election to Cooperstown and fans were proud that he would be the first player in the Hall who had spent time in Houston that would wear a Houston cap on his plaque. There was hope that his long time running mate and teammate Jeff Bagwell would earn the recognition in 2017. His vote total in 2016 left him less than 20 votes short of the 75% needed.

On the Field in 2015: Surprise, Surprise, Surprise

Gomer Pyle could not have said it better. With new manager A.J. Hinch at the helm, the Astros not only returned to contention for the first time since 2008, but made the postseason field for the first time since 2005.

They did it with overall improvement offensively and better pitching. Two improvements were massive, the homerun punch and the league leading pitching staff's 3.57 earned run average, but everything, especially from the bullpen, was considerably more efficient than in 2014. Offensively, the team produced the second best power numbers in franchise history. The club hit 230 homeruns, which was second best in the league to the Toronto Blue Jays. The offense was heavily all or nothing. The team got 17 percent of their total hits from homers. The team batting average was .250, which was tenth in the 15 team American League. They also had more strikeouts (1392) than hits (1363). Seven players struck out more than 100 times with part-time starters Colby Rasmus (154) and Chris Carter (151) leading the way.

The pitching staff was led by the big two: Dallas Keuchel and Collin McHugh. Keuchel was 20-8 with a 2.48 earned run average. That was good enough to win the team's first AL Cy Young Award. (Mike Scott and Roger Clemens had both won the award in the NL for Houston.) McHugh finished 19-7 with a 3.89 ERA.

Lance McCullers came up midway in the season and was impressive with a 3.22 ERA in 22 starts. Mike Fiers also joined the club mid-season and won two games. One of them was a no-hitter against the Dodgers. Both Scott Feldman and Brett Oberholtzer suffered injury-plagued seasons. The bullpen was solid, although fading slightly down the stretch. Luke Gregerson saved 31.

In addition to the homerun totals, the offense was again led by Jose Altuve who hit .313 and contributed to the power numbers with 15 homerun. He also stole 38 bases, but perhaps as impressive was his improvement in on-base percentage. Still not great for a .313 hitter, he was able to increase it to .353. Eleven players hit 10 or more homeruns. Designated hitter Even Gattis hit 27 homeruns and led the team with 88 RBIs. Rasmus and Luis Valbeuna both hit 25 homers.

But the next future superstar for the Astros, a player than many believed could join Biggio and Bagwell and possibly Altuve as the greatest Astros of all time, joined the club after the season began and made an immediate impression.

His name was Carlos Correa, the shortstop was drafted with the first pick in the first round in 2012—the first pick selected by the current Astro management.

Only twenty-years-old, Correa played in 99 games, hit .279 with 22 homeruns and 68 runs batted in. He played just over 61% of a full season and was so impressive that he was selected as the American League Rookie of the Year. The last Astro to be so honored? Jeff Bagwell in 1991 in the National League.

The Astros started the 2015 season hot under new manager A.J. Hinch. They were in first place for most of the season after a start that saw them 14 games over .500 on four occasions. The last was on August 26 when they were 71-57 after a 15-1 win over the Yankees in New York.

After that win, things started to tail off. Finishing 15-19, the team fell from first place and had to old off the Angels and Twins to clinch a post-season berth as one of the AL Wild Cards.

They would meet and beat the Yankees in a one-game wild card match. Dallas Keuchel, with some bullpen help, held New York scoreless in a 3-0 victory in New York. Homeruns by Rasmus and Carlos Gomez, who had been a mid-season acquisition, was enough for the victory.

Next up was the AL Central Champion Kansas City Royals, the defending American League champions. The Royals won the best of five in five. The Astros could have taken the series in four if the Royals had not staged two big innings in the eighth and ninth of Game Four. Houston led 6-2 with only six outs left. However, the Royals struck five straight singles and Correa made an error at shortstop on what might have been a double play grounder in which two runners scored. Later in the inning, the Royals added another run and took a 7-6 lead.

Kansas City added two more in the top of the ninth on a two-run homerun by Eric Hosmer. The Astros got only one hit, a single by Correa in the ninth, over the last two innings.

The next day the Astros led early, but by the bottom of the fifth, the Royals had taken a lead they would not relinquish and won entry into the ALCS with a 7-2 win. Houston was held to only two hits—one of them a two-run homer by Luis Valbuena.

The Astros packed up. The Royals ultimately went on to win the World Series. It was that close.

Still, Houston went from three straight 100-loss seasons to a postseason berth in only two years. Hopes for the future were bright. Even so, the era of Biggio and Bagwell will be hard to equal. However, for the first time since Houston's two Hall of Famers were at their peak, there is hope that the new glory era can be led by names like Altuve, Correa, Keuchel, and Springer. Time will tell.

2016 Fell Short but Not by Much

In 2016 the Astros got off to a slow start, lost 15 of 19 to the Texas Rangers, but were in contention for a wild card slot into the last week of the season. It was not as big of a step up as fans had hoped and the club finished with five fewer wins than in 2015 at 83-79. But the "next Biggio and Bagwells"—Jose Altuve and Carlos Correa—had fine seasons. Altuve won his second batting title while acquiring over 200 hits for the third time. Correa fell just short of driving in 100 runs.

The next big Astro news would be off the field in the first week of January 2017.

18 Bagwell Joins Biggio on Same Team Again

Courtesy of Arturo Pardavila III

"Its been a whirlwind. Its been fun and exciting. My family is very excited, too. I could not be more excited."

– Jeff Bagwell on how he felt about making the Hall of Fame

Biggio Was the First Astro in the Hall, but Bagwell Finally Joined Him

While the names of Craig Biggio and Jeff Bagwell are finally linked in the Baseball Hall of Fame in Cooperstown, NY, they have been linked since they both became stars in Houston for years. Biggio made the Hall in just his third year of eligibility after coming extremely close in his second. It just took Jeff longer. Upon his induction in the summer of 2015, Biggio made one of the Hall of Fame's best induction speeches:

"Thank you. This is pretty cool. What an incredible honor it is to be standing in front of these great men. I played against a lot of them. I admired a lot of them. But I respected all of them. Thank you Jane for this honor and all that you do for the Hall. I'd also like to thank Jeff Idelson,

Brad Horn, Whitney, and the Hall of Fame staff for keeping the integrity of the Hall of Fame. I'd like to thank the writers for the invitation to be part of the greatest team ever, the Baseball Hall of Fame. I am truly honored.

"What an amazing class to be part of. Big Randy J was a teammate and I tell you, man, he was a tremendous competitor. We had him for eleven games that season. I mean it was amazing to watch in 1998. John Smoltz, we had a lot of history together, but most of all I'll never forget when we finally beat you in the playoffs. Right? Finally, at least we got 'em twice, they sent us home three times. But he had the class and dignity to come into our clubhouse and wish Jeff and I good luck in the second round. That's just class, you don't teach that. Pedro you brought your A-game out there every time you pitched. You're a little guy, but you pitched like the Big Unit. These guys are Hall of Fame players, but they're better people. So the big question is, how do you get to the Hall of Fame? You've got to have a little bit of talent and you have to have a lot of help along the way.

"My journey started in the little town of Kings Park, New York, not too far from here (cheers). I hear you. (laughter) My mother Johnna Biggio and my father Lee Biggio were two hard working people who are no longer here. But I know they're watching.

"My father was an air-traffic controller who still hardly ever missed a game. One of the things that he used to do was take some rope, tie it around my waist and then tie it to the backstop and then throw me batting practice to keep me from lunging. It worked and I came home every day with rope burns around my waist. My mother, she never missed a game, and like in most homes, she's the rock. We spent a lot of time together traveling around from field to field. I know she's happy today. I miss you so much, Mom. And I really wish you were here today. My brother, Terry, my sister Gwen; we've been through a lot together. I loved you guys.

"My in-laws, Joe and Yolanda Egan, were a tremendous help along with their three kids, Joey, Timmy, and Kevin. I took their daughter to Texas twenty-five years ago and we had three kids there. I was very lucky to have a family that was so helpful and supportive as they have been throughout my life.

"Growing up in Kings Park, I had three responsibilities: school, sports, and I had a job. I had a newspaper route, OK? It was an afternoon newspaper, *Newsday*. Because most of the time I didn't get home till 7 or 7:30, that's when people on my route eventually got the paper, sorry about that.

But on my route I had a family, the family's name was the Albens. They had a boy, Chris, that came down with leukemia. It was right there and then that I realized what a family goes through day in and day out when somebody has to go through this. I made a promise to them that if I was ever in a situation or position to give back, I would. Thus, I'm the national spokesperson for the Sunshine Kids. It's an organization that helps kids with cancer and their families. The Sunshine Kids are a big part of my life and one of the reasons I stayed in Houston for twenty-plus years and continue to live there today.

"My memories growing up in Kings Park are great. I had a lot of great people around me.

My football and baseball coaches were hard-working and very supporting people. My first chance to get noticed by schools and scouts was when I played for a guy on Long Island named Marty Hasenfuss, who coached the Sachem A's, a Connie Mack team. He was an air-traffic controller like my father. Getting a chance to play for Marty was the first great opportunity I had to be noticed. I had a chance to be drafted out of high school by the Detroit Tigers, but I decided to go to college. I went to Seton Hall University where I met my future wife, Patty, and had three great years there. My college coach was Mike Sheppard. He was a tough man. He was a Marine. He was a disciplinarian. He kept you in line. Most of all, he loved his players and he had their backs no matter what. The man had 999 wins and hundreds of players get drafted. Coach Shep's motto was, 'Never lose your hustle.' Which is something I took to my pro career. I'm grateful I played for you, Shep, thank you.

"Ed Blankmeyer was the tremendous assistant coach and he was a tremendous teacher of the game; a man who's dedicated his life to college athletics and who's done an incredible job at St. John's University as the head baseball coach. Thanks, Blanky, and keep up the good work.

"Fred Hopke, who was the hitting coach, was a minor leaguer, career minor leaguer for ten seasons. He brought a pro-style approach to the program. He's the first person that taught me how to work myself through an at-bat. Thanks, Hop.

"Monsignor Sullivan was the baseball chaplain. He was my roommate on the road at times, but most importantly, he was my friend. He helped me with my conversion to Catholicism when I was going through a tough time in my life. I miss you very much.

"My teammates in my college, we had a lot of fun together the three years I was there. We had a good run, especially my last year. In a regional, we beat Frank Thomas's Auburn team, then lost to Billy Spiers's Clemson team 2-1, but then we lost to Frank's team. My memories in college are great.

"I had a man named Clary Anderson draft me for the Astros in 1987. Clary is legendary in New Jersey as a great football coach. He was our national cross checker for the Astros. He gave me a shot and I'll never forget that.

"I had two owners in John McMullen and Drayton McLane.

"John McMullen was more than an owner. He was like a father figure to me. We did a lot of things together off the field. Dr. McMullen kept baseball in Houston when the franchise was struggling. How many owners come to watch a prospect work out in a gym in the middle of the winter? McMullen and Hall of Famer Yogi Berra did that. I was drafted by the Houston Astros in the first round the following spring.

"And Drayton McLane, we spent seventeen years together and built the new stadium. We built a successful organization, but most importantly, I was able to stay with one organization for twenty years. I was loyal to Drayton and he was loyal in return. Drayton, you were my boss and my owner, but most importantly, you were my friend.

"I was lucky to have some incredible coaches and managers. Like a lot of successful organizations, you are only going to be successful with good people around you.

"One of those coaches was Hall of Famer Yogi Berra. Yogi was the smartest baseball man I was ever around. Although he is known for his Yogi-isms, his baseball intellect was second to none. Yogi would say things in a Yogi way, that he walked by, say some things and I'd be confused. And then the next inning one thing would happen, and then the next half inning, another thing would happen. And then I sat back down on the bench and said, 'Oh my gosh, I've got a lot to learn about this game.' Yogi used to say, said to me, you have to have an idea and a plan, but the end of the day keep it simple, stupid.

"And then there was Matty Galante, my coach for many years. Matty, where you at? Where ya at, Matty? Stand up, Matty! I'm not here without that man. Give him a round of applause, please. Matty, you're an incredible coach and teacher of the game.

"In the National League, you've got to play offense and defense or you don't play at all. I had just made the All-Star Game as a catcher, and the following year, the Astros asked me to go play second base, a position I had never played before in my life. We had six weeks to learn it in spring training, no pressure, huh Matt? Typical day with Matty is that we started at 7 a.m. and we go to a half field when the sun was coming up and we'd work for an hour and a half until 8:45 or so and go grab a sandwich. Then I'd go practice with the team from 9 'til noon. We'd go back to the half field for a while, and then I'd go back, play in the game and then head back to work out more in the back. We did that every day in spring training for six weeks. I thank God for Matt Galante and I'm so grateful. When I won my first Gold Glove, I gave it to him. Matt, thank you for everything. For being a great coach, great teacher, but a better person and friend.

"I want to thank all the clubhouse guys, the true heartbeat of the team. Dennis Liborio was the first man I met in the big leagues, truly one of my best friends. The first time I walked into the clubhouse and I asked him where Yogi Berra was, he said, 'Who the bleep are you? Your locker's over there,' and he turned and walked away. That was the beginning of our relationship. He can't be here today, I hope he knows in his heart how much I love him and miss him.

"I had some pretty special teammates over twenty years. Especially in my early years where they were the most impressionable. I was around guys like Nolan Ryan, Billy Doran, Buddy Bell, Terry Puhl. Being around those guys taught me how to respect the game and play the game the right way day in and day out. It was always about the team.

"Ken Caminiti was a great teammate and better friend and I miss him a lot. Nancy, Kendall, Lindsey, and Nicole, your father has given us an amazing relationship.

"Darryl Kile had the best curveball I'd ever seen. Brad Ausmus, a true friend. Moises Alou, one of the greatest hitters I ever played with.

"Jeff Bagwell, another east coast kid who just loved to play the game. We played fifteen years together and changed the culture in Houston by making it a baseball town. We both got to live our dreams together by playing in the big leagues side-by-side. Thanks for being here today, it really means a lot.

"I want to thank my agent, Barry Axelrod. One of the ingredients in success is your agent. We've been through a lot together over the last twenty-five years. I had great confidence in you. Your hard work and professionalism were part of my ability to stay with one team my entire career. Barry was always just a phone call away. Not just for me, but for all of his clients. I'm grateful for all they you have done and continue to do, but most of all, your friendship. John Palguta, my family and I cannot have done this without you, thank you, brother.

"To my close friends at St. Thomas and the late Monsignor Jamail, I want to thank you for supporting me in my personal and professional life.

"To the Astros fans, where you at? Let me hear you! Pedro's going to give you a run for the money! (BEE-GEE-OH chants from the crowd.) There you go! There you go! You guys are the greatest fans in the world, man. I love you guys. I want to thank you for the way you treated my family and I hope I earned your respect by the way I played the game and I never took that for granted. And I will never forget the playoff runs that we had and the twenty years of memories.

"To my family, the most important thing to me in my life. Conor, a graduate from Notre Dame and a four-year letterman on the baseball team, I'm so proud of the man you have become. And the man can type. He typed this for me in like twenty minutes!

"Cavan, I am so proud of you and your work ethic on and off the field. I'm so proud of the man you are becoming on the field and off as a student-athlete. Cavan just got here last night around midnight. He was very fortunate enough to make the Cape Cod League All-Star team and played in the game last night. I'm very proud of you.

"How lucky was I? I'll never forget the memories that we had traveling with the team when you guys were bat boys and enjoying the 3,000 hits on the field together. Memories of a lifetime.

"And to Quinn, you are beautiful and talented. Although you were young and don't remember my playing career, you sure play like you do. I'm looking forward to your bright future. You are a sweetheart and I love you very much.

"Saving the best for last, my wife Patty. You gave me three incredible kids. But most of all you gave me my best friend for the last twenty-five years. You are a great person. And our kids are who they are because of you. The baseball life is a great life, but it's a hard life. I was always in and out for eight months. You were the one who did everything for the kids. You were a mom, a dad, hitting coach, driver, the list goes on. But most of all, you were there and made things normal for our kids.

"And last, I gave the game everything I had every day. In baseball, tomorrow is not guaranteed and I tried to play every game as it was going to be my last. I want to thank the game for everything. The game has given me EVERYTHING. My family, my friends, respect, but most of all, the memories of a lifetime. Thank you very, very much, from the bottom of my heart."

– Craig Biggio, Cooperstown, NY, July 25, 2015

Baggy Had to Wait Mostly Due to One Word

On January 18, 2017 Jeff Bagwell finally got the call that his fans had been waiting for. He had been selected to be inducted into Cooperstown's Baseball Hall of Fame. While he would not be officially inducted until late July, it was time for fans to let the celebration begin. Not only were his fans overjoyed, but so were his former teammates. Lance Berkman told Jerry Crasnick of ESPN.com as much the day of the announcement. "I love Jeff. It did me a great service as a young player to watch how he conducted his business in the clubhouse and on the field. I think a lot of guys who played with him will make the effort to get up there [Cooperstown] and see him go in. We are all thrilled to death."

Berkman played with Bagwell the last five years of his career. Jim Deshaies was a teammate when Bagwell broke in and a television analyst for the rest of Baggie's career. "He was straight out of central casting. He just came in and played and never popped off. One thing I remembered him saying was, 'I won't hit a lot of home runs, but every now and then I'll get one and it will go a long way.' He hit an upper deck home run in Pittsburgh his rookie year and we were like, 'Wow, where did that come from?' You kind of knew it was in there." In other words, Bagwell always had power, but with a combination of old fashioned hard physical work and some tweaks in his swing by hitting guru Rudy Jaramillo to generate more backspin, the power came.

Jeff Bagwell needed six voting years to gain enough votes for enshrinement. Why the great discrepancy? In one word "suspicion." Too many Hall of Fame voters have cast a wary eye on all players, but especially power hitters who had big seasons during baseball's now notorious Steroid Era. Now mostly referred as the PED era for "Performance Enhancing Drugs," it was when some players discovered that augmenting their workout schedules with anabolic steroids, and later human growth hormone, gave them more strength and the ability to work out longer as well as recover from injuries more quickly. There were a couple of problems. First, many of the substances used were illegal for what they were being used for and certainly without legitimate medical reasons. One of the reasons some of the substances were illegal is they had not been properly tested and had some serious side effects.

There is little doubt the use of these performance enhancing drugs was popularized or perhaps even begun on the West Coast. They were not limited to there. There were connections to Mexico, Latin America, and dealers on the East Coast. The Oakland A's of the Jose Canseco-Mark McGwire years in the mid-1980s were in the middle of steroid's Garden of Eden. Canseco made it no secret that he was a user of the same sort of things used by body builders routinely for years. Canseco was even using needles to inject himself and other players that he actually named in a book he wrote. He wasn't just taking some questionable supplements. He was in the program big time.

During the early years, baseball ignored the rumors. The players who were going so far as Canseco and obtaining steroids from dealers tried to keep it a secret. Some things like creatine and androstenedione were in powder or tablet form, as was protein powder or amino acid supplements in gyms, health stores, and even the grocery vitamin shelf. A lot of players who wanted to be able to work out more and bounce back quicker after those workouts, or even the long day-to-day grind of the season, started visiting the health stores. What they bought off the shelf was legal. However, it didn't take long before the illegal stuff also entered baseball.

In the late 1980s, more and more players started hitting homeruns. Not only were the sluggers like Canseco, who almost everyone knew as using more than creatine and androstenedione, hitting the long ball, but so were players like Brady Anderson. Guys that already were known for power were hitting more than ever before.

When a reporter spotted a bottle of androstenedione in Mark McGwire's locker during the 1998 season as he was on the way to setting a new major league single season homerun record with 70, the door was open to the general public. It was no longer a hidden secret in baseball.

McGwire, who detested having to deal with the media, had to defend himself in the press and went so far as to say he was no longer taking andro, which was still legal, to set a better example for the youth. Still, the door was open and there were a lot of hidden skeletons in the closet.

As Canseco, a self-confessed steroid user, admitted in his book, both creatine and andro weren't really steroids. They were just supplements that would allow players to work out harder for a longer time. Their longterm effects were minimal. Conseco claimed that McGwire allowing reporters to see his bottle of Andro was perhaps only a ruse to keep them away from what he really used.

Baseball had been on a resurgence in interest that season as McGwire and Sosa went almost homerun for homerun. Sosa would also break the record, but fall short of McGwire's 70, but now the long ball was baseball's thing. "Chicks Dig the Long Ball" was a popular bumper sticker.

Soon, more and more players were trying to find the McGwire and Sosa secret. The problem now was that one of baseball's most cherished record, the single season homerun mark, had been broken by two players who were suspected of using anabolic steroids to help them get there. Unfortunately, there were other players who did not try the illegal steroid route that were lumped in with those that did give them a try.

Attendance was rising with more and more homeruns. Fans packed ballparks and the gates were opened early just so fans could see how far McGwire could hit balls in batting practice. But not all fans were happy with what was going on. Barry Bonds, already a Hall of Fame level player, reportedly was upset, too, when lesser skilled players like McGwire and Sosa were getting all the attention. He considered himself the best player in the game and would find the best "nutritional" advisors to help him claim that title.

A little lab in the bay area called BALCO came forward. As history records, Bonds broke all the homerun records McGwire and Sosa had established. He became physically huge. Even his head grew—which is one of the negative side-effects from steroid use. Bonds, unlike Canseco before him, however, always denied he took anything but natural and legal supplements. No one believed him and investigative reporting on the subject leads strongly against Bonds's proclamations. There was actual evidence in workout logs and usage schedules uncovered. Books have been written on this subject after the *San Francisco Chronicle* opened it up. Perhaps the best of those books, *Juicing the Game*, was written by Howard Bryant, who had been a reporter and columnist for papers in the Bay Area, New Jersey on the Yankees beat and Boston. Published in 2005, the book covers the history and growth of PED use in baseball, making references to the *Mitchell Report*, which had been commissioned by MLB to uncover the extent of illegal substance abuse in baseball. Names were being revealed with their ties to suppliers. Some protested. Others admitted. Baseball put a drug testing program in place and banned the use of hundreds of substances, many of which were not illegal to purchase, but were now illegal for players to use.

Astros owner Drayton McLane was not turning a blind eye. First of all, he admittedly was in the clubhouse himself for anywhere from 60 to 65 home games. And he told head trainer Dave Labossiere to let him know if he saw anything wrong. "Dave was an upright guy and I think if he had seen anything wrong, he would have told me 'cause I told him if he had any indication to let me know. And he never did."

The problem with the era was that everyone, even those who were never connected to using anything other than then legal supplements, was suspected along with those who had suppliers of anabolic steroids or human growth hormone. Those "suspected" even included players whose names had never come up in the *San Francisco Chronicle*, the *Mitchell Report*, or any other investigative report.

Jeff Bagwell was one of the latter. His name had never been linked with any illegal anabolic steroid use, but he was a power hitter who was built like a rock. Never mind that he claimed to have built that body the old-fashioned way. No one was in the Astro weight-room more often or longer than Bagwell. It was even unofficially named "Baggie's Gym." The fact is that an athlete on steroids, unless working for a body building competition, would not have to work out as much as Jeff did. Steroids build bulk faster, but don't require as much work to maintain. Bagwell always worked hard after every single game. Reporters missed some deadlines waiting for him to return from the gym after games. Astros' strength and conditioning coach Gene Coleman knew of Bagwell's dedication. "I can't tell you the number of times that Jeff was the player of the game on a get-away day and he would have to do the interviews. He would do them, but he would come in the clubhouse and always tell me, 'Hey, doc, I had to do the interviews, but I want to work out. Don't worry. They're not gonna leave us. They won't leave without me.'"

Bagwell was a workout freak, almost. "During the season I was able to supervise him most of the time," Coleman recalled. "In the offseason, that wasn't always the case. He had a guy he would work out with away from the ballpark, and some of the things he did, you know, by professional standards, were contraindicated. I can remember telling Baggy, that I'd like to come see him workout and he'd say, 'No, because you're not going to be happy with what I am doing.'"

Later, Bagwell would admit he may have been putting too much weight on his shoulder work that may have contributed to the injuries to both of his shoulders that shortened his career.

Still Jeff had to work out. Dennis Liborio, the Astros Clubhouse manager, was on duty all year. He would get Christmas off and he would shut the clubhouse up around December 20 and head to Boston where his relatives lived. Baggie always wanted to work out. As Gene Coleman remembered, "And so, for years since I had a key, Baggy would call me to let him in the facility on New Year's Eve, and then again at 10am on New Year's Day. Why? He wanted to have the last workout of one year and the first of the next."

The in-season work of Bagwell was also legendary. "He had a routine in which, the last workout before the season ended, he would bench press three hundred thirty-five pounds three times to prove to himself he was strong. He actually did it three times a year: once after spring training, once at the All-Star break, and once just before the season ended," said Coleman.

He also did it once to prove a point to some young Astros. As Gene remembered, "The team had played a long game in which they had been clubbed by the Cubs. I suggested we do his post-game weight work the next day. Jeff said no and furthermore he asked me to bring two of the Astros younger players, Morgan Ensberg and Keith Ginter, into the workout room and work out as well. So, I got both of them. I told them all they had to do was act like they were doing something, but to watch Baggy. So, as I prepared to spot for Jeff, he told me he had to do this to make an impression on these two young kids. So, I went over and told them that this guy [Bagwell] has been here since two pm. He played in a four-hour game. He took an oh-fer. The team was beaten badly. Can you believe how hard it is to press three hundred thirty-five pounds when fully rested? He is doing this to make an impression on you guys. You don't have to lift three hundred thirty-five pounds. You don't have to do all this stuff, but you have to be consistent. You have to show up and you have to do it. You have to be consistent in all aspects of your game."

Bagwell not only played and worked out hard, but he knew how to set an example for all his teammates.

Few outside the Astros' inner-circle knew half of this. To the doubters, he was a good friend with Ken Caminiti, who later admitted he had started using steroids after he went to the San Diego Padres in 1995. They worked for him. After never hitting more than 18 homeruns in a season with Houston over six full seasons, his years with San Diego saw him hit 26, 40, 26, and 29. After being an average offensive threat more known for his defense at third base in Houston, he was the MVP in the National League in 1996 when he hit 40 homers, hit .326, and drove in 130 runs. Caminiti admitted in a *Sports Illustrated* article that he first obtained steroids in 1995 during a trip across the border from San Diego into Mexico, where they were readily available. He wanted them to help him recover from a shoulder injury. When he saw what they did to him as a player, he was hooked on their use. But Caminiti had a weakness for addiction. As one baseball insider was quoted in *Juicing the Game* put it, "As drugs went, steroids were the least of Caminiti's problems." Continuing from Howard Bryant's book, "Ken went into a drug rehabilitation clinic in Houston twice for addiction to alcohol and painkillers, and would later be arrested for possession of crack cocaine. By 2001, he regularly sought psychiatric help."

The only thing Bagwell and Caminiti had in common outside of their being teammates and friends was that they both sometimes drank too much. Both underwent treatment to beat alcoholism. Caminiti, unfortunately, linked drugs, starting with pain pills but elevating to hard drugs after his career, with alcohol and anabolic steroids. On October 10, 2004, Caminiti was only five days out of the Harris County jail in Houston, where he had spent four weeks for violating his probation for testing positive for cocaine, when he was found dead in a Bronx, New York, apartment. Official cause of death for the forty-one-year-old former athlete was initially a heart attack. An autopsy showed a combination of cocaine and heroin in his blood. Ken Caminiti and Jeff Bagwell had been friends, but very different people.

Jeff Bagwell never denied he had used legal supplements for a time. Creatine, which was routinely available in MLB clubhouses for years, was used to help muscles recover. He also admitted using the stuff found in McGwire's locker, androstenedione. At the time, both were over-the-counter legal for the general public and for baseball players. He has always been adamant he never used either after baseball banned them or used anabolic steroids ever.

Gene Coleman knows Jeff was unfairly lumped by some Hall of Fame voters for years. "I think because of Jeff's physical make up and the fact that as a minor leaguer he was not a homerun hitter, and then he got big and he was guilty by association. That wasn't fair. There's always some external clues you can look for and Baggy never displayed any of them."

Whenever Bagwell's Hall of Fame credential came up after his unsuccessful six years on the ballot, the talk of his suspected steroid use was irritating. As Bagwell put in in 2009, "I know what I did; I know how hard I worked. If someone thinks I took crap because I was in that era, what am I going to do to show them I didn't? I can't go take a blood test now." As reported in an ESPN.com article in December, 2015, "I never used steroids and I'll tell you exactly why. If I could hit between thirty and forty homeruns every year and drive in one hundred twenty runs, why did I need to do anything else? I was pretty happy with what I was doing and that's the honest truth. All of a sudden, guys were starting to hit sixty and seventy homeruns and people were like, 'Dude, if you took steroids, you could do it too.' And I was like, 'I'm good where I'm at. I just want to do what I can do.'"

And for the record Bagwell never failed a blood test during his active career.

"I know a lot of people are saying, 'His body got bigger.' Well, if you're eating thirty pounds of meat every day and you're working out and bench pressing, you're going to get bigger. You can go to every single trainer I worked with and they'll tell you I was always the first guy in the weight room and last to leave."

That was not always a good thing. Bagwell started dedicated heavy lifting in 1995 after pitcher Mike Hampton thought he looked underweight and thin that spring. Bagwell had just gone through his first divorce and had a rough offseason. After a season that was not up to the standard he had set in 1994, Bagwell decided to work with a trainer and started lifting seriously.

The trainer was not in favor of all the lifting and body building Jeff was doing. He told him, "You have to stop doing those lifts behind your neck because it's going to hurt your arm. It's not normal." Bagwell protested that it felt so good, but the trainer pointed out Jeff was not a body builder, but a baseball player and in the long run it may hurt him. Now Jeff feels he was right.

Jeff actually began a rigorous training program after he had already had what would be the best season of his career. In 1994, he had hit .368 with 39 homeruns and 116 RBIs in only 110 games in the strike-shortened season. What working out he was doing then was for general conditioning. In fact, Phil Garner, who was a coach during Bagwell's rookie season, used to work out with him. "I worked out with Bagwell because I had always wanted to work out with weights. In those days, it was not fashionable to work out with heavy weights, but Bagwell enjoyed it and so did I so we would work out together. We had hard workouts. I began to respect Bagwell a lot on his work ethic and I always respected the way he played on the field."

Although Jeff used weights from the start, it wasn't until 1995 when Jeff really hit the weight room. His biggest gains were during the offseason after 1995. He gained 20 pounds by changing his diet and lifting weights. After Jeff built himself up, he wasn't putting up record-breaking homerun totals, but he had five more seasons of 39 or more homers. Of course, he was also in the chronological peak years of most careers—from 28 to 35.

Bagwell later confessed his extra and extreme weight work may have been a major reason why his shoulders started to fail him. His offseason work was not under the supervision of the Astros' Strength and Conditioning Coach, Dr. Gene Coleman, and included work not necessarily the best for baseball players. Weight-lifting can put a lot of extra stress on the joints. Sometimes the muscles become too strong for their supporting tendons and ligaments. Bagwell admitted that heavy weightlifting may have shortened his career. He told writer Jerry Crasnick, "I would come to spring training and couldn't throw the ball at all. And I played the last three and a half years in the most pain you can imagine just trying to throw a baseball."

By 2001, Jeff's shoulders were causing many problems. Most were unaware but it was Jeff's left shoulder that first needed surgery. It hurt when he reached for a throw and when he followed through swinging the bat. So after that season, he had surgery to extract bone spurs and repair a torn labrum. In the next year or so, his right (throwing) shoulder started to hurt. He had started to develop arthritis. The pain never got better without occasional cortisone shots. Fortunately, by now doctors knew to be careful with pain-reducing cortisone.

When Jeff's first college coach at Hartford, Bill Denehy, was pitching for the New York Mets, his shoulder pain that originally showed up when he tried to over throw a slider to Willie Mays, was kept under control with cortisone injections. Denehy received 57 injections during his career. Since then, it had been learned that ten or more over an entire career could lead to corneal damage and eventual blindness. Bill Denehy is now blind. His story, including his addition to alcohol and cocaine after he was fired from coaching at Hartford, are featured in his biography, *Rage*, co-authored with Peter Goldenbock. He had been let go at Harford in April 1987 after a bench-clearing brawl with Connecticut. He only coached Bagwell for part of one season, but he gave him a scholarship and made him a third baseman after Jeff got only a few looks out of high school.

Jeff won't wind up like his old coach. Drugs never caught him. He has had to work hard to get an alcohol problem under control, but always knew the dangers of anabolic steroid use was not just from the illegality, but from the possibility of what their use could do to the user's body down the road.

Jeff has always had a goal to have a good life after baseball. Getting inducted into the Hall of Fame was never primary. "I keep telling people this and people don't understand. Baseball does not define me as a person. It's what I do with my kids, and as a husband, that's going to define me. It'd be an honor, don't get me wrong, but I've got other things to do in my life, too," Jeff told USA Today reporter Ted Berg in 2015.

It hasn't been easy. He and his wife Rachel have both been married before. He and his first wife Shaune were childless, but he and his second wife Ericka had a fourteen-year marriage with children. The blended family of Jeff and Rachel has five children to care for, and taking care of and raising them is Jeff's greatest goal. He has had chances to return to the field as a coach, or even work more with the club. He worked Sunday home games on TV for one season. He tried being a hitting coach for part of one season. Being away from home as much as he was as a player, which could have contributed to two failed marriages, was not for him. Former teammate and close friend Brad Ausmus even felt him out about joining him in Detroit with the Tigers. Jeff's answer was essentially thanks, but no thanks.

When the current ownership of the Astros took over, they purged many long time employees from the team, from batting practice pitcher Stretch Suba, to traveling secretary Barry Waters, and many scouts and staffers from the front office. At that point, Bagwell had no interest in continuing an association with the club. However, owner Jim Crane and the team's second President, Reid Ryan, urged Bagwell to return to the team in some capacity. Jeff accepted the chance to return as an advisor and part-time spring training instructor.

Much more introverted than most super stars, Jeff was a quiet but very effective leader in the clubhouse during his playing days. His work effort in the gym and on the field was legendary. As former teammate Geoff Blum put it in the Houston Chronicle in 2002, "It's pretty impressive when you watch a guy like him. He knows what he has to do, and he puts his mind to it and does it."

Another former teammate, Mike Hampton, in a SABR Bio Project report from multiple sources, showed that separating Craig Biggio and Jeff Bagwell from Astro history is almost impossible. Bagwell was "the ultimate teammate. Bagwell and Biggio let it be known there was an Astros way of doing thing. The Bagwell and Biggio way was to demand accountability, starting with themselves. Bagwell was particularly quick to deflect credit for his success explaining, 'that's my job,' and to readily accept blame—often for the failures of others that weren't even his. His ability to connect with teammates knew no barriers, racial or otherwise."

I have one special memory of Jeff's leadership. I had arranged for Derek Bell to spend some time with me to tape an interview for the Astros' TV pre-game show. But when the time came, Bell had an excuse and couldn't do it right then. He said he would do it later. Later came, and he was out of time. I went over to Jeff and asked him if he could fill in since my scheduled guest had stood me up. Jeff immediately asked me who left me hanging. I said it was Bell. I remember Jeff scanning the field and glaring in the direction of Bell. Then he said he'd do it. I know he wasn't happy being asked with such late notice, but I watched Bagwell head to the outfield where Bell was hanging out. I never had another problem getting Derek Bell to do an interview after that.

For all his leadership qualities, Rookie of the Year and MVP honors, career statistical achievements, or even the success the Astros had during his career, Jeff was denied the Hall of Fame honor until 2017 in his seventh year of eligibility. He came close in 2016 with 71.6% of the 75% vote needed. As a player and leader, he was a Hall of Famer from the day he retired.

Astro fans hope some from the nucleus of the team that made the postseason in 2015 will form the next "Golden Era" of Houston baseball. If that happens, the team will need some future Hall of Famers like Craig Biggio and Jeff Bagwell to get it done.

Craig Biggio
Lifetime Statistics

Hall of Fame Induction Vote: 454 of 549 Ballots (82.7%)
Positions: Second Baseman, Catcher, Center Fielder,

Bats: Right
Height: 5' 11"
Signed: June 8, 1987
Debut: June 26, 1988

Throws: Right
Weight: 185 lbs.
Team: Houston Astros 1988-2007
Last Game: September 30, 2007

Left Fielder, Right Fielder
All-Star Games: 1991, 1992, 1994, 1995, 1996, 1997, 1998
Gold Gloves: 1994, 1995, 1996, 1997
Silver Sluggers: 1989, 1994, 1995, 1997, 1998

Career Totals

Games Played: 2,850
At Bats: 10,876
Runs: 1,845
Hits: 3,060
Doubles: 668
Triples: 55

Homeruns: 291
Runs Batted In: 1,175
Strikeouts: 1,753
Putouts: 7,156
Assists: 5,671
Errors: 201

Led the National League

1992: Games Played (162), Plate Appearances (721)
1994: Doubles (44), Stolen Bases (39)
1995: Plate Appearances (673), Runs Scored (123)
1996: Games Played (162)
1997: Games Played (162), Plate Appearances (744),
      Runs Scored (146), Times on Base (309)
1998: Plate Appearances (738), Doubles (51)
1999: Plate Appearances (749), Doubles (56)
2004: Errors as Outfielder (9)

Jeff Bagwell
Lifetime Statistics

Hall of Fame Induction Vote: 381 of 442 Ballots (86.2%)
Position: First Baseman

Bats: Right
Height: 6' 0"
Signed: June 10, 1989
Debut: April 8, 1991

Throws: Right
Weight: 195 lbs
Team: Houston Astros 1991-2005
Last Game: October 2, 2005

All Star Games: 1994, 1996, 1997, 1999
Gold Gloves: 1994
Silver Sluggers: 1994, 1997, 1999
MVP: 1995

Career Totals

Games Played: 2,150
At Bats: 7,797
Runs: 1,517
Hits: 2,314
Doubles: 488
Triples: 32

Homeruns: 449
Runs Batted In: 1,529
Strikeouts: 1,558
Putouts: 17,546
Assists: 1,705
Errors: 129

Led the National League

1992: Games Played (162)
1994: Slugging Percentage (.750), Runs Scored (104),
    Total Bases (300), Runs Batted In (116), Runs Created (137)
    Extra Base Hits (73), Times on Base (216)
1996: Games Played (162), Doubles (48), Times on Base (324)
1997: Games Played (162),
1999: Games Played (162), Runs Scored (143),
    Bases on Balls (149), Times on Base (331)
2000: Runs Scored (152)
2006: Salary ($19,369,019)

Bibliography

In addition to the books listed, the help from web sites such as base-ball-reference.com; mlb.com; and sundry other websites and news outlets, including those available through newspapers.com, were invaluable in researching stats and historical notes. Magazine and newspaper articles credited in the text were also very important in compiling this volume.

Bouton, Jim. *Ball Four*. Champaign, IL: Sports Publishing, Inc., 1970.

Brown, Bill and Mike Acosta. *Houston Astros: Deep in the Heart*. Houston, TX: Bright Sky Press, 2013.

Bryant, Howard. *Juicing the Game*. New York, NY: Viking Press, 2005.

Canseco, Jose. *Juiced*. New York, NY: Regan Books, 2005.

Denehy, Bill and Peter Golenbock. *Rage: the Legend of Baseball Bill Denehy*. Las Vegas, NV: Central Recovery Press, 2014.

Direker, Larry. *This Ain't Brain Surgery*. New York, NY: Simon and Schuster, 2003.

Fainbaur-Wada, Mark and Lance Williams. *Game of Shadows*. New York, NY: Gotham Books, 2007.

Footer, Alyson and Terry Lawrence. *Inside the Magical Seasons*. Houston, TX: Tate Publishing Co., 2006.

Houston Astros. *Houston Astros Media Guides*. Houston, TX: Houston Astros Ball Club, 1962-2012.

Izenberg, Jerry. *The Greatest Game Ever Played*. Houston, TX: Henry Holt and Company, 1987.

McTaggart, Brian. *100 Things Astro Fans Should Know*. Chicago, IL: Triumph, 2016.

Miller, Jeff. *Going Long*. New York, NY: McGraw-Hill, 2003.

Morgan, Joe and David Falkner. *Joe Morgan: A Life in Baseball*. New York, NY: Norton and Company, 1993.

Ortis, Jose de Jesus Jr. *Armed and Dangerous*. Champaign, IL: Sports Publishing, LLC, 2006.

Pirkle, John. *Oiler Blues*. Houston, TX: Sportsline Publishing, 2006.

Radomsky, Kurt. *Bases Loaded*. New York, NY: Hudson Street Press, 2009.

Ray, Edgar. *The Grand Huckster.* Memphis, TN: Memphis State University Press, 1980.

Reed, Robert. *Colt 45s: a Six Gun Salute*. Hosuton, TX: Gulf Publishing, 1999.

Siroty, David. *The Hit Men and the Kid Who Batted Ninth*. Lanham, MD: Diamond Communications, 2002.

Tan, Cecilia ed. *Baseball in the Space Age*. Phoenix, AZ: Society for American Baseball Research, 2014.

Titchener, Campbell. *The George Kirksey Story.* Austin, TX: Eakin Press, 1989.

Watson, Bob and Russ Pate. *Survive to Win*. Nashville, TN: Nelson Publishing, 1997.

Wynn, Jim and Bill McCurdy. *Toy Cannon*. Jefferson, NC: McFarland Publishing, 2010.